POSTGRADUATE STUDY IN THE UK
THE INTERNATIONAL STUDENT'S GUIDE

NICHOLAS FOSKETT AND **ROSALIND FOSKETT**

SAGE Publications

London • Thousand Oaks • New Delhi

SAGE Publications Ltd
1 Oliver's Yard
55 City Road
London EC1Y 1SP

SAGE Publications Inc.
2455 Teller Road
Thousand Oaks, California 91320

SAGE Publications India Pvt Ltd
B-42, Panchsheel Enclave
Post Box 4109
New Delhi 110 017

British Library Cataloguing in Publication data

A catalogue record for this book is available from the British Library

ISBN10 1 4129 0718 7   ISBN13 978 1 4129 0718 7
ISBN10 1 4129 0719 5 (pbk)   ISBN13 978 1 4129 0719 4 (pbk)

Library of Congress Control Number: 2006923438

Typeset by C&M Digitals (P) Ltd., Chennai, India
Printed on paper from sustainable resources
Printed in Great Britain by The Cromwell Press Ltd, Trowbridge, Wiltshire

SUMMARY OF CONTENTS

CONTENTS

PREFACE

This book has been written to meet the needs of students from around the world who are either considering taking a Masters degree or a Doctorate at a university in the United Kingdom, or are already on a Masters or Doctoral programme. It provides a single source of guidance on the whole process of becoming and being a postgraduate student, from the initial idea to beyond graduation. There are many sources of information about being a postgraduate. However, these are either about the application process and moving to and living in the UK, or they are about how to study for a Masters or a Doctorate. In this book we cover both these aspects as we believe they are strongly inter-connected.

The book is divided into four parts. The first part (Chapters 1–3) looks at the nature of postgraduate study in UK universities and considers the processes of choosing and applying for a programme. The second part (Chapters 4–7) considers everyday life as an international postgraduate student, and looks at a range of issues from accommodation to finance to student life in the UK. The third part (Chapters 8–11) concentrates on studying, and looks in detail at teaching, learning, assessment, assignments, examinations, managing your study time and research. The final part (Chapter 12) looks at life beyond your postgraduate programme, at issues such as graduation, finding a job and returning home. We have tried in this way to look at all parts of the 'student life cycle' for international postgraduate students.

The book is intended for all postgraduate students. Whether you are planning to take a Masters degree or to undertake a PhD or taught Doctorate, many of the issues you will face are the same. However, throughout the book we have included clear sections that relate specifically to either Masters or Doctoral degrees where this is appropriate. For example, Chapter 8 is about taught postgraduate courses and is therefore mainly for Masters students and those on taught Doctorates.

The book has been written from a student's perspective. Much of what is written elsewhere about choosing a UK programme is basically marketing literature from institutions or organizations seeking to persuade you to come to the UK or specifically to their university or programme. We have tried here, though, to work through the questions you will be asking as a potential or current postgraduate student and to provide honest, informative and realistic answers to those questions. While we believe very strongly that a UK postgraduate programme is an excellent choice for many international students, we are also keen that you make a well-researched and carefully thought through decision. If a UK postgraduate programme would not be right for you then we would rather you make a different choice of what to do next. To support this approach you will find three distinctive features of this book:

- Most of the sections are focused on key questions that postgraduate students will want to ask. We have tried to cover most of the frequently asked questions (FAQs) and have arranged the material so that you can look at the contents list and find the question that you want to ask at any particular moment
- We have included in every chapter a feature called '*Pause for thought*'. These are sections that are designed to encourage you to spend time thinking about your own views, needs and ideas on the topic that is being covered. These will help you make better informed decisions and plan carefully how your individual needs can be met.
- At the end of each chapter we have included a section entitled '*Key risks and how to avoid them*'. This presents a brief summary of the main things you need to be aware of and to think about. The list has been created from the experiences of current or recent students and identifies those things you need to be most watchful and careful about. The list is not designed to frighten you! It is, rather, designed to reassure you so that you can check that you have not forgotten to think about something that is important to your success.

We have worked for many years with international postgraduate students as tutors and supervisors and this has given us a considerable amount of experience and knowledge about the issues they face and the choices they make. We have also been actively involved in academic research on student choices and decision-making, and have published research in this field. We have met with international students in the UK and also at universities in many other countries, and we have attended international recruitment fairs. All of this knowledge has been important in helping us to write this book. However, we have relied much more on the direct comments and views of students we have talked to in the preparation of this book. Many students from a wide range of institutions and programmes have talked to us openly and in detail about their choices, their life in the UK and their experiences as postgraduate students. It is their knowledge, insight and experience that is at the heart of this book.

We would suggest you might use this book in two ways. If you are setting out to think about applying for a postgraduate programme in the UK then you will find it useful to read it right through in order. This will take you through each step of the path to becoming a postgraduate and identify all of the issues to think about. The second way of using it, though, will be for those already in the UK on a postgraduate programme. For these students it will be a useful reference book to be 'dipped into' when particular questions or issues arise.

There are a few important things you need to be aware of as you read this book. The first is that while we have of course tried to make the information as accurate and up-to-date as we can, detail changes quite rapidly. Universities change programmes and procedures as do government departments and agencies both in the UK and in your own country. We have therefore, as much as possible, written this book so that you understand the issues and principles on each theme and then have details of other places and sources where you can check the latest situation and detail. We cannot accept any responsibility for the accuracy of the information in this book. The responsibility lies entirely with you to check situations and information.

The second is that you should not read any information in this book as endorsing or supporting any particular choice, institution or programme. We have used many examples to illustrate the points we make, and this includes examples of particular institutions or programmes. These examples are not recommendations or endorsements. Our aim throughout has been to enable you to make the choices that are right for you, and wherever we have used examples there will almost certainly be many other choices you could consider which may or may not suit your needs better.

Finally, we hope that you enjoy the book and find it helpful in your thinking. It reflects many years of very positive experiences for us working with international students. We hope it will provide the basis for many positive experiences for you too.

Nick Foskett and Ros Foskett
Southampton, UK

ACKNOWLEDGEMENTS

This book reflects the experiences of a large number of international students in the UK and of many of their tutors and supervisors. We would like to acknowledge the willingness and enthusiasm of many students, from a wide range of countries, to answer our questions and provide thoughtful comments and insights into life as an international postgraduate in the UK. They are too numerous to name individually, but many will recognize their experiences within the advice and guidance contained in this book.

PART 1
CHOOSING A PROGRAMME AND HOW TO APPLY

CHAPTER 1
WHY DO A POSTGRADUATE DEGREE?

- Why choose to do a Masters or Doctoral postgraduate programme?
- What is a Masters degree?
- What different types of Masters degree are there in the UK?
- What is a Doctoral degree?
- What challenges will face me in my postgraduate study?

First thoughts

Becoming a postgraduate student is the start of an exciting phase of your education. The decision to start a Masters or Doctoral programme is a commitment to study at a high level and shows your wish to achieve significant academic success. Choosing to do your postgraduate studies in the United Kingdom (UK) is a decision to spend at least a year in a country and culture that is new to you with the excitement and challenges that will bring. This book is about these choices. Its main purpose is to help you reach a decision about postgraduate study that is right for *you*. That decision has several elements. First you need to decide whether you will choose to undertake postgraduate study. Secondly, if you have decided to do so, you will need to decide whether to study in your own country or to move to another country for your postgraduate programme. Thirdly, you need to choose a programme and subject of study. Finally, you need to choose where to study – which university and which town or city to move to.

Each of these challenges will be considered in detail in this book, but with a focus on choosing a postgraduate programme in the UK. We shall look at what postgraduate study requires from you and the different types of programme that are available. We shall then consider life as a postgraduate student in the UK, including both academic life and day-to-day living. This will cover questions ranging from how to move to the UK, to money and finance, to shopping, to writing assignments and taking examinations. Finally, we shall look at issues about returning home after your postgraduate programme and the career opportunities open to you. However, here in Chapter 1 we shall start at the beginning of the process by looking at a very important question – *why do a postgraduate degree?*

Why choose to do a Masters or Doctoral postgraduate programme?

For most readers this question is probably one you have already thought about – and answered! If you are reading a book about choosing a postgraduate programme in the UK it is likely that you have already spent some time deciding that you want to undertake study at postgraduate level, and that you are seriously considering doing this in the United Kingdom.

But what exactly is postgraduate study? Simply, it is study to a level that is higher than a first degree. A first degree in most countries is referred to as a Bachelors degree and is awarded at the end of an undergraduate programme of three to five years' full-time study (or longer if you have studied part-time). The number of people worldwide who complete an undergraduate programme has increased rapidly in the past two decades. This is partly because governments have been trying to raise the level of educational achievement in their country by encouraging more people to go to university. It is also, though, because many young people and their families recognize that a university degree is an important step to better job and life prospects. The Organisation for Economic Co-operation and Development (OECD) has shown from its own studies that those with a degree will earn on average 159% more in salary than an average non-graduate over their lifetime, even though by studying they will start to earn a little later than if they had left school and entered a job straight away. The advantages of undergraduate study are clear therefore – but what is the benefit of continuing to study beyond your Bachelors degree? Following a Masters programme will take one or two years full-time study to complete, while a Doctoral programme will take at least three further years. Anyone choosing to follow this path will want to be sure that the benefits of study will outweigh the challenge of several years without starting a career and earning a salary.

There are many reasons to become a postgraduate, and for each person the reasons will be individual and probably quite complex. However, the main reasons for taking a postgraduate degree are the following.

For the intellectual challenge

Perhaps the most obvious reason for postgraduate study is the stimulus of the intellectual challenge. You need to like working with ideas, stretching your mind by working with new concepts, developing skills of analysis and investigation, and debating and arguing issues and approaches. The challenge of making a contribution to knowledge, however small, is an exciting prospect for those who have enjoyed study at school and as an undergraduate. The chance to work alongside some of the cleverest students, academics and researchers in your chosen field and to work with them on the ideas that are at the cutting edge of that field is very appealing to many. This may not, of course, be the most important reason for you to follow a postgraduate programme. However, it must be at least a part of your reason, for without being excited by the prospect of the intellectual challenge you will certainly find it very hard to stay motivated or to achieve a good result at the end of your studies.

For the personal challenge

This is the wish to challenge yourself at an individual level. Even if you found study at undergraduate level quite easy you will be aware that studying at a higher level will be more challenging. It will stretch your skills, challenge your ability to work with more complex ideas and give you the opportunity to see how you compare with the brightest and best brains in your field. It will also test you in other ways. While undergraduate study develops your study skills and ability to work independently, at Masters and Doctoral level independence and personal organization are very important. At undergraduate level, providing you follow the detailed instructions and guidance from your teachers you will probably succeed. At postgraduate level, you have much more responsibility and independence for planning what and how you study and for managing your own learning and the creation of new ideas. Your success will depend on you working *with* your tutors and professors rather than working *for* them.

For improved career prospects

As increasing numbers of people graduate with a first degree so the numbers qualified for the best jobs (whether that means the best paid, the most interesting or the highest status jobs) has increased. As a result many jobs now prefer applicants to demonstrate their achievements at postgraduate level, either as a requirement for entering the career or as a necessity to secure promotion to more senior levels. Having a Masters or Doctorate on your curriculum vitae (CV) can improve your job prospects substantially, and give you the edge in a competitive job market.

As an essential career requirement

Some jobs require a level of expertise or knowledge which it is not possible to acquire from an undergraduate degree, and so insist on a Masters or Doctoral degree as an entry requirement. For those working in the field of science or engineering and looking for a career as a researcher, obtaining a PhD is almost an essential entry requirement, for example. Similarly, many professional fields have established specialist postgraduate programmes with universities that are designed to meet their specific professional needs. Entrants to those professions may either need to obtain such a degree at their own cost before entering the profession or be required to do such a programme by an employer as the first stage of their professional training.

To enter an academic career

Many high achievers at undergraduate level aspire to a career as a university teacher or researcher, perhaps with the ambition of becoming a professor. In a survey conducted for *The Times Higher Education Supplement* (THES, 12 August 2005), nearly two-thirds of all postgraduates indicated that moving into an academic career was their main reason for taking a higher degree. In many countries an academic post at a university is a high-status position (although not always a well-paid one!). In addition, though, the prospect of a career researching and teaching in the subject that you love is very appealing. Increasingly, following an academic career within a university means that having a postgraduate degree is essential, and in many countries such a position will not be possible without a Doctorate. The rapid expansion of higher education in many countries, therefore, means that the demand for those educated to Doctoral level is growing enormously.

● ● ● *Pause for thought* ● ● ●

Before going any further through this book you may like to spend a few moments thinking about these reasons for undertaking postgraduate study. You do not need to match all the reasons – in fact if you can put a tick against any of the reasons then that is sufficient to indicate that postgraduate study is a good choice for you. However, if none of the reasons applies to you then you should think carefully whether postgraduate study really is the best pathway for you to follow.

Most people who choose to do a postgraduate degree complete it successfully and enjoy the experience. But through many years of working with postgraduates it is clear to us that some of those who do not succeed or who do not enjoy the experience had chosen a postgraduate programme for the wrong reasons. The list below indicates some of these reasons. If your *only* reason(s) for thinking about being a postgraduate is in the list below rather than in the list of factors covered above then, we would respectfully suggest that you think carefully about whether this really is the best pathway for you:

- I can't think of anything else to do when I've finished my undergraduate programme.
- My brother/sister/father/mother did a postgraduate degree.
- My family is pressurizing me to do a postgraduate degree.

- Many of my friends are doing a postgraduate degree.
- I enjoy the freedom of lifestyle of being a student.
- It delays having to find a job for another year or two.

Of course, even if these views apply to you, you may find that once you start a postgraduate programme then the other factors begin to be important to you, and that you enjoy and are successful in your programme. Below is a more specific list of factors that would suggest a postgraduate degree is not a good idea:

- You found it difficult to cope with the demands of undergraduate study and although you were awarded a degree it was not of a high grade. If you struggled with your first degree you will find a higher degree even harder. Most Masters programmes require you to have a good grade of first degree, and most Doctoral programmes require the same or a good grade of Masters degree as an entry standard. This does not mean that you have to have been the top of your year group academically or the genius amongst your peers. Many postgraduates have not been identified as future stars but are still good achievers. Some who have been modest achievers as undergraduates find they blossom personally and intellectually as postgraduates. There are examples in every discipline and every university of very successful professors whose undergraduate degree was modest in quality, although they probably will not admit it!
- You are not self-motivated, and usually require teachers and professors to pressurize you to produce work and assignments. The increasingly independent nature of postgraduate study requires you to be a self-starter, and most postgraduate programmes will expect a reference from your undergraduate tutor indicating that you are well-organized and self-motivated.
- Your academic subject does not excite you. Of course you may be choosing to do a Masters degree or Doctorate in a different field (for example, a Masters in Business even though you have a first degree in History), or you may be choosing a programme in the one aspect of your subject that does excite you (for example a Masters in Meteorology when your first degree was a broad-based Physics programme). But if you did not get excited by your undergraduate subject, will you really be motivated to engage fully with a postgraduate programme?
- Your chosen career does not value a postgraduate qualification. Postgraduate degrees are not seen by all employers as a good thing in themselves. In some careers there is not a tradition of taking postgraduate Masters or Doctoral programmes before entering the career, and if you apply with such a qualification you may be regarded as 'over-qualified', 'too academically minded' or simply as a threat to less-qualified peers and senior colleagues. In many countries, for example, a Doctorate would be seen as a positive disadvantage to anyone entering secondary or primary school teaching as it might be questioned how well you would understand the learning needs of children who are in the early stages of learning your subject. You should certainly check this out with those working in the career that you might like to enter eventually.

Making the decision about postgraduate study, therefore, is one that does require some careful reflection. However, if you can read the sections above and identify the positive reasons for going further with your study career then it is likely that a postgraduate programme is right for you. If it is, then you will be making a decision to undertake one of the most rewarding, stimulating and satisfying phases of your education that will prepare you strongly for a successful career and a rich insight into both your own discipline and the higher levels of understanding about knowledge and knowledge creation.

What is a Masters degree?

Masters degrees are an award higher than a Bachelors degree. Under the European Union's Bologna Agreement of 1999, Masters degrees are what have been called 'second cycle higher education', where the first cycle is the Bachelors degree. In many countries of the world Masters degrees are awarded after two years of study beyond a Bachelors degree, while in the UK, because of the ways in which the programmes are designed, they are normally achieved after a full year of full-time study.

The difference between a Bachelors degree and a Masters degree is easy to understand. While a Bachelors degree requires detailed and systematic knowledge and understanding of a general subject area, a Masters degree requires, in addition, *critical* skills and understanding, and a thorough knowledge of current trends and issues at the forefront of a specialist academic discipline. In the UK the national agency for academic quality and standards, the Quality Assurance Agency (QAA), describes a Masters degree as one that requires:

- A systematic understanding of knowledge and a critical awareness of current problems and/or new insights, much of which is at or informed by the forefront of the academic discipline, field of study or area of professional practice
- A comprehensive understanding of techniques applicable to independent research or advanced scholarship
- Originality in the application of knowledge, together with a practical understanding of how established techniques of research and enquiry are used to create and interpret knowledge in the discipline
- Conceptual understanding that enables the student to evaluate current research and advanced scholarship in the discipline and evaluate methodologies and develop critiques of them and, where appropriate, to propose new hypotheses.

While this is a very formal description of a Masters degree it paints the picture of bringing you to the cutting edge of your academic field in terms of knowledge, skills and criticality.

What different types of Masters degree are there in the UK?

The word 'Masters' really refers to an academic level of study rather than a particular course with a standard organization and structure. Within the UK there are three main types of Masters degree, but there is also quite a large range of other programmes that are taught at Masters level but do not lead to a Masters degree. Let us look at the three main types of Masters degrees first.

Traditional Masters degree

The traditional Masters degree is a taught programme of one year's full-time study (or two years part-time) which leads to the award of an MA or MSc degree. The MA is a Master of Arts degree and is normally awarded for a programme in an arts, social sciences or humanities subject – for example an MA in Victorian Literature or an MA in Criminology. The MSc is a Master of Science degree and is usually awarded for a programme in a science or technology discipline – for example an MSc in Software Engineering or an MSc in Environmental Management.

Some universities use other Masters degree titles to show the specialist area of study rather than just using MA or MSc. The best known is probably the MBA, or Master of Business Administration, which is for those specializing in a programme in business, management and administration. Other examples include MSc(SocSci) for programmes in the social sciences or MEd for programmes in education.

Within the UK these programmes have very similar ways of being organized. All will include a number of specialist taught courses (or units), each of which will be assessed in some way, perhaps by an examination or by the submission of a project or coursework. The taught course will make up two-thirds of the overall assessment of the programme. In addition, though, every student will undertake an individual dissertation or project requiring a final report of usually 15,000 to 25,000 words, which makes up the other one-third of the overall mark. It is usual for the taught courses to be undertaken during the earlier parts of the programme and for the dissertation or project to be the final task, but this pattern may vary between programmes.

Most Masters degrees are designed for students who have just completed a Bachelors degree, and the only academic entry requirement is that applicants must have a good overall grade in their first degree by the time they start the Masters. Many students apply during the final year of their Bachelors degree and may be offered a place on the Masters on condition that they complete their Bachelors degree at a certain level of achievement. This is known as a **conditional offer** of a place. Others apply a few years (or sometimes many years) after completing their first degree.

Some Masters degrees, though, are intended as professional development programmes for those working in particular professional fields. The MBA degree in most universities is described as 'a post-experience programme', for example, in that those on the course will be expected to draw on experience of working in business or commerce. One of the entry requirements for such courses may be a minimum period of work experience, typically between two and five years. Similar entry requirements may apply to Masters programmes in the fields of education, health, law or social work, where the Masters programme is both an academic and a professional development course.

Integrated Masters degree

Integrated Masters degrees are not free-standing Masters programmes, but are undergraduate programmes extended by one year to enable students to reach Masters level. These programmes are usually four-year courses. By the end of three years of full-time study students will have reached the level of a Bachelors degree, and if they choose to do so can complete their programme at that time and leave with a Bachelors degree. Providing they have reached a suitable standard of achievement, though, students can study for a fourth year for a Masters degree, where the academic level of work in the fourth year is at Masters rather than at Bachelors degree (called Honours) level. These programmes are normally found in science and engineering academic disciplines, and the usual degree awarded is MEng (Master of Engineering), or a named integrated Masters degree such as MPhys (Master of Physics) or MChem (Master of Chemistry). It is not usually possible to enter the fourth year of these programmes with a Bachelors degree from another university, so those who are seeking an integrated Masters degree will need to apply for the full four-year programme.

Masters degree by research

Masters degrees are normally described as 'taught' programmes, even though they include a 'research' dissertation or project, because most of the course is through taught units of study. In some subjects, though, it is possible to study for a Masters degree which is largely a research programme, in that most of the assessment and credit is achieved through a research dissertation. This will be a single large independent research study, typically of 30,000 to 35,000 words, at Masters level, and will be for the award of an MRes (Master of Research) or MPhil (Master of Philosophy) degree. In many ways an MRes or MPhil programme is more like a PhD – the main work is an individual project, working with a research supervisor. The difference from a PhD is in the academic level of the study (i.e. it is a Masters level of study) and in the size of the dissertation, which is much shorter than for a Doctorate. Most Masters degrees by research will include some taught courses, normally on research methods, but the assessment for the degree will be only through the dissertation.

While some students choose to take an MPhil degree for its own sake, the main feature of an MPhil is that it is a stage on the pathway to a Doctorate. Many universities register PhD students first of all for an MPhil and then, if they are making suitable progress, change the registration to PhD. MPhil will often be awarded therefore to those students who either decide not to progress to PhD or, occasionally, where the standard of the PhD thesis was not high enough for the award of a Doctorate but was judged to be of Masters standard (see Chapter 11).

Postgraduate Certificates and Diplomas

We have looked so far at the range of Masters degrees awarded in the UK. However, as we said earlier, 'Masters' is a level of study, not in itself a degree award, and there are a number of postgraduate awards at Masters level which are not actually called Masters in their title. These are programmes that are at Masters level (i.e. they make the same academic challenges as a Masters degree) but are shorter programmes. They are usually courses leading to a Postgraduate Certificate or a Postgraduate Diploma, and may be available in almost any academic field. To understand these awards you need to understand a little about the structure of a UK Masters degree.

The UK government's Quality Assurance Agency (QAA) rules on a Masters degree are that a full Masters is valued at 180 Masters level (M-level) credit points. Normally 120 points can be awarded for the taught part of a programme and 60 points for the dissertation or project. A Postgraduate Certificate (PGCert) is an M-level programme worth 60 credit points. It will therefore normally be awarded for a taught course which is equivalent to one-third of a full Masters degree, or one-half of the taught part of a Masters. A Postgraduate Diploma (PGDip) is awarded for 120 M-level points, which is equivalent to a full Masters but without the dissertation.

Many universities offer free-standing PGCert and PGDip programmes, often with a particular title – for example a PGCert in Statistics. Alternatively they may use these as alternative awards for students who started a full Masters programme but chose to complete only a part of the full programme. A PGDip will usually be awarded to a student who has completed the taught part of their Masters degree successfully, but whose dissertation is not of a high enough standard (see Chapter 11).

But Beware!

There are three important things to be aware of in the UK Masters degree scene.

The first is that, as we have said earlier, 'Masters' refers to a level of study. Simply because a course is taken after you have completed a first (Bachelors) degree does not mean it is at Masters level. Some courses are postgraduate in time (they take students after they have completed a first degree), but are not postgraduate in level (the award they give is at a lower level than Masters). An example of this is the PGCE – Postgraduate Certificate in Education – which is the standard route for graduates to enter a career in school teaching in the UK. A PGCE is postgraduate in time (only graduates can take the course), but is not necessarily at postgraduate level. Some universities offer a PGCE which is genuinely at Masters level (for example the Universities of Birmingham, Durham and Southampton) and give 60 M-level credits. Others are taught at the level of a final year undergraduate Honours course and give only 120 undergraduate credit points. More properly these latter courses should be called *Professional Graduate Certificates in Education*, but may still use the title PGCE. It is important to check the level of your proposed course!

The second is that most universities in Scotland award an MA as their first degree, and postgraduate Masters degrees will be MSc, LLM etc. rather than MA.

The third is that some universities award MA degrees that require no formal study at all. This is the tradition at the Universities of Oxford and Cambridge where an MA is awarded to any individual who already holds a Bachelors degree from the university seven years after they first enrolled as an undergraduate student. These awards are therefore not an indication of academic study, or of a course, and are only available to Oxford or Cambridge graduates. In some respects MA(Oxon) and MA(Cantab) should be regarded as honorary degrees.

What is a Doctoral degree?

For many students the award of a degree that enables them to use the title of Doctor (Dr) in front of their name is the ultimate academic achievement. For some, being called Dr is the principal reason for following a Doctoral programme, for it brings prestige and social status. Doctoral programmes are what has been called by the Bologna Declaration 'third cycle' programmes, because they are a third phase of academic study following the first cycle (Bachelors degrees) and the second cycle (Masters degrees), although in some circumstances it is possible to progress straight from a first degree to a Doctoral programme.

The main feature of a Doctorate is the Doctoral thesis. This is a substantial research project on a specialist topic within the student's chosen academic field, written as a thesis of between 40,000 and 120,000 words, depending on the exact Doctoral programme. This is the size of a medium to large academic book. The QAA explains what a Doctoral candidate must demonstrate in their thesis: that they can . . .

- create and interpret new knowledge through original research or other advanced scholarship of a quality to satisfy peer review, extend the forefront of the discipline and merit publication
- systematically acquire and understand a substantial body of knowledge which is at the forefront of an academic discipline or area of professional practice

- conceptualize, design and implement a project for the generation of new knowledge, applications or understanding at the forefront of the discipline, and to adjust the project design in the light of unforeseen problems
- show a detailed understanding of applicable techniques for research and academic enquiry.

This is a detailed description, but in simple terms a Doctoral student has to show that they can contribute new knowledge in a field where they already have substantial existing expertise through a well-designed research project so that the findings will be judged by their academic peers as worthy of publication.

The exact way in which a Doctoral programme is organized may vary, and within the UK there are a number of different types of Doctorates. All will expect you to take between two and four years' full-time or between three and six years' part-time study to complete your thesis. All will include some element of taught research training courses in the early stages of your research. Most will require you to have a Masters degree before you start your Doctoral programme. The main types of Doctorate are described below.

PhD or DPhil

The PhD degree is the traditional UK research degree. The degree title comes from the Latin for Doctor of Philosophy (**Phi**losophiae Doctoris). In a small number of universities, for example the University of Oxford, the equivalent degree is called a DPhil (Doctoris **Phi**losophiae). The British PhD is similar to those in other European countries, but is different in structure to PhD programmes in the USA. It requires you to do a single research project that leads to the writing of a thesis, under the supervision of an academic who is an expert in the field. In some areas of creative or performing arts the thesis may be replaced by the production of an artefact or performance with a written commentary. Traditionally a PhD had no formal taught courses or units as part of the programme. However, in recent years it has been recognized that all new researchers need training in the use and selection of research methods, so that all PhD programmes now include some taught units on research methods. While studying these units may be a requirement for completion of the programme, however, the judgement about whether the Doctorate is awarded or not is based only on the quality of the final written thesis. This is the distinctive character of the British PhD.

Integrated PhD

In contrast to the British PhD, the American PhD model is one that has always included taught and assessed course units within the programme. This includes taught units both on research methods and on topics in the field in which the research is being undertaken. Indeed, an American PhD does not require substantial focus on the research thesis topic until the later stages of the programme, and the thesis will not be as long as a British PhD. Recognition that for some students including such taught elements in the programme and that the opportunity to build relevant professional experience and skills (in addition to straight academic skills) would be helpful led to the development of a new and alternative form of PhD in the UK. This is known as the Integrated PhD, or is still sometimes called the 'new route PhD'. An integrated PhD requires a longer period of study than a traditional PhD, with a usual minimum of four years' full-time study or six years' part-time study. The integrated PhD has three elements:

- A taught element of course units in both research methods and skills and in subject-specific or inter-disciplinary topics, which are all formally assessed
- A professional and transferable skills element, including training in a range of skills appropriate to the professional field of the Doctorate but also of a more general nature, which is also assessed
- A research element, which involves undertaking a research project and writing a thesis.

While the final award of the Doctorate depends on the research thesis and its quality, students on an integrated PhD need to complete the other two elements successfully before being permitted to start their thesis.

Professional Doctorate

Professional Doctorates are more similar to the integrated PhD than to the traditional PhD. They include a compulsory programme of taught units in the early stages of the programme. These units include both research methods units and units in the broad subject area of the field of study. Successful completion of the taught units is a requirement for progressing to the research project phase of the programme. Most professional Doctorates have developed in academic fields with a strong professional dimension, and the Doctorate normally includes an indication of the professional field in its title – for example in education a professional Doctorate is called an EdD, in business and management it is called a DBA (Doctor of Business Administration) and in engineering it is called an EngD or DEng. Professional Doctorates have emerged in the UK in the past two decades and are now a well-established form of Doctoral programme.

Progressing to the Doctorate

One of the important features of a Doctoral programme that you need to remember is that at some stage part way through your programme you will have to go through what is called an upgrade or transfer process. The step up from Masters to Doctoral level is quite large, so part way through your programme you will be expected to show that you are able to work at Doctoral level. In many cases this will come at a stage when you have written part of your thesis and done some of the data collection – probably during your second year of study if you are doing a PhD full time, or during your third year of study if you are following a professional Doctorate or integrated PhD programme.

Normally this will involve submitting a sample of your work for review by a panel of academic staff within the department or school you are working in, and attending a *viva voce* meeting. A viva voce (usually just called a viva) is an interview at which you will be asked questions by the panel of staff reviewing your work and will be able to discuss the work you are doing and your plans for completing the research. Following the viva, the panel will decide whether the work you are doing is likely to reach Doctoral standard or not. If it is, then you will be allowed to progress to submit your work for a Doctorate. If it is not then you can usually try to be upgraded at a later date when you have progressed the work and made the changes the panel recommends. However, if you are still not permitted to upgrade then you will normally be allowed to submit your work for a research Masters degree such as an MPhil.

With some professional Doctorate programmes the upgrade process happens at the end of the taught element of the course. At this stage your assignments and written work and the detailed proposal you have written for your research project will be considered to enable a decision to be made about whether you can upgrade to a Doctoral pathway.

What all this means is that although you plan to achieve a Doctorate at the end of your programme you will normally start off by registering for a Masters research degree. This is why most universities advertise their research programmes as being MPhil/PhD programmes.

● ● ● *Pause for thought* ● ● ●

*Think through what type of postgraduate degree will suit **you** best. Are you thinking about a Masters programme or about a Doctorate, or perhaps you are planning to do a Masters followed by a Doctorate? If you are planning a Masters degree then draw up a list of the advantages and disadvantages to you of an MSc, an MA or a named Masters such as an MBA. If you are planning a Doctorate then produce a similar list for each of the main types of Doctorate – PhD, integrated PhD or professional Doctorate. If you are planning a Masters followed by a Doctorate then do this for both programmes.*

What challenges will face me in my postgraduate study?

This book seeks to provide a balanced view of becoming a postgraduate student in the UK. In the chapters that follow we shall explore each of the main challenges you may face and provide some ideas about how you can deal with them and try to ensure that your time as a postgraduate student is happy and successful. The issues we shall deal with are those identified by a significant number of current international students in the UK, and they are covered in the following chapters.

In the rest of Part 1, Chapters 2 (British Universities and International Postgraduate Students) and 3 (Choosing a Postgraduate Programme) look at the range of universities and colleges that provide postgraduate degree programmes, the procedures for applying and getting a place, and how to choose the university and programme that is right for you.

In Part 2, Chapters 4 (Studying in the UK) and 5 (Financing your Postgraduate Programme) look at what it is like to be a postgraduate student in the UK, and at how you can find financial support for your postgraduate studies. Chapters 6 (Moving to the UK) and 7 (Living and Working in the UK) then look at the issues around moving to the UK and at the main challenges of everyday life living and working there.

In Part 3, Chapters 8 to 11 look in detail at studying for a postgraduate degree. Chapter 8 (Studying for a Taught Postgraduate Degree) concentrates on Masters degrees, while Chapter 9 (Planning and Writing your Research Thesis) is about the work of producing a research thesis. Chapter 10 (Tutors, Supervisors and Student Support Systems) considers how you can make best use of the academic staff and university support services, while Chapter 11 (Examinations and Vivas) looks at the topic that often causes most concern for students, the important issue of examinations.

The final part, Chapter 12 (Beyond your Postgraduate Degree) looks at life after your postgraduate degree and considers issues like getting a job and returning to your own country.

KEY RISKS AND HOW TO AVOID THEM

We shall end each of the chapters in this book by summarizing some of the key risks that you need to think about in deciding about a postgraduate programme in the UK. These are not necessarily problems – they are simply things that you need to have thought about in your planning. For each one we suggest an approach to reduce the risk, the things that you can do to try to ensure that your postgraduate choice and course work out well for you. In this chapter we have looked at what you need to consider as you ask the question 'Why do a postgraduate degree?'. The main risks that we have discussed and the possible ways of avoiding them are presented here.

Risk 1: *Not considering both the advantages and disadvantages of a postgraduate programme before you make a decision*   It is important to realize that choosing to do a postgraduate programme will have some disadvantages as well as advantages. Make a list of the advantages and disadvantages for you.

Risk 2: *Thinking that a postgraduate programme is similar to an undergraduate programme*   The subject area might be the same as your undergraduate studies, but postgraduate programmes will require more detailed knowledge, more advanced skills and, most of all, critical and creative skills.

Risk 3: *Choosing to do a postgraduate degree if it will be a handicap to your intended career*   Some careers do not value a postgraduate qualification and may think you are too academic or over-qualified if you have one. Check the expectations for any career you think you may want to enter.

Risk 4: *Doing a postgraduate programme because somebody else wants you to*   A postgraduate programme must be your choice, not the choice of your parents, brothers or sisters or anybody else. Be sure that *you* want to do the programme.

Risk 5: *Doing a postgraduate course because you cannot think of anything else to do*   It is easy to move on to a postgraduate programme without thinking what else you might do, so think through what other options you might be interested in – look at possible jobs, careers or travel for example.

Risk 6: *Choosing a postgraduate programme when you found undergraduate studies difficult*   If you found it difficult to complete your undergraduate programme either because it was difficult or you were not motivated to study, then you will not enjoy a postgraduate course. Think carefully about how you feel about academic study and whether you really want to spend one to three more years studying.

Risk 7: *Not being self-motivated and well-organized*   Postgraduate studies require you to be more independent as a learner than undergraduate programmes, so you need to be well organized. Think carefully about whether you are, or could be, well organized and whether you can motivate yourself without pressure from teachers.

Risk 8: *Not being excited by new ideas and different ways of thinking*   Postgraduate study is about dealing with challenging ideas, looking at existing ideas in new ways and creating new knowledge. You need to be excited by all this if you are going to be successful, so be sure that you enjoy developing your mind in this way.

Risk 9: *Not looking widely at possible postgraduate programmes and universities*   There is a wide range of possible postgraduate programmes as we shall see in Chapter 3. You may just want to continue studying your undergraduate subject, but do explore widely the possible courses and universities you could choose.

Risk 10: *Being afraid to take the risk of doing a postgraduate degree*   Choosing to do anything new has some risks, and choosing to become a postgraduate will be no exception. But if you have the ability to study at this level it may be a bigger risk to decide *not* to continue with your studies – later in life you may regret the missed opportunity. So do not be deterred but rather be prepared to take the risk and go ahead with studying for a postgraduate degree in the UK.

CHAPTER 2

BRITISH UNIVERSITIES AND INTERNATIONAL POSTGRADUATE STUDENTS

- What are the different types of university in the UK?
- Who are the students?
- How many international postgraduate students are there and where do they study?
- How can I find information about individual universities?
- What are the benefits of postgraduate study in the UK?

First thoughts

When you have decided that you are very interested in becoming a postgraduate student in the UK, an important question is *'Where shall I study?'* This is partly an academic question about where the programme you want is available and which university might be the most suitable for you. It is also, though, a geographical and social question, for you will need to decide which part of the UK you want to live in. Which region, town or city will you choose to make your home in for the period of your programme? The UK is a very diverse country, with large industrial and commercial cities, large and small regional towns, and extensive rural areas. And because there are so many institutions and so many locations it means you will be faced with real *choices* about where to go to study. In this chapter we shall look at the variety of universities in the UK, and also at the reasons why international students often choose to go to the UK for their postgraduate studies.

What are the different types of university in the United Kingdom?

Ask almost anybody around the world and they will be able to name one or two famous universities in the UK. The list will almost certainly include Oxford and Cambridge, but other universities such as Imperial College, London or Edinburgh University may also be mentioned. However, these are just a few amongst many. The UK has over 400 institutions that offer higher education programmes (although not all of these are universities) and there are very few parts of the UK which do not have an institution offering degree programmes. These range from the internationally renowned universities to small colleges which offer just a few undergraduate programmes but whose main purpose is lower-level vocational or academic courses. If you choose to go to the UK to study for a postgraduate degree, however, then the number of institutions you can choose from is much smaller. About 140 offer programmes at this level and have the legal power to award Masters or Doctoral degrees. Most are universities, although as we shall explain below, there are other types of institution that offer postgraduate programmes. To keep things simple we shall use the word 'university' throughout this book to mean any institution that offers postgraduate programmes. So what are the main types of higher education institution in the UK?

Universities

The UK has 113 institutions that have the title of university. A university has been granted authority by the government to award degrees and to design and validate its own degree programmes. This means that your final Masters or Doctoral degree will be awarded by the university itself, and the university is responsible for the quality and organization of the programme.

Each university is different from every other one. Each has its own range of degree programmes, its own character and its own reputation for subjects that it is regarded as being good at teaching and researching (and, of course, those where it may not be as strong!). They are different, too, because of their size, location, buildings or campuses and also in the sorts of student they see as their main market. Some see research as a very important part of their work. Others see teaching as the most important activity and may not be quite so concerned about research. In fact, the diversity of UK universities can be one of the most difficult factors in making a choice of where to study. It is important therefore to think carefully about what it is that you need or want from the university you choose – we will look at this issue a little later in this chapter.

To help understand the types of university, though, we can group them in a number of ways. The simplest grouping is into what are called 'old universities' and 'new universities'.

'Old' universities Old universities are those that were called 'university' before 1992. It includes some that are among the oldest in the world. Despite the name, though, not all of these universities have long histories, and there are a number of types of 'old' university.

The **ancient universities** are those founded more than 150 years ago, and this group includes only five institutions – Oxford (founded in 1096), Cambridge (1209), Edinburgh (1583), London (1826) and Durham (1832).

The University of London is not really a single institution. It is made up of a number of colleges, each of which can be regarded as a separate university, and some of which have large numbers of students. Some provide a broad-range of programmes, for example University College or King's College, while others have a specialist subject focus – for example, the School of Oriental and African Studies (SOAS), the London School of Economics (LSE) and the University of London Institute of Education.

An important feature of Oxford, Cambridge and Durham universities is the individual colleges which make up the university. A college (for example, Balliol College Oxford, Trinity College Cambridge or Hatfield College Durham) is a small separate institution that recruits its own students, but who are then automatically students of the university. Most take both male and female students, although a few remain as single sex colleges (for example St Hilda's College in Oxford and Newnham College Cambridge are only for women). The colleges provide accommodation, social and study facilities in their own right and are small communities, usually in distinctive and attractive ancient buildings. Some teaching is undertaken by the colleges, but most is provided by the academic departments of the university. The university is responsible for examinations and standards and provides the degree award at the end of a programme. Students in such a college environment often have a very strong allegiance to their college as well as to the university overall.

In the late 1800s, universities began to be recognized as important in providing the knowledge on which economic growth depended and as a symbol in themselves of knowledge and power. Several of the large cities in the UK established universities at this time. In many cases the money to establish them came from the wealthy industrialists and business communities in these cities, and the universities that date from this period are known as **civic universities**. They include the universities of Birmingham, Bristol, Leeds, Liverpool, Manchester, Sheffield and Glasgow, and The Queen's University in Belfast in Northern Ireland. All were founded close to the city centre and are characterized by many large Victorian buildings of dark stone or brick.

Between 1900 and 1960 a number of other cities developed universities with the same characteristics, including Leicester, Nottingham and Southampton. This whole group of universities are sometimes referred to as 'redbrick universities' because of their distinctive architectural characteristics.

During the early years of the 1960s a British government report (the Robbins Report) recommended that the UK needed to increase the number of its universities to support economic growth. As a result many new universities were created. Some of these **1960s universities** were established from new, built on greenfield campus sites, such as the universities of Bath, Essex, Keele, Lancaster and Warwick. Others (often called technological universities) were created from already existing colleges of advanced technology. These included the universities of Aston, Brunel and Bradford, with specialisms in technology-based subjects such as engineering, computer science and applied science. Most of these universities are based on specialist campuses and are characterized by 1960s architectural designs using concrete and glass.

'New' universities   The 'new' universities are those institutions given university status since 1992. Many are not 'new' in a strict sense as they have been educational institutions for many years, some with histories that date back into the eighteenth century. Most are what were known in the 1970s and 1980s as polytechnics. Polytechnics were founded as colleges for technical education by the local government of cities and to meet the need for technical education for local people. During the 1960s and 1970s, as part of the push to expand higher education following the Robbins Report, many of these colleges developed undergraduate degree programmes in technical and vocational subjects and took on the title of Polytechnics. By 1990 there were over 30 Polytechnics. In 1992 the government decided to give the polytechnics the same powers and status as universities, and as a result a large group of new universities was created, including for example, the universities of Hertfordshire, Luton, Portsmouth, Plymouth and Sunderland.

There is not a simple difference between old and new universities. Old universities often have a stronger tradition of research, but many new universities have excellent research records, and some are the leading research universities in particular subject areas. New universities are often thought of as placing more emphasis on teaching than research, but the teaching in many old universities is usually of a high quality too. For these reasons it is important to choose between universities not on the basis of whether they are old or new but according to which one meets your own particular academic and personal needs.

University colleges and colleges of higher education

University colleges and colleges of higher education are small to medium-sized institutions, often with a narrower range of academic disciplines than universities. Almost all were originally teacher training colleges, which during the 1980s and 1990s widened their range of degree programmes to include, often, combined subject undergraduate degrees. Many are notable for their small campuses with a distinct sense of community. They often have only a few postgraduate degree programmes with relatively small numbers of Masters and Doctoral students. More importantly, though, the degrees they award will not be their own – they will be degrees validated by a university, but taught in the college. Remember that only universities can award and validate their own degrees.

The number of university colleges and colleges of higher education (CHEs) has declined since 1992. Many CHEs have been awarded the title of university college, and some have been given full university status. Some of the newest universities in the UK were until recently CHEs and university colleges. King Alfred's College, Winchester, for example, became University College Winchester in 2003 and then the University of Winchester in 2005.

Specialist colleges

A small number of higher education institutions are highly specialized in that they only provide programmes in a small range of subject areas. These include specialist agricultural colleges (e.g. Sparsholt College in Hampshire) and those with a focus on the creative or performing arts. The Central School of Speech and Drama in London, for example, specializes in drama and the creative arts.

Colleges of further and higher education

Across the UK most vocational education for 16–19-year-olds has traditionally been provided by colleges of further education, and most large towns will have at least one 'FE college'. Since 1992 a number of these colleges have started to provide some courses at undergraduate level, often in collaboration with a local university and with the degrees awarded by that university. There are over 300 such colleges in the UK and most now provide some form of higher education – in some cases this has become enough for them to change their name to become colleges of further and higher education (CFHEs). It is rare for such colleges to provide postgraduate programmes however, and so they will not be within our focus area throughout most of this book.

Other university groupings

While you may read descriptions of UK universities that describe them in the way we have indicated above (for example as 'new' or 'old' universities), a number of other groupings have become established to represent the interest of particular types of university or for marketing purposes. The following are some of the main groups you may come across.

- **The Russell Group** (www.russellgroup.ac.uk): an informal group of 19 universities which regard themselves as the premier research universities in the UK.
- **The 1994 Group** (www.1994group.ac.uk): a group of 19 research-led 'old' universities.
- **The Coalition of Modern Universities** (www.epolitix.com): a group of 29 'new' universities.
- **International groups:** many universities in the UK have a high status and standing around the world, and a number of international groupings have been established between leading universities in many parts of the world to promote their own research and academic interests. Two such groups are the Worldwide Universities Network (WUN) (www.wun.ac.uk) and Universitas 21 (www.universitas21.com).

Membership of any of these groups by a university is not in itself an indication of the quality of a particular programme that it might offer. Rather it indicates the aims and mission of the university and the position it is choosing for itself in the UK and global higher education market. It may indicate something of the priority the university places on research or teaching and how far it is part of national and global networks of researchers – but it should be used with caution in choosing where to study for your Masters or Doctoral degree.

● ● ● *Pause for thought* ● ● ●

Although you will need to look at the exact nature of any university you are considering applying to, you probably have some ideas of the sort of institution that you would most like to study at. Does it have to be one of the world's top research universities? Must it be one that is very well known in your own country? Would you prefer a university that is very large or one that is smaller? Take a few moments to write down your thoughts about your ideal UK university.

We will use these thoughts in the next chapter when we look in detail at how to choose.

Who are the students?

A key part of the character of any university is the students. Most students at UK universities are British, of course, and most are on undergraduate programmes. Over 40% of young people in the UK now go on to university, which means the students come from a wide range of backgrounds and experience. Overall there are approximately 2,400,000 students in UK universities, and some 525,000 of these are studying postgraduate programmes. Of course, the universities vary very much in size. The largest universities have over 20,000 students (for example, the University of Leeds) while some of the smaller institutions may have only between 2,000 and 5,000 students.

The number of postgraduates in the UK has increased by over 20% since 1997. Overall, the numbers of postgraduate students is generally larger in the 'old' universities than in the 'new' universities, although the numbers in 'new' universities have been increasing much faster than in the 'old' universities. By 2003 the 'old' universities had 66% of all the UK postgraduate students while the 'new' universities had 34%. In 2002/03 the ten universities with the largest number of research students were Cambridge, Oxford, Birmingham, Nottingham, University College London, Sheffield, Edinburgh, Manchester, Leeds and Newcastle. The ten universities with the most taught postgraduate students were The Open University (all part-time, distance learning students), Westminster, City, Birmingham, Strathclyde, Leeds, Warwick, London Metropolitan, Manchester Metropolitan and Sheffield Hallam.

How many international postgraduate students are there and where do they study?

In reading this book you will already have made a decision to consider studying for a postgraduate degree outside your own country. While there is some movement of students between most countries, there is a clear pattern in the international market. The provision of postgraduate programmes for international students is dominated by a small number of countries. The USA receives almost 60% of international students and the UK approximately 20% each year. Most of the rest of the market is dominated by Australia, New Zealand and the countries of Europe.

In 2004 there were approximately 80,000 international students studying a Masters-level programme in the UK and 17,000 studying for a Doctorate. This number has been growing steadily for more than thirty years, and has doubled since 1999. International students now represent over 63% of all Masters students and 34% of all Doctoral students in the UK. And they come from all over the world, with virtually every country being represented in that international community. Most of the students come from a relatively small number of countries. China is the largest, mainly because it has the world's largest population, but the biggest providers also include the countries of Western Europe, Asia and the Middle East.

The largest numbers are in the largest universities, but even smaller institutions have significant numbers of international postgraduate students. In 2002/03 (the most recent year for which national data are available) the universities where international students make up the largest proportion of the whole student body were:

London School of Economics	42%
Cranfield	32%
Essex	23%
University of Manchester Institute of Science and Technology (now part of the University of Manchester)	18%
Oxford	16%
Cambridge	15%
Imperial College, London	15%

A large population of postgraduates or of international students may, of course, be an attractive or unattractive feature of a university for you. Large numbers may indicate a great strength in meeting the academic needs of postgraduates and may provide a large international community, but may lead to an individual student feeling almost lost amongst those large numbers and perhaps having less access to tutors, or perhaps experiencing teaching in large classes. Small numbers, though, may enable strong individual support to be provided and a strong and intimate sense of community to be developed – but that may mean there are smaller classes and a narrower range of programme options. Remember that a large part of your learning as a postgraduate student will come from the other students, so you may want to find a programme or university with a lively postgraduate community. You need to decide what suits you and your needs best of all.

How can I find information about individual universities?

We have shown here the range and variety of UK universities. To find out information about them individually there are a number of good sources.

- **The HERO website**. HERO (Higher Education and Research Opportunities) is an organization funded by all of the main organizations involved in higher education in the UK, including the funding bodies, the universities themselves and the government. Its website (*www.hero.ac.uk*), therefore, is an official source of key information, and provides a lot of detail about universities and postgraduate study in the UK. Of particular use is its map and database of UK universities. This enables you to find the location of every university or HE institution and to find a full profile of its size, expertise, programmes, campus and facilities.
- **University websites**. Every university has its own website, which will provide in-depth information about every aspect of the university, its programmes and its application procedures. We have included a full list of university website addresses in Appendix L.
- **Handbooks, guides and other websites**. In the appendices we have included details of a range of published handbooks and guides to postgraduate study and also websites with similar information. Most of these contain descriptions and profiles of each university.

Every university, of course, also produces a prospectus that provides considerable detail about the university, its programmes and student life. Most universities will have a specialist Postgraduate Prospectus that you should certainly read for those universities you are seriously interested in. You can obtain the Postgraduate Prospectus using the university's website. In addition, though, it is worth reading the Undergraduate Prospectus for each university you are considering, as this will add more to your image of what the university is like. The problem with prospectuses, of course, is that they are marketing documents, and will not tell you the disadvantages or problems of the university. It is helpful therefore to try to find an 'Alternative Prospectus' for the university. These are produced by the Student Union, written by students for students, and will give a very clear view of the university from a student perspective. The Student Union part of the university website should have details about how to obtain an alternative prospectus.

What are the benefits of postgraduate study in the UK?

So why do so many international students choose to come to the UK? The precise motivation for choosing will always be highly individual for every student, but overall there appear to be a number of reasons why postgraduates choose the UK to study. The list we give here has been produced by asking international postgraduate students why they chose to come to the UK to study, and it reads a little like an advertisement for British universities! Clearly, those who chose to go to other countries will have equally good reasons why they preferred those destinations, but since this book is about postgraduate programmes in the UK it is reasonable to focus solely on the UK here.

1   There are a large number of universities and higher education institutions which provide postgraduate programmes at Masters and Doctoral level.
2   Many of the universities have an international reputation for the quality of their programmes.
3   The international research world has a very high profile of UK academics who are researching and publishing in their specialist fields and are therefore well known internationally.
4   British universities have a reputation for the high quality of their programmes.
5   British universities have actively marketed their programmes to international students over the past two decades.
6   British degrees have a good reputation in the employment market, whether that is for jobs in business or the public service sector or in the academic world.
7   British universities have a long history compared to many. They have built up strong relationships with national governments, with schools, colleges and universities in many countries, and particularly with those countries that are now part of the Commonwealth.
8   English is one of the main international languages of the world, both in the business and academic communities. This means that many potential students find it easier to study here, and also that the experience of studying in English provides an invaluable transferable skill.
9   The UK has a reputation for a tolerant, open and welcoming approach to international visitors and students.
10   British history and culture is known throughout the world and many students are attracted by the possibility of combining their postgraduate studies with a period living in the UK and experiencing British culture first hand.

● ● ●   *Pause for thought*   ● ● ●

*Think about how important for **you** studying in the UK will be. For each of the ten reasons for studying in the UK listed above decide whether it is:*

(a) *Very important to you*
(b) *An interesting but not very important aspect of coming to the UK*
(c) *Of no interest to you*

Score three points for every (a), two for every (b) and one for every (c). If you score 25+ then the UK should probably be your choice for your postgraduate programme. If you score 20–24 then coming to the UK will still probably be a stimulating and valuable opportunity. If you score less than 20 then you might feel that a different country would be a better choice.

KEY RISKS AND HOW TO AVOID THEM

Making the right decision about where you want to study is crucial to having a good postgraduate experience and ensuring that you gain the best advantage from it. This list of key risks identifies what you should be careful to avoid when making this decision.

Risk 1: *Thinking there are only a few universities in the UK for postgraduate studies* It is not unusual to hear of international students who thought there were only four or five universities in the UK where they could study – Oxford, Cambridge, London and one or two others. In reality there are about 140 that offer postgraduate programmes and degrees. Check the range of handbooks and websites listed in Chapter 3 and the Appendices to find out about them all.

Risk 2: *Not understanding the differences between the main types of university in the UK* The number of universities means that there are many different types of institution. After reading this chapter you should be able to identify the main groups and differences between them.

Risk 3: *Thinking that the quality of your programme is dependent on the type of university you choose* The UK has national systems for checking the quality of programmes at universities, so you can be sure that all programmes are of a satisfactory quality. Just because a university has a good overall reputation, of course, does not necessarily mean that a particular programme is excellent – and lower 'status' universities have some excellent postgraduate programmes. You need to check out the quality of any individual programme you are considering, and we will explain in the next chapter how to do that.

Risk 4: *Thinking that international reputation is the only important factor in choosing a university* Reputation may be important to you – you may feel that you only want to go to an internationally famous university. But be aware that just because a university is famous does not necessarily mean that the individual programme you are looking at is the best one in the field.

Risk 5: *Choosing a university of the wrong size* Think about your own needs. Will you be happiest in a very large university or in a small community? Remember you could feel 'lost' in a large institution or it could provide a stimulating wide range of opportunities. Think this one through carefully for yourself.

Risk 6: *Not understanding that UK universities are international communities*   Do not expect to be the only international student in your university. UK universities are international communities, so it will be a chance to meet not just UK students and staff but also people from around the world. Be ready for this.

Risk 7: *Choosing a university just because it has a large international student community from your own country*   While it may be reassuring to know that there are other students from your own country, there is always a risk that you will not mix with UK and other international students. Think carefully about how big an issue this might be for you.

Risk 8: *Not recognizing that UK universities are British*   This will sound strange – but it is important to realize that UK universities are British in culture, and will be different from the university you have experienced already as an undergraduate in your own country. If you go to a UK university, see it as an opportunity to sample British life and not as a cultural threat to try to keep at a distance.

Risk 9: *Not considering a range of national settings*   Be sure that you have considered other national settings as well as the UK. Can your own country's universities provide what you need? And what about other countries?

Risk 10: *Forgetting that UK universities are good at marketing to recruit international students*   The ethical standards of UK university marketing are very high and you can be confident that you will be given honest and truthful information to help you make a good choice. But as with all marketing, the universities will emphasize their strengths and keep quiet about their less attractive features. It is important therefore that you find information from many different sources and not just the universities themselves.

CHAPTER 3
CHOOSING A POSTGRADUATE PROGRAMME

- How can I get general advice about applying to the UK for a postgraduate programme?
- How do I find out what programmes are available?
- How do I choose between the programmes?
- What should my programme include?
- How good are the programmes?
- What qualifications will I need?
- Where do I want to live?
- What social and cultural facilities do I need?
- What should I do if I have a disability?
- How do I apply for a place?

First thoughts

In the first two chapters we have looked at some of the general reasons why you might choose to become a postgraduate student, at the range of programmes that are available and at the different universities in the UK. Now that you have a general understanding of postgraduate study in the UK you can start to make the detailed choice of programme and university. Many students make their choices quite quickly, using only a limited amount of information to make their decision. However, by thinking carefully about what is on offer and about exactly what your needs and wants are in a postgraduate programme you can make a choice that will suit you even better. While such careful thought can take longer, it is more likely to find you a programme and university that will better meet your needs – and that means your chances of successfully completing the course will be higher. In this chapter we shall look at this process of choice and suggest a range of ways that can improve your decision-making.

How can I get general advice on applying to the UK for a postgraduate programme?

Most students thinking of applying to the UK for a postgraduate programme will feel they need some advice and help to do this. While the choice, decision and application must be done by you, very helpful support can be obtained from a number of sources. First, of course, the main aim of this book is to provide you with general advice and guidance on applying to the UK for a postgraduate programme! In addition, though, the most useful source of guidance is probably The British Council. The British Council has offices in almost 150 countries and provides support and information on all aspects of British life and culture. One of its key roles is to promote UK education internationally, and it does this through its brand of EducationUK. Initial advice can be found directly on The British Council websites (*www.britishcouncil.org* or *www. educationUK.org*). On the website you will find access to education advice for applicants from your own country. This contains contact details and website addresses for The British Council in your own country, and information on how to make an appointment with a British Council Education Officer.

You should also visit the website of UKCOSA, which provides excellent detailed guidance and advice. UKCOSA is an organization established specifically to provide information, advice and support to international students and their website address is *www.ukcosa.org.uk*.

How do I find out what programmes are available?

The first stage in making your choice is to find out which universities offer programmes in your field. For well-established subjects there may be 40 or 50 universities offering a suitable Masters course, and for research degrees most universities will take Doctoral students in most subjects. For highly specialist programmes, though, there may be only one or two universities that offer a suitable course – so you will need to plan your search very carefully.

There are a number of important sources of information that you can use for this process.

Internet Search

The internet will give you access to information on every programme that is available, since all UK universities will have programme details on the internet.

There are two ways in which you can use the internet to help you. The first is to use a **search engine** such as Google or Yahoo! and enter the key words for your subject. For example you could use the search terms 'Masters + degree + Software + Engineering' to search for a Masters degree in software engineering. This will provide a list of websites with information on programmes in this field.

The second approach you can use is to visit some of the established **websites** with information on postgraduate degrees, and which have assembled much of the information you might need. Websites such as these are listed below, and each has a searchable database of postgraduate programmes.

- **The British Council Website** (*www.educationUK.org*). This is the official website of The British Council, funded and supported by the UK government.
- **The UKCOSA website** (*www.ukcosa.org.uk*). This is the website of the independent UKCOSA organization, which provides support and guidance for international students.
- **The Hobsons website** (*www.postgrad.hobsons.com*). Hobsons is a commercial organization with a long history of providing detailed programme and careers information to students in the UK.
- **The Prospects website** (*www.prospects.ac.uk*). UK Prospects is operated by a partnership of UK educational organizations, including government departments, funding bodies and university groups.
- **The Association of MBAs website** (*www.mbaworld.com*). This site provides detailed information on MBA programmes in the UK.
- **The Studylink website** (*www.studylink.com*). This site provides listings of postgraduate taught programmes.
- *The Guardian* **Education website** (*www.EducationGuardian.co.uk/courses*). This website provides information on taught postgraduate programmes and has a separate section on MBA programmes.
- **The Hotcourses website** (*www.hotcourses.com*). This site provides course and scholarship information.
- **The FindaMasters/FindaPhD website** (*www.FindAMasters.com* and *www.Find APhD.com*). These websites advertise programmes only for those universities which choose to use them.

Postgraduate study guides

There are a large number of publications which have been produced to provide information on postgraduate programmes in the UK. These can be found in the library of your own university or in the offices of The British Council. There are two sorts of guide, and it is important to know the difference between them.

Official guides are those produced by UK organizations representing the British government, universities, professional or charitable organizations such as The British Council. They will contain information on all the programmes that they know of, and do not charge universities for including information about their courses. These publications include:

- **The British Council Guide to UK Education – Postgraduate and MBA**. This is a large handbook containing detailed information on all postgraduate programmes and universities in the UK, together with advice on many aspects of life and study in the UK.

- **The Prospects Postgraduate Directory**. This is available as a complete directory or in separate parts for Arts and Humanities (Volume 1), Science and Engineering (Volume 2) and Business and Social Sciences (Volume 3).
- **Postgraduate UK**. This is produced jointly by ProspectsUK and The British Council and is a guide to life and study in the UK as a postgraduate.
- **The Official MBA Handbook**. This guide is produced by the Association of MBAs, and includes information on accredited courses at MBA, DBA and PEMM (Pre-Experience Masters in General Management) level.

Unofficial guides are those which are produced by commercial businesses. They may charge universities a fee for including their programmes in the lists of courses, and they may not provide a full list of all the courses in a particular subject area. They are nevertheless a very useful source of information. These publications include:

- **Postgrad UK.** This is published by Hobsons and provides information on postgraduate and research programmes in the UK.
- **The Hobsons MBA Guide.** This provides specific information on MBA programmes.
- **The *Guardian* Guide to Postgraduate Courses.** This is published annually in The *Guardian* newspaper in June.

Personal contacts

A good source of information will be the academic staff in your current university. They will have a good knowledge of their subject area and may well know which universities offer programmes in the subjects that you want to study. The advantage of using such personal contacts is that they may know the staff who teach on some of the programmes either personally or through their publications and research, and so can give a very detailed insight. The disadvantage is that they may not know *all* the programmes available, their information may not be up to date and they may not know of new programmes that have been started. Also, if you are an excellent student they may have a vested interest in your staying on at your current university!

Education agents

Another source of information is through education agents. Agents provide information and support for students seeking to study abroad, and will have access to many sources of useful information. Agents earn their income by either charging applicants for assisting them to apply or by charging a fee to the university with which you finally register. This means they will have a commercial relationship with a selected number of universities. They may, therefore, not necessarily provide information on all the universities and programmes available and may encourage you to apply to those that will provide the agents with the best financial benefits for themselves.

Students are often wary about the advice and help they receive from education agents. However, most are very reputable and provide a useful and professional service to both students and universities. You can check whether the agent you are considering using is registered with the national agents' association in your own country by looking on the English UK website at *www. englishuk.com/students/agent_associations_list.pdf*. This will give you contact details of registered agents, and while it does not provide any guarantees of quality, it at least indicates whether the agent is recognized in their own country.

If you use some or all of these information sources you will produce a list of most of the suitable programmes that there are in your chosen specialist field. However, you need to be aware of two important issues – new programmes and programme titles.

Most universities introduce new programmes each year, as new subjects or fields or topics become important or because they feel there is a market for a particular new programme. These programmes might be too new to appear in some of the publications and directories, so it is important to use the internet to search as well as using other sources.

It is also important to think broadly about the titles of programmes that you might be interested in. Although you may be looking for a Masters programme or a PhD programme in Urban Planning, programmes in this field may have a wide range of titles – for example, Urban Management, Planning and Society, Geography and Planning, Urban Design. It is important, therefore, to search using as wide a range of titles, names and key words as you can think of. It is also important to consider how a programme with a general title might have options or specialist pathways within it that enable you to focus on your particular interests. For example, an MA in Theatre Studies may enable you to focus on Elizabethan Theatre, Costume Design or Production. It is always helpful, therefore, to look at exactly what is covered and what the options may be within a programme with a general name.

How do I choose between the programmes?

When you have a list of the possible programmes available you can move to the second phase of choosing, which involves a careful comparison of the programmes and the universities. It is helpful to think about what you are looking for before you begin the comparison stage so that you know what is important for you. However, you should also be aware that there may be aspects of a programme or a university that you had not thought about but which are quite attractive when you discover them.

So, what factors should you consider in choosing? Choosing a university and programme is very much an individual decision, and will depend on a wide range of factors that you might want to take into account. Broadly, though, the factors to consider can be divided into two groups: the academic factors, relating to the programme and the university, and the personal factors, relating to what is important in your own life and experiences while you are in the UK.

Academic factors

The main academic factors relate to the content and organization of the programme and its quality. If you are looking for a Masters degree then you will need to decide whether you want to do a general programme in your subject, which will probably allow you to take some specialist topics of particular interest, or whether you want a programme that is highly specialized. This will determine whether there is a wide or narrow choice of programmes open to you. If you are looking for a Doctoral programme the same is true – but the choice is likely to be quite narrow because the academic staff with expertise in your specialist area who can supervise your research may be found in only a small number of universities.

Whether there are large numbers of programmes in your field or only one or two, you will want to identify which is the 'best'. But 'best' is a difficult idea, for it depends on how you measure it. Does 'best' mean the one that has most applicants or is the most difficult to get a place on, or does it mean the one whose graduates all get good jobs afterwards? Does 'best' mean the one that is taught by academic staff with an international reputation for their research, or does it mean the one with the teachers who spend more time working to support the students on the course? Does 'best' mean the one with the state of the art computing equipment or the one with the excellent modern library facilities? Does 'best' mean the programme at the university with the greatest international reputation, or might it mean a programme in an excellent department at a university that is less well known? All this means that you have to decide what makes a programme 'best' for you. The list below shows some of the academic factors that might be important in deciding which programme is 'best':

- The programme is in one of the most prestigious universities.
- The programme is taught by well-known researchers.
- The programme has a high reputation for the quality of teaching.
- There is a good ratio of staff to students.
- The programme has excellent teaching resources (e.g. computers, workshops).
- The programme has access to an excellent library.
- Graduates from the programme mostly get excellent jobs afterwards.
- The programme attracts large numbers of students.
- The programme has many specialist options within it.

In addition, for a Doctoral programme you might want to add the following to the list:

- All students have their own desk and computer.
- There are several research students each year working in your particular field.
- The research training programme has good ratings and a strong reputation.
- The department has a number of students with prestigious scholarships, indicating it is highly regarded for research training.

We shall look at the issue of quality in more detail later in the chapter.

Personal and social factors

These are the factors that are much more personal, and depend on how you want to live your life and spend your time while you are a postgraduate student. It includes factors to do with housing, social life, cultural life in the university and the nature and character of the town or city that the university is in. The following is a list of some of these factors:

- Does the university have accommodation in university residences available for international postgraduate students?
- Does it provide accommodation for students who have their families with them?
- How close to the university will you be able to live?
- Does the university have a large community of international students?
- Does it have a large community of students of your own nationality/faith?
- Does the university and the department have good social facilities and arrangements for postgraduate students, e.g. common rooms, eating facilities, clubs and societies?
- Does the university have specialist facilities for your preferred cultural needs (e.g. a Muslim prayer room)?
- Do you want to live in a large city, a smaller city or a smaller town or rural area?
- Do you want to live in or close to London?
- Do you want to live in a historic city or a modern or industrial city?
- Do you want to live with good access to attractive countryside and/or the coast?
- Will the cost of living in a particular town or city be relatively high or low?

Of course, although you can get the factual answers to many of these questions from prospectuses, handbooks and websites, bear in mind that what often makes a place a happy one is the chance set of friendships that you will make and the general feel and comfort of the place. A university that answers 'yes' to every one of your questions may still not be the best place to go – and often students who have by chance gone to a university that at first sight did not seem to meet many of their criteria have a wonderful experience as a student. To get the full picture it is always worth asking people you know – wherever you are in the world you will find people who have attended particular universities, and many universities have alumni societies in other countries who can arrange for you to meet and talk with a former student. Details will be on their website or in their prospectus.

To help you to explore these academic and personal/social factors for yourself we shall now look at five key questions. In each case we shall suggest that you think through the questions and what you are looking for so that you can then compare different universities and programmes more carefully. The five key questions are:

- What should my programme include?
- How good are the programmes?
- What qualifications will I need?
- Where do I want to live?
- What social and cultural facilities do I want my university to have?

What should my programme include?

In some ways this is an easy question, as you are probably clear about the broad subject area that you want to study – Music, or Civil Engineering for example. However, it is in the detail that you will discover that every programme is different. If you want to do a Masters in Music do you want to focus on composition, music theory, musicology, performance, contemporary music, music and business, or another aspect of academic music? Do you want a broad programme or one focused on just one of these areas. And there is then a wide range of issues about the teaching methods and the facilities that will be available to you. To help you decide on what you are looking for, work through the *Pause for thought* below.

● ● ● *Pause for thought* ● ● ●

(a) *If you are looking for a Masters programme write down the topics/subjects that you would like to have in your programme, and against each one indicate if it is an essential (E) or only desirable (D) part of the programme.*

(b) *If you are looking for a Doctoral programme write down the research fields or topics that you are interested in working on.*

(c) *Write down the skills that you want your programme to include (e.g. specialist computing or design skills), and against each one indicate if it is an essential (E) or only desirable (D) part of the programme.*

(d) *Write down the facilities you expect your programme to make available to you. Don't include things like a library, as all universities will have this, but do include things like access to your own individual computer or your own desk or your own area of lab space or easy access to practice studios.*

(e) *Who do you want to be taught or supervised by? Do you want to work with well-known international names in your field? The list below is a range of situations – write down which one is the minimum you require for your programme:*

- *The department has many international names, and they contribute to the teaching of the programme*
- *The department has many international names, although they may not contribute to the teaching of the programme*

- *The department has one or two international names, and they may contribute to the teaching of the programme*
- *The department has no names I know, but the staff who teach on the programme have a good record of research and are well-qualified*
- *The department has no names I know and few staff in my field have a good record of research, but the teaching is of good quality*

(f) *What size department or programme do you want to be in? Write down whether you want there to be a large or small number of postgraduate students.*

When you have completed the exercise in the *Pause for thought* you can look in detail at the prospectuses or websites of the programmes and universities that you identified from your general search. This will enable you to narrow the choice down to a small number of programmes that seem to meet your needs quite closely. This is your short list of places to consider applying to.

How good are the programmes?

The standard of British postgraduate programmes is very high. The quality and standards of every programme are controlled in a number of ways, in part by each university itself and in part by quality assurance systems of other organizations. Every university, for example, has to meet the standards imposed by the national Quality Assurance Agency (QAA), which sets out general standards about Masters programmes and Doctorates. These standards are checked in universities by inspection visits, known as audits, and the results are published on the QAA website (*www.qaa.ac.uk*).

In addition, any programme that has a professional component (for example in teacher training, or in engineering or medicine) has to gain approval from a relevant professional body. For example, a postgraduate programme in Marketing will be accredited by the Chartered Institute of Marketing (CIM) as well as leading to the award of a university Masters degree. Similarly, if you are considering an MBA programme, then the accreditation of the programme will be an important aspect of your choice. There are three main accreditations that MBA programmes may receive:

AMBA – accreditation by the Association of MBAs
EQUIS – accreditation by the European Quality Improvement System
AASCB – accreditation by the Association to Advance Collegiate Schools of Business

Each has its own detailed requirements and tells you something different about the programme and school. For details of the differences and their meanings look at the website at *www.mba-central.com*.

Following a programme accredited by a professional organization can be important in getting a job after you graduate, and if you want to take a programme in a professional field you should check which professional accreditation is essential and which is advisable. You can do this by checking with the relevant professional body in the UK (use the internet) or, if there is one, the equivalent professional body in your own country.

Thirdly, all programmes are checked for standards by a system of external examiners. External examiners are usually academic staff from a different university who look at the work of students on the programme and write an annual report on the quality and standards of the programme. From September 2005 these reports have to be published on the QAA website at *www.tqi.ac.uk*, and you can look for yourself at what the external examiners say about the programme. In addition universities are required to publish on this website a range of information about the nature, quality and character of each degree programme, and you can search the site by university and programme.

And then there are the league tables! Over the past ten years the British media have started to produce performance tables to compare universities. These are *not* official publications, for they are not produced by the universities themselves or by the UK government. They are produced by national newspapers using data that are available from official sources. The most well-known league tables are:

- **The Times League Tables**. These are available at *www.timesonline.co.uk*. There are two main types of tables – tables of overall university gradings and tables of gradings subject by subject.
- **The Sunday Times League Tables**. These are different from *The Times* League Tables but are also available at *www.timesonline.co.uk*.
- **The Times Higher Education Supplement League Tables**. These are available at *www.thes.co.uk*. In addition to the standard two forms of tables, the THES has produced in 2005 a league table of the world's top 200 universities, which enables you to compare UK universities with other internationally known universities. It has also produced a league table based on the National Student Survey, published in September 2005, which shows the satisfaction of students with the experiences they had at their university.
- **The Guardian League Tables**. These are available at *www.EducationGuardian. co.uk/guides*.

How helpful are league tables? They have the advantage of giving a quick impression of relative quality and can certainly help you distinguish the very best from the very worst. But they need to be read with care and not used as the only source of information, because they have a number of problems:

- Each newspaper calculates its table in its own way using a complicated formula that balances academic achievements and facilities, and it is not always easy to know exactly how the calculation has been done. The newspapers producing the tables are often trying to emphasize particular aspects of universities – for example *The Guardian* tables put very little weighting on a university's research income and achievements but put more weighting on its undergraduate teaching achievements.

- The data used are not always up-to-date.
- In most tables the 'score' difference in the table is quite small. This means that there may be very little difference between universities that are separated by many places, and year by year universities can move up or down a long way with only a small change in their data.
- The data in the tables are mainly about research and about undergraduate programmes, so they may not be very helpful in choosing a postgraduate programme. It is now possible for you to make your own league table using the weightings that you think are important to you. This facility is available on *The Times* newspaper website at *http://www.thegooduniversityguide.co.uk/* – but remember that the basic data in the table is still that used to make *The Times* league table.

So, you should treat league tables with caution, and look at several before you decide what the tables are telling you about a particular subject in a particular university. On the other hand, the universities take the tables seriously, know that potential students use them to help in their choice and make great efforts to ensure the data on which the tables are based are as advantageous as they can be. Universities at the top of the tables will say how useful they are – universities near the bottom will say they are of little importance!

There are two other official sources of information that can be used to help to judge the quality of a university or a subject within a university – the results of the Research Assessment Exercise (RAE) and the results of Quality Audit by the QAA. The RAE is undertaken by the Higher Education Funding Council every few years (1992, 1996, 2001 with the next one in 2008) to judge the quality of research being undertaken in universities. Its exact methods and results are changed each time, which makes it difficult to use the information, but the results are published and can help to compare universities. In 2001 each subject discipline in each university that undertakes research in that field was graded on a six point scale (1,2,3,4,5,5*), taking into account publications and research in the previous five years. Those graded 5 and 5* ('five star') are those with a strong international reputation for their research quality, while those graded 4 have strong national and international research. Those graded 1–3 have some good research areas but not with the same international profile. You can find all the 2001 RAE research ratings by looking at the website at *www.hero.ac.uk/rae*.

If you are applying to do a postgraduate programme then the quality of research in your subject at the university will be of interest to you. You will certainly believe that those universities with the best research record will have the expert academic staff to provide you with the best programme. In addition it is likely that gaining a Masters or Doctorate from a highly rated university will be seen as a better achievement. This is largely true, of course, but the RAE rating is not an assured guarantee, for a number of reasons:

- The grades are now five or six years old and staff move on or retire. The next RAE is in 2008, and will also use a different scoring method and rating than the 2001 RAE.

- Academic staff in a department that is strongly research-driven may spend their time doing their own research rather than teaching on programmes or supporting research students. You may be taught or supervised by a more junior member of staff or even by other research students. So, while you may be able to work alongside the world-famous professor, you need to be sure whether this is really the case.
- Research ratings do not tell you anything about teaching standards. You need to check teaching standards from examiners reports or other sources.

Some national governments insist that they will only give their own scholarships and support to students who go to study in a department rated at grade 4 or above (or sometimes grade 5 or above). Clearly this may mean that you have no choice. But, if you do have a choice, be prepared to consider other universities, since RAE ratings are not everything. And remember that even grade 1 rated departments may have individual staff with great expertise either as researchers or in teaching at Masters or Doctoral levels, and even grade 5 rated departments may have staff who are less good researchers or teachers.

Some guide books, and some of the published league tables, make use of Teaching Quality data from the QAA. These data are based on individual inspections of subject departments in universities, and give a score out of 24 for the quality of teaching. Most departments score 18–24 marks. The quality inspection system has now changed, so that it does not use a scoring system at all, and the data used are from the period 1992–2002 – some may therefore be over ten years old. We would not recommend placing any reliance on such data to indicate teaching quality.

What qualifications will I need?

An important question every potential postgraduate will ask is 'Will I have the qualifications to be offered a place on the programme?' Qualifications are important, of course, but universities make their decisions about whom to accept onto their postgraduate programmes on a range of factors. Some of these will be formal educational qualifications that you either have or expect to have, but others will include your English language skills, and what is said about you in the references that you provide. Others will depend on the university's judgement about whether it can provide you with a suitable programme. So, for example, many postgraduate programmes will have quotas – a maximum number of students that can be accepted on to the programme, which is affected by the number of teaching staff available and the teaching resources such as computers and library resources that are provided. In addition, it will also depend whether your individual specialist needs can be met. For example, if you are applying to do a Doctorate it will depend whether the department you are applying to has a member of academic staff who can supervise your research project. Let's look at each of these factors in detail.

Academic qualifications

Whatever the postgraduate programme you want to apply for you will need to have, or expect to get before you join the course, a first or Bachelors degree of a good standard. If you want a place on a Doctoral programme you will probably also need, or expect to have, a Masters degree of a good standard.

Every country in the world has its own school system, higher education and academic qualifications, and while there are very many similarities between the systems, each is unique in detail. One of the issues in higher education is that the title and academic level of first-degree qualifications varies between countries, and in some ways an academic qualification is like currency for international travellers – the currency has to be acceptable in the country where you want to spend it, and it will have a value which reflects the international exchange rate.

When universities in the UK indicate that they require a good first degree as an entry qualification to a Masters degree what they really mean is either a degree from a UK higher education institution or a qualification from another country that is at the same level and standard. So, the key thing is to know whether your degree is seen as equivalent in standard to a British first degree. There are two parts to this. The first is whether the level of your qualification is equivalent to a British Bachelors degree at Honours level. The second is the level of your final achievement in that qualification. Many countries now assess their degrees using grade point averages (GPAs), which is the average score achieved across all the courses within the degree programme. While there is now some early discussion about whether British universities should use the same system, they currently use a degree classification system. This means that the final degree a student is awarded is graded as follows:

A *first class honours* degree is the highest level of achievement, normally representing an overall mark of at least 70%.

An *upper second class honours* degree (usually called a 2:i – 'a two-one') represents an overall mark of more than 60%.

A *lower second class honours* degree (usually called a 2:ii – 'a two-two') represents an overall mark of 50%.

A *third class honours* degree normally represents an overall mark of 40%.

A *pass degree* normally represents an overall mark of 35%.

To be accepted on to a Masters programme you will normally need the equivalent of at least a lower second class honours degree, and for popular and competitive programmes this will normally have to be at least an upper second class honours degree. To be accepted on to a Doctoral programme you will normally need to have a Masters degree already, although exceptionally a student with an excellent Bachelors degree may be accepted.

Most universities have long experience in knowing what the equivalence is within this system of most qualifications from other countries. In most cases this equivalence is widely published and is the same for each British university, and the universities will provide you with information about the equivalence of your qualifications. If you would prefer to do this yourself you can refer to the website of NARIC (the National Recognition Information Centre), at *www.naric.org.uk*. They will provide an individual report for you at a cost of £30.

There are, however, two important things to be aware of. The first is that there are so many qualifications from around the world that most universities will only list a few on their website. If your qualification or country is not listed you will need to check its equivalence from one of a number of places:

- You could ask the universities you are considering applying to, probably by e-mail. Their website (see Appendix L) or prospectus will have the name and e-mail contact details of somebody to ask.
- You could ask the British Council office in your own country. You may need to do this by telephone or by e-mail.
- You could contact NARIC (see above).

The second consideration is that the decision on the equivalence of your qualification is entirely up to individual universities. There are no national regulations on this, and the acceptability of some qualifications does vary between universities. So, in the end, the only certain way to get an answer to this is to find out from the university you want to apply to.

If you wish to apply for an MBA you may also be asked to show that you have passed the Graduate Management Admissions Test (GMAT). Details of the GMAT test can be found on the website of the Graduate Management Admissions Council at *www.mba.com*.

If you are applying to do a Doctorate you will usually need to have or expect to get a Masters degree before you can start the programme. As with a first degree, what UK universities are really asking for is a UK Masters degree or its equivalent, and they will have considerable experience in understanding which international qualifications have this equivalence. Knowing how well you achieved in a Masters degree is more difficult with a British Masters, as many are only awarded on a pass/fail basis and do not have different levels of achievement of passes. Some, however, do award a Masters degree with Merit for any student achieving an average of more than 60%, and a Masters degree with Distinction for those achieving an average of more than 70%. To enter a Doctoral programme it is usually necessary to be able to show that you achieved quite a high standard in your Masters degree, and this will be judged normally from either a GPA score or from the comments your referee makes about your achievement. However, as with first degrees, it is essential that you check with the universities you are thinking of applying to whether your own Masters qualification will be regarded as an equivalent to a UK Masters degree.

Professional experience

Most postgraduate degree programmes do not require you to have professional experience as well as academic qualifications. However, in some fields, such as medicine, education, social work or business, you will normally be expected to have between two and five years of experience in your profession before entering a Masters programme. This is because the programme is focused in part on practice, and is regarded as both a higher degree and as a postgraduate professional development programme.

English language expertise

All degree programmes in the UK are taught in English. This means that you will need to be able to show that you have a good enough knowledge of English to be able to understand and follow the programme, to be able to read academic literature in English and to be able to write your assignments and dissertation/thesis with an acceptable standard of English. There are normally four indicators that show you have an acceptable standard of English language:

- If you come from a country where English is the everyday language, and where the education system operates in English, for example Australia, Jamaica, most of Canada.
- If you have completed your first degree at a university in which the language of teaching is English, for example if you are a student from China who has completed their first degree at a university in Australia or the United States.
- If you attend an interview for the programme and can demonstrate that your spoken and written English is of a high enough standard.
- If you have a formal qualification in English language that meets the minimum standard the university requires.

For most international applicants it is the fourth of these that is the usual way of showing English language competence. Each university sets its own minimum standards, so you will need to find out from the university website or from their prospectus what those standards are. However, there are some common standards used by most universities and these are minimum levels achieved in recognized international tests of English language ability. Figure 3.1 shows what these standards are.

There are many other English language qualifications so if you have a different qualification from those listed you will need to check how acceptable it is to the university you are applying to.

If you do not have a suitable English language qualification then you will need to make arrangements to take one of the tests. You will be able to find out about the arrangements for these tests by enquiring through one of the following:

Qualification	Normal minimum standard
AEB Test in English for Educational Purposes (TEEP)	Grade 3
ARELS Oral Examinations	Pass
British Council/Cambridge International English Language Test (IELTS)	6.0–7.0
Cambridge (UCLES) Certificate in Advanced English	Grade C
Cambridge (UCLES) Certificate of Proficiency in English	Grade C
NEAB University Entrance Test in English for Speakers of Other Languages	Pass
London Certificate of Attainment in English	Levels 5–6
Oxford Higher Certificate in English as a Foreign Language	Credit
Pitman Examinations Institute ESOL examinations (higher)	Pass
TOEFL	600
CBTOEFL	250
Trinity College Examination in Spoken English	Grades 10–12

FIGURE 3.1   *Normal minimum English language qualifications for a postgraduate programme*

- Your local or national British Council office
- A local specialist English language school
- The national or local representative of the testing organization
- The website of the testing organization.

There are a few important things to be aware of with English language testing:

- You will have to pay for the test yourself.
- You are advised strongly to arrange for an English language course before you take the test, even if you feel your English is quite good. It is very difficult to reach the standards required without careful teaching of English and without guidance and practice in the tests. English language courses are easily available in almost every part of the world through specialist language schools or through ordinary schools and colleges, and you will be able to identify such a course from advertisements in your own local area. Be careful though to use a reputable school or course – choose one that is recommended or approved by The British Council, or by your local or

national government education authorities, and which can demonstrate that it is successful in teaching people to reach the standard of English for entry to a UK university.

- Allow plenty of time to take the test and get the results before you need to start your postgraduate programme. Although you will only need to have the qualification by the time you enrol at your UK university, and not necessarily at the time you apply for a place, it can take several months to undertake a course, take the test and receive the results and the certificate. In particular you need to have enough time to retake the test if you are not successful first time.

- If you have very little English language understanding then you should consider taking a longer course before taking the language tests. Language schools offer courses at all levels, from complete beginners to quite experienced speakers, and will be able to advise on the level of course that you need. You might wish to take such a course in your own country before you apply for a postgraduate programme. Many students consider spending time at an English language school in the UK, though, since this has the advantage of learning English in the context of the British culture.

To find out more about English language schools in the UK there are two invaluable sources. The first is The British Council, which inspects and accredits English language schools in the UK. A school which has British Council Accreditation is one that has demonstrated it meets high standards of teaching and student support. The British Council gives details of its accreditation scheme and full information about all schools in the UK that are accredited on its main website. This website (*www.englishinbritain.co.uk*) allows you to search for a suitable school to meet your needs in terms of cost, location and length and level of course. The second is the English UK website (*www.englishuk.com*) which has a searchable database of accredited English language schools.

To assist students who have some knowledge of English but who do not have a qualification at the required level, most universities can make arrangements for you to take a language course either at the university or at a local English language school before starting your academic programme. These 'pre-sessional courses' vary in length according to your needs, and you will need to pay the additional fee required for this course as it will not be included in the standard university fee. Reaching the required standard by the end of the course is also a requirement for starting your academic programme – if you do not reach the required standard you will not usually be allowed to start your postgraduate course. You will be able to find out information about these courses from the universities you are thinking of applying to.

A good personal statement

To apply for a place on a postgraduate programme you will need to fill in an application form for each university (details of this process are covered in a later section). Most universities include on their form a section in which you are asked to make a personal statement about why you are applying for the course and why you feel you are a good applicant for the programme. This will be read carefully by the admissions tutor for the programme, particularly where there is strong competition for places on the programme.

You will need to show in this statement that you have a good academic record, that you are a well-motivated, well-organized and hard-working student, and that you have good reasons for wanting to do the course. It will also be a way in which the admissions tutor checks your standard of written English. The things you should write about in your personal statement therefore are:

1 Your own academic achievements – what degree programme you studied, what you specialized in within it and what grades you achieved. If you achieved any particular distinctions, such as being the top student in your year or in a particular course, or if you were awarded a prize, then include this.

2 Your special academic interests. Explain what motivates you about your subject or discipline, and what parts of the subject interest you most (and why).

3 Why you want to take the postgraduate programme you are applying for. Explain your personal, academic and career reasons for taking the programme, and explain what you hope to do in your career after completing it. Make sure that this part is about the specific programme you are applying for – do not just write a general statement that you could include in an application for any course in the field. You need to explain why *this* programme at *this* university is the one for you.

4 What you will contribute to the programme. You will obviously bring your own academic knowledge or professional experience but try to show how you will contribute, for example in seminars, practical work, discussions etc.

5 If you are applying for a Masters programme, then explain what you think at this stage you might want to study for your research project for your dissertation. This might change at a later stage, but its good to show you have thought about this before you apply.

You do not have to be able to show in your personal statement that you are the world's best potential postgraduate student! You simply have to show that you are motivated, enthusiastic and have the academic background, skills and commitment to complete the programme successfully. Spend time drafting and redrafting this statement and ask somebody else to check your English and comment on what you have written.

Good references

You will be asked on the application form to give the details of two or three people who can write a reference about you that supports your application. Some universities then write directly to those people asking for a reference, but some may send you a form to give to your referees for them to complete and send back directly to the university. Some applicants will already have references that they can send with their application. The important thing, though, is to check first how the university you are applying to organizes references, and follow their requirements.

One of the most common reasons for a university not being able to send you an offer of a place quite quickly is that referees take a long time to send back their references. It is a good idea, therefore, to ask your referees well in advance so they can prepare a reference ready for when they are asked to provide it, and to politely remind them to respond to a request quite quickly. If you know that one of your referees will be away on leave or on sabbatical, then you may prefer to choose somebody else to be your referee.

Who should you ask to be your referee? They need to be people who can write about you as a student and about your academic achievements. Most applicants choose two people from the university where they studied their first degree or, if they are applying for a research degree, their Masters degree. Typically this will be their own personal academic tutor and either the head of the programme that they studied or another member of academic staff who they worked closely with and knows them quite well. If it is some time since you were at university you should still use one referee from your university, but you might want to choose a second referee who has known you well since then. This needs to be somebody who can comment on your skills and intellectual ability and make a judgement about whether you will cope well with a Masters or Doctoral degree. Your employer might be fine, particularly if he or she is a senior professional and either has a higher degree or understands the nature of postgraduate degrees. Do not, however, use family or personal friends since their judgement will not be seen as objective.

A good research proposal

In many academic disciplines, if you apply to join a Doctoral programme you will be applying to undertake a research project that has already been chosen by the department you are joining. This is particularly true in science or engineering subjects, where postgraduate students undertake research that forms part of a larger-scale project; they will be working as part of a research team led by a senior member of academic staff. In these circumstances you will need to be able to show in your application that you have the background, skills and knowledge to undertake the specific research project you would be allocated.

In other disciplines you will normally apply to undertake a research project on a topic of your choice, and in this case your application will need to include an outline research proposal. This is more often the case in social science, humanities or arts disciplines such as history or business. A research proposal is simply an outline of what you intend to do for your research, and will include:

1 A proposed title or subject for the research
2 Some background and context to explain why this is an important topic to research

3 A suggestion for the research methodology you will use, and how you plan to organize your research. This might include some idea of what data you need to collect, how you will collect the data and how you might analyse the results.

It will normally be 1,000–2,000 words in length, and it is important to understand what the university will be looking for in this:

- It will *not* be looking for the *perfect* research project that is going to transform the world with its discoveries. That would be nice, but is not very realistic.
- You will need to show that you have done some initial reading about the subject and thinking about the research, so it should include a few relevant references – equally, you do not need to show that you have already read everything there is to read on this topic.
- You will need to show that you have got some ideas about research methods, and what might be appropriate and what might not. Once again, you should include some evidence that you have read something about research methods.
- It does not need to be an absolute commitment to researching this topic in this way. You will almost certainly want to change your ideas once you have started the Doctoral programme, and change slightly or even radically what your research is about. The proposal is just to show that you have some initial ideas.
- The university will need to be sure that it is able to support your research effectively, and that it has academic staff with expertise in the broad field you are researching and the methods you plan to use to be able to supervise you properly. It is very helpful therefore if you can show in your proposal how your proposed research links to the expertise of the department and to one or more academic staff. Careful study of the university website will help you identify the academic staff and their research interests, and may save you from submitting a proposal that they will not be able to support (however good it is!). It is quite common, and certainly recommended, that before you write your research proposal you make contact with the most appropriate academic staff at your chosen university, perhaps by e-mail or telephone. By doing this you can discuss your research ideas and, probably, show an early draft of your proposal to them. This can then be adjusted so that you can be confident your proposal is one that they are likely to accept.

Where do I want to live?

If you become a postgraduate student in the UK then you will spend between one and four years living in the country. It is quite important to think about the sort of place that you would like to live, for there are universities in almost every part of the country. Some are located at the heart of large cities or in smaller towns. Some have their own campus, which might be on the outskirts of a city or in a rural location. By thinking in advance about the sort of place in which you might wish to live you can see whether the universities you have listed as meeting your academic needs will also be the sort of place you would like to live. You might want to think about how important some of the following things are for you: access to city social life or large city services (entertainment or shopping for example); city landscapes or rural landscapes; living in a large community or a small community. The *Pause for thought* here will enable you to think through where you would like to live.

● ● ●   *Pause for thought*   ● ● ●

What sort of place would you like to live in and what would you like your university to be like? Write down your thoughts on the following questions:

(a)   *Do you want to live in:*

- *London*
- *A large city other than London (e.g. Manchester, Leeds, Glasgow)*
- *A smaller city (e.g. Nottingham, Newcastle, Plymouth)*
- *A medium-sized town (e.g. Worcester, Northampton, Oxford)*
- *A rural campus (e.g. Lancaster, Keele)*
- *Near to the coast (e.g. Bournemouth, Brighton, Swansea)*
- *Near to upland areas (e.g. Bangor, Stirling, Sheffield)*

(b)   *Do you want to live in:*

- *A campus university, where the teaching, and student accommodation and facilities are all together on a single site (e.g. Warwick)*
- *A precinct university, where the teaching and student accommodation are close together within a town or city (e.g. Southampton Solent)*
- *A city centre university, where the teaching accommodation is in the city centre but the living accommodation may be elsewhere in the city (e.g. most London University colleges)*
- *A suburban university, where the facilities of the university are in a suburban area a little distance from the city centre (e.g. Birmingham)*

What social and cultural facilities do I need?

The final key question is about the wider social and cultural facilities that you would like your university or university town to have. We shall be looking in Part 2 of the book at what it is like to live in the UK as an international student, and some of the detail in those chapters will help you think more carefully about what you would like. However, it is worth giving some thought at this stage to some of the things you will want or need, and the *Pause for thought* below will help you to think this through.

● ● ● *Pause for thought* ● ● ●

Think through and note down your ideas about the following aspects of life as a postgraduate student:

(a) *Do you want to live in:*

- *A hall of residence.*
- *University accommodation but not a hall of residence (e.g. a flat).*
- *Accommodation that you must find for yourself.*
- *Accommodation where you can live with your family.*

(b) *Do you want to live in:*

- *A university with many international students.*
- *A university with many students from your own country.*

(c) *Do you have particular needs, perhaps related to a disability – for example, will you need easy wheelchair access to facilities?*

(d) *Do you want to live in a university which has any of the following social or cultural facilities:*

- *Facilities to enable you to follow your own faith (for example, a Muslim prayer room).*
- *Good social facilities for postgraduate students, including postgraduate cafeterias or common rooms.*
- *Societies or organizations to support your personal and leisure interests – for example, a good cricket club, a Chinese society/club, a strong drama society, a windsurfing society or a chess club. You should note down the sort of social organizations or societies you would like to be part of so that you can check against the list of societies and clubs on the university's website.*

What should I do if I have a disability?

'Disability' could be anything from a serious mobility problem, for example if you need to use a wheelchair, to a sensory disability (e.g. visual or hearing problems), to a health disability (e.g. insulin dependent diabetes), to a learning disability (e.g. dyslexia). UK universities are required by law to enable students with any disability to study, and to try to meet their accommodation, teaching and study needs. Every university has a disability officer who will be able to discuss with you what your needs may be and how they might be met. If you have any disability that will impact on your studies then you are advised to discuss this by e-mail or telephone with the disability officer at the universities you are considering *before* you submit an application. You can find their contact details on the university's website or in the prospectus or from the admissions tutor for the programme you are considering.

How do I apply for a place?

By working through the questions within this chapter and looking at the detailed information about each university and programme that is available on websites and in prospectuses you should be able to identify a list of between one and ten programmes you would like to apply for. So how do you apply for a place on the programmes of your choice?

Each university has its own admissions system for postgraduate programmes, and you will have to apply separately for each university. There is no limit to the number of programmes or universities you can apply to, but it is difficult to apply to more than between five and ten because of the time it takes to complete the applications. All universities have their own official application form that you will need to complete fully. Some universities deal with applications centrally for the whole university, while others deal with applications in the Faculty or department that you are applying to. Some have application forms available on their website, and some are now able to accept forms that have been submitted electronically. This means that you need to check the exact system for each university. The list that follows, however, indicates the steps you need to take to apply for most postgraduate programmes.

1 Study the website of the universities you are interested in applying to, and also study carefully the printed prospectus (catalogue) for each one. Some universities have their prospectus on their website, but for others you will need to look at a hard copy version. You can obtain the prospectus by:

- Ordering one online through the website.
- Writing to or e-mailing the postgraduate admissions office.

You can also look at the prospectus in the library of many organizations – for example, the British Council offices, the library or careers office of your university or language school. This will provide you with the information you need on the application procedure for that particular university.

2 Decide who you are going to ask to be your referees, and ask them if they are willing to do this. Respectfully check that they are not going to be away at the time any request for a reference may come to them, and also remind them of the need to respond quickly to a reference request.

3 Complete an application form and send it to the university you are applying to, using the system it describes on their website or in their prospectus. You need to do this very carefully, because if you forget to send a document that they are asking for then this could delay the processing of your application. The key documents are likely to be:

- The application form itself, which has been completed and signed by you.
- Evidence of your qualifications – copies of your degree certificates or transcripts and your English language qualifications: if these are not in Roman script

(for example, if they are in Chinese or Urdu or Cyrillic script) then you will need to send a translation of your certificate with an official certificate indicating the translation is correct.

- Details of your referees: this may simply be their contact details, but it may be the references themselves.

4   You should receive an acknowledgement from the university when they receive your application, and some indication of how long it will be before you hear from them again.

5   If you are already living in the UK or are going to visit the UK then the university may ask you to an interview. Some universities will also interview postgraduate applicants either by telephone or video link if that can be arranged. The advantage of an interview is that it gives you the opportunity to find out more about the course and the university but also about the academic staff who you will be working with.

6   Finally, you will need to decide which university offer you wish to accept. If you have several offers then you will be able to choose which one best matches your needs and interests. When you have decided you need to inform the university of your choice, but you also need to inform those universities whose offers you will not be accepting, because this means that a place on a programme could then be offered to somebody else. A common problem that universities complain of is that applicants do not tell them if they are rejecting an offer. When the UK government's new visa regulations are introduced (probably in 2008, see Chapter 6) you will have to choose the offer you wish to accept before you apply for a visa as you will only be issued a visa to come to the UK to study one specific programme.

KEY RISKS AND HOW TO AVOID THEM

The key risk in choosing a programme and a university in the UK for your postgraduate studies is that you are unhappy and uncomfortable in that choice and do not get the most out of your period of study. Those students who do not complete (a small number, fortunately) usually fail because their choice has been poor. The list of risks we identify here is intended to enable you to make the best choice for you.

Risk 1: *Not searching widely for information to help you choose*   Search as carefully and thoroughly as you can so that your choice is made on as much real information as possible.

Risk 2: *Making your choice on only one source of information*   Do not rely on any single piece of information to make your choice. One person's advice, or a single website or only one league table will only give you a partial picture.

Risk 3: *Forgetting that personal and social factors are as important as academic ones in choosing the best place to go*   Before you compare the programmes available think through carefully what is important for *you* in your choice, and find the universities or programmes that meet as many of your needs as possible. Do not necessarily choose the programme at the most prestigious university.

Risk 4: *Trying to find the perfect choice*   Remember that there is no perfect choice. Whatever you choose will have some advantages and some disadvantages. You need to be sure, therefore, that the choice meets all your essential factors and excludes any things that it is essential you avoid, and that overall the advantages far outweigh the disadvantages.

Risk 5: *Letting others make your choice for you*   Remember that the choice is very individual. What is best for you may not be what is best for your friend, and may not be what your current university tutor or your parents would choose for themselves. Take their advice – but do not let others make your choice for you.

Risk 6: *Not having a high enough standard of spoken or written English*   You do not have to be able to speak English perfectly but you do need enough English to cope with your programme. The standards universities set for English language are there to ensure you can cope, not to try to prevent you joining the programme. If the standard of your English is poor, think about attending an English language course before you apply for postgraduate study.

Risk 7: *Choosing referees for your application who will not send a reference in good time*   The main delay in the application process in most universities is the delay in receiving references from students' referees. So choose your referees carefully and politely remind them of the timescales they need to keep to.

Risk 8: *Submitting a poor application form*   Do not jeopardize your application by submitting a poorly completed form. Plan carefully what you will say in each section of the form and ask somebody else to check both what you are saying and your English language.

Risk 9: *Leaving your application too late*   Popular programmes or attractive scholarships are very competitive, so it is important to apply as early as you can. While many universities will accept applications until the day the programme starts it is much better to get your application in at least six months before then. Allowing plenty of time for applications and choices will be even more important once the UK government's new visa regulations begin (probably in 2008). This is because you will have to have chosen the offer to accept as a visa will only be issued for you to come to the UK to study a specific programme at a specific university. You will need to avoid having to accept the first offer you receive simply because you have left your visa application too late. Give yourself time to receive ALL your offers so you can decide carefully which one to accept before you apply in good time for your visa.

Risk 10: *Trying to apply to too many programmes*   You will need to apply for several, if there is more than one suitable one, to ensure you get a place. But do not apply to more than between five and ten universities, as you will find it too difficult to 'manage' the forms and application process.

PART 2
EVERYDAY LIFE AS A POSTGRADUATE STUDENT

CHAPTER 4
STUDYING IN THE UK

- How do postgraduates spend their time?
- What academic work will I be expected to do?
- What learning resources and study space can I expect?
- What are relationships with academic staff like?
- How can I best prepare myself for postgraduate study?
- How can I get help with my English?
- Will I be offered living accommodation?

First thoughts

By the time you begin to consider a postgraduate programme you will already be an experienced student. Through your time in school and through your experiences as an undergraduate (and possibly as a Masters student) you will have developed a wide range of skills to enable you to work through a Masters or Doctoral programme. Being a student is very similar wherever in the world you study – you will know about attending lectures, taking notes, organizing reading in your own time or in the library and, if you are a student of science or engineering or the creative or performing arts, spending time in practical classes or workshops. If you have been successful so far as a student then you are well equipped to be a postgraduate student in the UK.

However, there are important differences between universities and academic programmes in different countries, too. Every university and education system partly reflects the culture(s) of the country in which it exists, and has developed over time to meet the needs of the political, social and economic systems of that country. The UK education system, and the UK university system, therefore, have many characteristics which are unique, and are different from the way things are organized elsewhere. Understanding how studying as a postgraduate student in the UK will be different to studying in your own country is important, therefore, so that you understand what you might expect to experience if you come to the UK.

In this chapter we shall look at how postgraduate programmes are organized for students, how you might expect to spend your time and what expectations you might reasonably have.

How do postgraduate students spend their time?

The first difference you will notice about becoming a postgraduate student is that it becomes a full-time activity for the whole year. As an undergraduate you will have had long vacation periods during the academic year, so that the amount of time you spent at university was only typically 30–33 weeks each year. As a postgraduate student the programme fills the whole year and you will spend most of your time at university. As a Masters student, although the *teaching* programme will only take place during semester time, the assignments, projects and dissertation tasks will require you to study throughout the year. You will only be able to take short periods of holiday, in the same way that you might if you were working in a normal job as an employee. As a Doctoral student you will be expected to continue your research and studies throughout the year, with only a few weeks' holiday. By becoming a postgraduate student you have become a full-time academic.

In addition to working longer during the year, you will also have much more responsibility for how you organize your time during the working week. As an undergraduate student you will have had a timetable, which meant that you were programmed for much of the week to be in lectures, seminars or practical classes. The amount of time this filled varies between subjects, but typically you may have had between 15 and 25 hours per week of timetabled activities. As a postgraduate student you will probably have rather less formally programmed activities and rather more time for reading and individual work.

Masters programmes vary considerably in the amount of teaching time they require. Some, particularly in the sciences, business or vocational disciplines such as Law, may have programmes similar to undergraduate timetables, with 10–20 hours of programmed activities each week. Others, particularly in the humanities or social sciences areas, may have only 5–10 hours of teaching each week. You may ask, therefore, how programmes with such different amounts of teaching can all be at Masters level. The answer is that what matters is the total amount of study time involved, whether this is in lectures, seminars, lab classes, fieldwork, private study or assignment/project preparation. In the UK the national qualifications framework indicates that a Masters-level programme requires 180 credit points at M-level, with each credit point representing about 10 hours of study time. The project or dissertation must be worth 60 of these 180 credit points, so the pattern of work for a Masters programme will be approximately:

(a)   The 'taught' component – 120 credit points, or 1,200 hours of study time. Most universities have programmes where each 'contact' hour (teaching, seminar, lab class) expects 3–4 hours of individual study time to support it, so typically this part of the programme will involve about 200–300 hours of contact time.

(b) The 'dissertation' component – 60 credit points, or 600 hours of study time. Much of this will be individual study time, involving data collection in the lab or in the field or in the library and the planning and writing of the project. It will include some direct tutorial supervision, too, but mostly it will be individual work.

Since Masters programmes in the UK are one-year programmes, this means that an average week will involve about 35–36 hours of work – or approximately the hours you would work in a typical professional job.

For Doctoral students taking a PhD the time allocation will be different. In the early stages of a Doctoral programme there will probably be formal taught classes focused on research methods and techniques, although these will occupy a fairly small amount of time – perhaps 5–6 hours per week for your first year of study. The rest of your time will be focused on your own research project. For those working in science, engineering or other practical/lab-based fields this research time will need to fit with the demands of the project you are working on and the availability of lab time etc. Most science and engineering Doctoral students, for example, are working on a project that is part of a rather larger programme of work, and so the time you need to be in the lab will be organized as part of that project. For other Doctoral students, however, there will be considerable flexibility around how you organize your research time, and you will have most of the time in most weeks to plan for yourself.

For those taking 'taught' Doctorates, then the pattern of time allocation will be similar to that of Masters students during the taught part of the programme, and similar to that of PhD students during the research project phase.

Clearly, organizing and managing your time is your own responsibility. Every student has a preferred way of working – some prefer to study starting early in the morning, others work better later in the day or during the evening. Most universities have study facilities available for most of the day, with libraries open for extended periods including weekends – in some universities libraries are open 24 hours per day. You will need therefore to plan your time around:

- The fixed times of classes or lab times.
- The opening hours of facilities such as libraries, ICT facilities and study space such as student offices.
- Your own preferred pattern of working.
- The need to work 30–40 hours per week as a full-time academic student.

What academic work will I be expected to do?

The exact work you will have to do as a postgraduate student will depend fundamentally on the programme you are following. Every academic programme and every student's individual work programme will be different. However, there are a number of aspects of postgraduate work that will almost certainly be part of your programme – we shall distinguish here between those activities typical of a Masters programme and those found in a Doctoral programme.

Masters programmes

Lectures   You will be familiar with the idea of lectures, with a single lecturer providing instruction on a specific theme. Lectures vary in the number of students present, from 10 to 200 or more. Individual participation by students is not always easy, but there will usually be an opportunity for questions, and some lecturers may ask students to undertake brief discussion activities with those around them, or may ask questions of the students present.

Seminars   Seminars involve a small group of students and a tutor. Either the tutor or one or more of the students will talk about a topic, which will then be discussed by the seminar group. Every student in the seminar group will be expected to participate in the discussion and to take their turn in leading discussion or presenting a paper.

Workshops   Workshops are essentially seminars focused on a practical activity. For example, engineering students may work as a group on a practical problem, drama students may work on a performance, or education students may work on a role play activity about teaching. As with seminars, all students will be expected to participate and to take their turn in leading.

Practical classes   Practical classes are an important part of many programmes, and focus on the development of skills – an MSc in Geographical Information Systems, for example, will include a considerable number of 'hands on' classes using GIS software.

Fieldwork   This will be important within environmental or earth science programmes, but also as part of the data collection part of preparing for dissertations in many social science or business fields.

Tutorials   Tutorials are meetings with a tutor, either individually or in very small groups. In some programmes you may have an individual tutor (or personal tutor) who has responsibility for you for the whole of your programme, and may talk with you about both academic and personal or pastoral issues. You will also have tutorials as part of some taught courses, where the course tutor will meet with you to discuss assignments or practical work. You will also have a tutor to support you in your project or dissertation, and this will usually be a member of the academic staff who has specialist knowledge in the field which you are researching.

Reading   For most Masters programmes reading will be one of the most important parts of your learning. A Masters provides you with the opportunity to read widely and in depth around your specialist field to bring your own knowledge to the cutting edge of that field. You should expect, therefore, to spend considerable amounts of time in the library or reading materials borrowed from the library or available on-line, whatever your specialist discipline.

Assignments   Unfortunately, all of these stimulating courses and units will be assessed in some way, and it is increasingly common for this to be through an assignment rather than an examination. Assignments vary greatly in size and scope, from research essays to small practical projects to seminar presentations, but all will require considerable individual preparation and work.

Examinations   You will be very used to examinations, and many Masters programmes are still assessed using traditional two- or three-hour written examinations. These may occur at the end of the taught programme or spread throughout the course with some at the end of Semester 1 and some at the end of Semester 2.

Dissertation   The dissertation, or project, will be a major part of the Masters programme, worth one third of the assessment total. We shall look in detail in a later chapter (Chapter 9) at how to plan and manage a project, but typically it will be a project of between 15,000 and 25,000 words in length that you plan and undertake on your own. Although you will have a nominated supervisor, it will be expected that you show considerable independence in choosing, planning and writing up the project.

Doctoral programmes

Taught course units   Within 'taught' Doctorates much of the first one or two years will involve taught courses. These will include units on subject-based topics, units on professional subjects and units on research methods and skills.

As with Masters programmes, these units will include a wide range of teaching methods varying from lectures to workshops to seminars and practical classes. All will be assessed, typically through an assignment.

Increasingly, PhD programmes include taught units as well. These are normally research methods and skills units, providing you with the practical and intellectual skills to plan and undertake a Doctoral research project. These may include 'hard skills' such as computing or statistics, as well as softer skills such as writing and presenting academic papers. PhD programmes recognized by the UK Research Councils and for which the councils will provide funding for some students are all required to include such taught units as part of the research training of Doctoral students.

Tutorials You may be supported through tutorials during the taught part of a doctoral programme, but during the research project phase tutorials are a critical part of your study time. We shall look at the nature and purpose of tutorials at this stage in Chapter 9, but, as a full-time student you should expect to meet your supervisor for a tutorial on average every two or three weeks during your Doctoral programme.

Individual research Individual research is the key feature of a Doctoral programme. Whether your research is entirely of your own creation or whether you are part of a large research project team, it is your research that will be your main focus of work. The work will include planning the research, undertaking the research, by whatever method is appropriate (from library research to interviews to laboratory experiments), analysing your data and writing your research project up as a final thesis. It will occupy you for between two and five years and will become the main focus of your life and study – you will live, eat and breathe your project. Although you may be able to share your ideas with other members of the research team and your supervisor, or with colleague Doctoral students, your project and your thesis will be your 'baby', needing nurturing, absolute preoccupation and complete attention.

● ● ● *Pause for thought* ● ● ●

*In recent years there has been a lot of research on student learning styles, and it is recognized that students work in different ways. How do **you** prefer studying and learning? How do you manage your study time? Are you someone who prefers studying through lectures or do you prefer to be involved in discussion or practical activities? Are you a visual learner or do you learn better from words and language? At what times of day do you learn best? Write down your thoughts on each of these questions.*

What learning resources and study space can I expect?

Universities in the UK have high standards of learning facilities for all of their students. These include general facilities such as libraries and computers and also specialist facilities for particular academic disciplines. You can expect that you will have access to a well-stocked library with up-to-date books and journals in your field, and to a computer network that includes on-line learning services and access to the internet. Many programmes now make use of virtual learning environments using software systems such as Blackboard or WebCT, which means that you can access resources for your programme, communicate with tutors and other students and find details of teaching sessions, notes and assignments through the computer network. It is now very common for access to the network to be available from student rooms in halls of residence or through wireless technology.

You can also expect good facilities for the study of your subject or programme, whether this involves laboratories, specialist technical facilities or simply teaching rooms and lecture theatres. However, this varies from university to university and from programme to programme in detail, so you will need to check through prospectuses and the website to find out exactly what the facilities are really like. Some questions you might like to think about include:

- What is the ratio of computers to students? If it is 1:2 that is good, if it is 1:10 then you may find access limited.
- What are the library opening hours? A library that is open 24 hours a day is probably more useful for your studies than one that is only open from 9 am to 5 pm.
- Are there any negative comments about learning resources and facilities either in independent guidebooks about the university or in the external examiner reports on the web?

Study accommodation refers to the facilities within the university that are available to postgraduate students. Once again, this will vary between universities. For Masters level students few universities will provide you with your own dedicated desk/workspace or computer, and you will be expected to use the general study facilities of the university – workstations, libraries, study areas etc. Some academic departments may have shared rooms equipped for Masters students to use with suitable study and ICT facilities and, possibly, some social facilities, but this is quite rare. This means that you should identify from the prospectus, the website and perhaps from student publications or independent guide books what the study facilities are like for Masters students.

For Doctoral students the study facilities will probably be somewhat better. In many cases full-time research students will be provided with their own desk and, probably, their own or a shared computer, probably in a shared office or open-plan area. This is because research students are often regarded as being almost part of the academic staff of the department and so have access to facilities similar to those for full academic staff. However, the exact arrangements vary between universities and often between departments and disciplines within the same university – so you need to check the information in the prospectus or on the website.

What are relationships with academic staff like?

As you become more specialized in your studies, the number of academic staff you come into contact with becomes fewer. As an undergraduate you may have been taught by 20 or 30 different staff, but on a Masters programme it may be only four to eight, and as a Doctoral student it may be even fewer – and you will have much of your 'teaching' from your research supervisor. Getting on well with them will be important, both to make sure you progress well but also so you have a pleasant experience as a student.

The culture of universities varies enormously around the world. It may be that your undergraduate studies have been in an environment where you hardly knew the academic staff outside lectures and where you had a very formal relationship with them – addressing them as 'Professor', only meeting them at formal appointments or tutorials, and being expected to show deference to them. In most universities in the UK relationships between students and staff are quite informal – staff will call you by your preferred name and will probably expect you to call them by their first name. It can be quite daunting at first when a world-famous professor whose eminent work you have read introduces themselves to you and says 'call me Sue'. Most are very approachable, and will be keen for you to join in with both the academic and, probably, the social life in the academic department or faculty. They will expect you to be active in your interaction with them – to stop them in the corridor to speak, to be relatively informal in your dealings with them and to try to make your work with them an enjoyable and positive experience. Remember that most will be delighted that you are as interested and excited in the same things as they are and that you are somebody else who they can have serious academic discussion with in their specialist field. Being friendly, warm and approachable does not mean that they will not expect the highest of standards of academic work from you, though – indeed, it is one of the ways they hope that they can make this possible, and respect will be based on how you work and how you engage with your studies.

How can I best prepare myself for postgraduate study?

Being prepared for postgraduate study has two parts – being prepared academically and being prepared personally. To be academically prepared you need to have the right academic entry qualifications, to have done as much reading as you can in the field that you will be studying and to have a sufficient level of English language skills to cope with the course.

To be prepared personally is a much wider issue, for it means that you must be ready to deal with the challenges of living and working as a postgraduate student. Most important is probably having the skills of organization and time management to be able to cope with the demands of the programme timetable and managing your individual study time. This is something you will have developed as an undergraduate or Masters student. You need to be able to organize your own work in an environment where you will have a lot of time that is not formally timetabled, and you will need to be happy to work independently on your own assignments or projects. The best way of preparing for this is probably to talk with those who have had experience of being a postgraduate student – friends, family, colleagues at work or your current university who have studied for a postgraduate degree fairly recently.

You also need to be prepared for some of the personal challenges. Most important is certainly the financial issue, for you need to be confident you have or can earn enough to finish your programme without having to worry too much about money and without having to work such long hours for money that it risks damaging your study – it may be better to delay your programme for a year so you can earn and save some money rather than suffer financially by taking a programme immediately.

And then there are the issues of living away from home, perhaps away from friends or family and possibly in a new culture for one to three years. Be aware, in particular, that you may find the first few weeks or even months quite challenging until you have made new friends and settled into your new environment, and while this can be very exciting and stimulating, almost everybody will feel a little alone or homesick at some stage in their early days. So, be ready for these feelings and think through how you might cope with them – weekly phone calls home, a visit home at the end of your first semester, joining societies or groups or new activities to help you settle in.

● ● ● *Pause for thought* ● ● ●

Which of the following aspects of being a postgraduate student do you feel confident about, and which do you need to spend more time thinking and planning for? For those you don't feel confident about try to write down exactly what your concerns are. When you have thought about this, you can then read in detail the sections on these issues in the chapters indicated:

• *Planning your own time*	*(Chapters 8/9)*
• *Financing your studies*	*(Chapter 5)*
• *Being away from home*	*(Chapters 6/7)*
• *Working for the whole academic year*	*(Chapters 8/9)*
• *English language skills*	*(Chapters 3/4)*
• *IT skills*	*(Chapter 8)*
• *Planning and writing a dissertation or thesis*	*(Chapter 9)*

How can I get help with my English?

If English is not your own first language then you will have had to demonstrate that you have a suitable level of English language skills before you could enter the programme. However, many students whose English is quite good still feel the need for support with language skills, perhaps because of the technical language needs of their subject or because they feel that the quality of their writing and reading could be even better if they had more training. There are several ways of getting help with your written or spoken English:

- You could do this informally, through the network of friends and colleagues that you will form. International students often help each other with language skills, and UK students are often happy to help their friends with their writing or reading skills. This can be very helpful in the early stages of a programme, perhaps when you are preparing your first written assignment or the first drafts of parts of your thesis or your first lab reports – many international students ask friends to read through their written work and help them improve their English in this way.
- You can do it formally. All universities will have continuing courses in English for international students, and, although you will need to pay the fees for such courses, they can be very helpful to continuously improve your language skills.
- You can do it commercially. This means that you can pay to attend a course at a separate English language school. Most towns or cities in the UK have English language schools, and will offer courses at a range of levels.

The best advice, though, is to use English as much as you can. If you are one of many postgraduate students from your own country it is easy just to mix with them and speak your own language with them. However, if you mix with a wide range of people you will have to speak English – and, of course, you could agree with your friends that you will only speak English most of the time, saving your own language for specific occasions or one day of the week (perhaps Saturdays). Also, by reading English magazines and newspapers, watching UK television or listening to the radio your language skills will improve quickly.

Will I be offered living accommodation?

An important part of being a student is your own accommodation. Many international students feel that it is an important help in moving to a new country and a different culture if the university provides living accommodation for them, perhaps in a student hall of residence or flat. In some universities international postgraduate students are offered university accommodation, but there is considerable variation between universities. This means that it is very important to check in the prospectus or on the website of each university exactly what their policy on accommodation for postgraduates is – this can vary from a guarantee of a student room in a hall of residence to all postgraduate international students, to a situation where very few postgraduates can be accommodated. Some universities have only limited accommodation for postgraduates, but give priority to international students. Most have only limited amounts of accommodation for students with families, so it is particularly important to check the arrangements if you will wish or need to bring your family with you. Whatever the arrangements, though, every university in the UK has an accommodation office whose role is to help students find accommodation, and all have expertise in helping international students whether they need a place in a university hall of residence or whether they wish to rent a room, a house or a flat in the private sector. You should make contact with the accommodation office as soon as possible after you have decided to accept a place at a university. We shall look at issues of accommodation and housing in more detail in Chapters 7 and 8.

KEY RISKS AND HOW TO AVOID THEM

We have tried to paint a broad picture of what it is like to be a postgraduate student in the UK in terms of the life of being a student. We shall look at each part of this in more detail in later chapters. The important thing is to understand something of the nature of postgraduate study, how you might expect to spend your work time and what resources or facilities will be available to you. Before you apply, think about what is important for you and be sure that you identify a programme and a university that meets these needs. The key risks to avoid are:

Risk 1: *Not understanding how studying will differ from your experiences so far*   If you are just finishing your undergraduate course, then you need to be aware of how a Masters course will be different. If you are completing a Masters, then be aware of what a research degree programme will be like.

Risk 2: *Not realizing there will be a period of transition and adjustment*   Starting a new programme is like starting anything new in life – you will need to adjust to the new way of life and of doing things. When you do this, and combine it with moving to another place or country, this can be even more challenging. Be prepared for a period of change and uncertainty and develop strategies to cope with this.

Risk 3: *Not developing your English language skills continuously*   See it as a challenge to make your English as fluent and sophisticated as you can, and continue to learn and practise for the whole of your programme.

Risk 4: *Not being organized and self-motivated*   As a postgraduate student you are expected to be able to organize yourself and your work and not to need constant guidance and direction from tutors. See this as an exciting opportunity and not a frightening responsibility, and see it as an opportunity to be in control of your own life and destiny!

Risk 5: *Not taking responsibility for your own learning*   As a postgraduate student you will need to be sure that you find ways of learning and studying effectively. Learning is *your* responsibility. Take opportunities to improve your study skills if there are classes or courses available.

Risk 6: *Not having enough money to support yourself during your studies*   If you have very little money or have to work very long hours to earn enough you will not enjoy being a postgraduate student. You do not have to be wealthy – student life can be relatively low cost – but you do need enough to be comfortable. Plan your finances before you embark on a postgraduate programme.

Risk 7: *Not developing a positive relationship with your tutors*   University communities in the UK are quite informal in their relationships, and it is easy to get to know people well and quite quickly.

Risk 8: *Mistaking informal relationships as low expectations of academic work and standards*   Do not allow yourself to think that a relaxed approach means that tutors will be relaxed about work deadlines or standards. They will not.

Risk 9: *Not developing your IT skills throughout your studies*   The better your IT skills the easier you will find studying and the more successful you will be. Make the most of the many opportunities that will arise to use and build your IT skills in ways relevant to your subject.

Risk 10: *Not seeking your tutors' guidance and support*   Tutors have much experience in helping postgraduate students. Do not fail to make use of this resource. Raising any issues with them at an early stage will help you make good progress on your programme.

CHAPTER 5
FINANCING YOUR POSTGRADUATE DEGREE

- How much will it cost me for fees?
- How and when do I pay fees?
- How much money will I need to support myself?
- How much does it cost for medical care, childcare and schools?
- How can I find out about studentships and scholarships?
- How can I transfer money to the UK?
- How easy is it to get a job?
- Are there any other ways of reducing costs or earning money?
- What if I get into financial difficulties?

First thoughts

For most people the most important issue in thinking about taking a postgraduate degree is the cost, and concerns about how to find the money to pay for it. This is true wherever you are thinking of studying. Even if you plan to stay in your own country, attending a local university and living at home, the cost will be quite high. If you are considering studying in another country then you will certainly have concerns about how you can afford it.

Most potential students understand that a postgraduate degree is a long-term investment. They expect, quite rightly, that it will lead to improved prospects for employment which will certainly lead to economic benefits over their lifetime, and may well lead to a much improved income quite soon after graduating. But the challenge is how to find the funding to pay for the programme and for the cost of living while a student – in other words, how to raise the money to invest in their own education. This chapter will look at the issues involved in funding your programme and your time as a student – and how some of the challenges this raises can be met.

How much will it cost me for fees?

Universities charge fees for all their postgraduate programmes to cover the cost of tuition and the use of the university's study facilities, such as the library or the IT network. The fees are decided by each university, but most are close to the recommended figures that are published each year by the government. The fees vary between programmes, so that, for example, science-based programmes that include a significant amount of laboratory work will be more expensive than classroom-based subjects. The annual fees for 2005/06 are shown in Figure 5.1. Remember that you will have to pay these fees for each year of study – so for a typical doctoral programme you will need to pay this amount three times.

Arts, Humanities and Social Science Subjects	£6,250–8,500
Science and Engineering Subjects	£6,500–10,000
Clinical Subjects (e.g. Medical Subjects)	£7,000–18,000
MBA	£12,000–20,000

FIGURE 5.1   *Typical 'Overseas' postgraduate fees for 2005/06*

To find out the exact fees for a particular programme you will need to check in the university's prospectus or on its website. When you look up this information be sure to find the fees for international students. The UK government contributes to the total fee costs of students from the UK and students from the European Union (EU) through direct funding by the Higher Education Funding Council (HEFC). As a result, the fees charged to UK students (or 'home students' as they are usually called) and students from the EU are less than for other students. An important issue for every international student, therefore, is to be clear about their own fee status. Most students from outside the EU will fall into the category of 'overseas' fees as they will not be eligible for the lower 'home/EU' fees status. To qualify to pay home fees as an international student you will need to fall into one of the following categories:

- If you have been permanently resident in the UK for at least three years.
- If you have been granted refugee status by the UK government.
- If you have applied for asylum in the UK.

If you are not sure of your fee status then you will need to check this with each university you will be applying to, as the final decision rests with the university.

The fees that are charged will cover the cost of tuition and supervision. However, in some subject disciplines, particularly in science, engineering, medicine or the creative arts, you may be charged an additional fee known as a bench fee, to cover the cost of materials you may use in your work. You should check whether your university will charge a bench fee for your subject, and if so how much. If they do charge, it is likely to be between £200 and £1,000, so you will need to budget for this.

How and when do I pay fees?

There are many different ways of paying your fees, and you will need to check the system used by the universities you are thinking of applying to. The list below is of some of the most common ways of paying – but these are not all available at each university, so do check!

- **Payment of a deposit**. Some universities may ask you to pay a small proportion of the total fees when you accept their offer of a place on the programme. This is usually between £100 and £500, and may not be refundable if you do not finally register for the programme.
- **A single payment**. This means that you pay the whole of your annual fees in a single payment, usually close to the start of the academic year in October or November.
- **Two or three payments**. Some universities ask you to pay your fees in two or three instalments, usually either at the start of each term (October, January, April) or at the start of each semester (October, February).
- **Monthly payments**. An increasing number of universities will allow you to pay your fees monthly, usually through eight to ten monthly payments each year.

With multiple payments, most universities will ask you to complete a bank instruction to make the payments (by Standing Order or Direct Debit) at the right times. Some universities will allow you to pay using a credit card, but in this case may charge you a small fee for this. Equally, some may give you a small discount (typically 1–2%) if you pay your fees in a single payment at the start of the year.

To avoid bringing large sums of money to the UK to pay your fees you might prefer to arrange to pay your fees in advance by direct bank transfer from your own bank in your own country. The university will be able to provide details of how to do this. Alternatively, you could arrange to bring a cheque or banker's draft with you, payable to your university.

How much money will I need to support myself?

The fees at UK universities do not include any charge for accommodation or living expenses. This means that you will need to have enough money to pay for all of your other expenses, including accommodation, food, clothes, travel, books and entertainment costs. As a postgraduate student you will probably already have had some experience of managing your own money, working out a budget and living within the budget you set, so this will not be a new or strange experience. However, the costs of all these parts of your budget may be very different to what you are used to – some items that are quite low cost in your own country may be relatively expensive in the UK, while others may be relatively cheap.

It is not easy to indicate an exact amount for how much you will need to support yourself each week or each month. This is partly because everybody's lifestyle, priorities, needs and costs are different. However, it is also because there are quite significant differences in costs in different parts of the UK. Accommodation rent may be much higher, for example, in London than in some other cities or towns. Travel costs may be higher in large cities where you may need to live at some distance from your university. Even the cost of food and entertainment varies from place to place.

The costs in Figure 5.2, therefore, are intended to give you a general picture of the cost of living, in London and in other parts of the UK.

	London	Elsewhere
Weekly rental costs	£100–£140	£75–£120
Food	£45	£40
Transport	£15	£10
Clothes/books	£10	£10
Entertainment	£20	£15
Total	**£210**	**£165**

FIGURE 5.2   *Typical weekly costs for a postgraduate student*

For a full year in the UK you will need to budget for about £11,000 if you are going to live in London and about £9,000 if you are going to live elsewhere. For a more detailed picture of the cost of living in each university town or city you should refer to the Royal Bank of Scotland Student Living Index. This was devised in 2004 by the bank to help students use cost of living information in choosing where they might go to university. Although aimed at undergraduates, it is useful in providing a general picture of costs for a postgraduate. The website for the Index is

http://image.guardian.co.uk/sys-files/Education/documents/2004/08/23/bank.pdf

Whether these prices seem expensive or not, of course, will depend from which part of the world you are coming to the UK, and on the exchange rate of your own currency with the pound sterling.

These costs are, of course, for you as an individual student. If you are going to come to the UK with your family then there will be additional costs to support them too, and it is reasonable to estimate that you will need an additional £5,000 for your husband or wife and £2,000 per year for each of your children.

There are a number of websites that have been designed to help you plan and organize your finance and budget, and these are listed in Appendix I. Typical is the Studentmoney website at *www.studentmoney.org*, which has a wide range of information on all aspects of student finance, including banking, loans, fees and the cost of living.

One cost that many students forget to include when thinking about the budget for their postgraduate programme is the cost of travelling to and from the UK. You will certainly need to pay for transport to the UK at the start of your programme and home again at the end of it. However, you may feel that you will want to return home to visit friends and family during your studies. If you are taking a one-year Masters programme then you may feel you will not need to do this, but if you are coming to the UK for a Doctorate and will be here for three years you may want to visit your home perhaps at the end of each year. Although travel can be expensive, if you plan carefully and a long time ahead you may be able to find quite low cost airfares.

And then there is the cost of some of the opportunities that will be available for you in the UK. You will certainly feel that you want to see something of British life, culture and landscape while you are here, so you might want to budget for a number of visits to other parts of the UK – perhaps to London for a weekend, or to Edinburgh or Oxford, or to some of the attractive landscapes in Wales or Scotland. This can often be arranged quite cheaply through student travel organisations in the UK, which you will find out about from the Student Union in your university (see also Appendix K). Overall, though, you will not want to return home after your studies feeling that you have seen nothing more than life in the university town or city that you chose to study in. So, you need to budget for this.

How much does it cost for medical care, childcare and schools?

There are some costs that you will be hoping that you do not need to pay, for example for medical treatment, and others that may only be necessary if you come to the UK with your family, such as childcare. For international students registered on a postgraduate course you can have free access to the services of the UK National Health Service (NHS). This means that you can register with a local doctor (called a general practitioner, usually referred to as a GP) either at the University's Health Centre (they all have one) or in the nearby community, and will have access to free medical services. In the case of emergencies or serious illness you will also be able to use local NHS hospitals. In both cases the standard of medical treatment is very high. There are some services, however, that are more difficult to access or for which you may have to pay. At the present time, for example, it is not always possible to register with an NHS dentist, and therefore if you need dental treatment you may need to pay the full fee for the service to a private dentist. You will also have to pay directly for a number of services – for example for the cost of spectacles if you have to replace them or find you need them while you are in the UK, and a contribution to the cost of any medicines prescribed by a doctor. Most of these services are free for children or for women during pregnancy.

If you have children of school age then you will have to place them in a suitable school. School is compulsory in the UK for all children between the ages of 5 and 16, but is provided free by the government. Although there is no direct charge for education, there will be some costs you face. For example, many schools have a school uniform that children are required to wear, and this could cost between £50 and £200 per child per year, although many schools arrange 'second hand' sales of uniforms to keep costs low. In addition, most schools organize educational visits and activities that they are able to ask parents to pay for. This might include visits to local museums or field trips. While in theory it is not compulsory for you to pay for such activities, there is an expectation in practice that parents will pay. However, most schools are able to provide funding to cover these costs for families who are in very difficult financial circumstances. The cost of these additional activities may be as much as £100–£200 per year, particularly if your children are at secondary (high) school.

If you have children younger than 5 years of age then you do not need to send them to school – but you may want to send them to a local nursery or preschool (kindergarten), either part-time or full-time. Most universities have their own university nursery for children from 6 months to 5 years old, and these are of a very high standard. You will, however, have to pay for them. Costs are often reduced for students, but you will probably have to pay between £15 and £25 per day for a place. It is important to contact the nursery as soon as you know that you are going to the university, as demand for places is high. In addition to the university nursery, of course, you will find that there are local nursery schools, pre-schools and playgroups, and you can seek a place for your child in these in the same way that any other local parent can.

● ● ● **Pause for thought** ● ● ●

What finance will you have available when you start your postgraduate degree? Add together the amount you will have in savings and the amount that your family will be able to give you. Find out the current exchange rate between your own currency and sterling, and then see how much you will have in sterling. If you are a single student you will need about £15,000 per year for most courses, and if you have a family you will need an additional £5,000 for your partner and £2,000 for each child. How much will you need, therefore, and how much extra do you need to find?

How can I find out about studentships and scholarships?

Many students wll find themselves unable to afford a postgraduate programme unless they are funded through a studentship or scholarship. This means that finding a place on a postgraduate programme is only part of the search; finding a scholarship may be a much bigger challenge.

Scholarships may be called different things – scholarships, studentships, bursaries, sponsorship, for example, but we will call them all scholarships here. What they all mean is that some or all of the cost of being a postgraduate student is paid for you. The best scholarship will be one that pays your full fees and then pays you a monthly amount that covers all your living costs. This is often called a full scholarship, and means that you will not have to find any funding from any other source. These are quite rare, however, and most scholarships will provide just some of this finance – some may pay your fees but no contribution to your living expenses, for example, or perhaps just some contribution to your fees.

So how do you get a scholarship? For any scholarship you will have to make a formal application, usually by filling in an application form. Depending on the scholarship, this may be a simple or very extensive form. Since there are always more people seeking scholarships than the number of scholarships available, there will then be a selection process by the organization providing the funding. In most cases scholarships are awarded to the most academically excellent applicants, and this is usually the only selection criterion. However, some will be restricted to the best candidates in particular categories – perhaps for those from a particular country or seeking to study a specific subject or from a particular background (perhaps from a poorer family) or with a particular talent (for example, sport or music). There are a few key 'rules' about applying for any scholarship.

1 Read the regulations and criteria for the scholarship very carefully and make sure you meet them all. Make sure you are not applying for a specialist scholarship that does not apply to your field, such as a science scholarship if you want to study drama, or for a scholarship that does not apply for come other reason, for example a scholarship for mature students if you are aged only 23. Otherwise you will waste your own and other people's time.

2 Make sure you meet the application deadline. This will vary between scholarships, but is usually quite early in the year, before the date you want to start your programme.

3 Fill in the application carefully, providing all the information needed.

4 Try to 'sell' yourself. Remember that scholarships are very competitive, and you need to show that you are an excellent applicant. Evidence that you were one of the top 5% of students in your first degree (i.e. undergraduate) course for example, that you were awarded one of the top '1st class' degrees from your university or that you have received prizes or previous scholarships in your field will all help.

5 Choose referees who will support your application strongly and who will stress your excellence – but be careful, for many scholarships require very particular people to write a reference, such as the Head of Department of your undergraduate degree programme or your personal tutor on that programme.

Because of the competition for scholarships you also need to apply for as many as possible and to be prepared for rejections, even if you know you are an excellent student. To be rejected is not a sign of failure, just an indicator that many people are seeking to study for a postgraduate degree.

So how do you find out what scholarships are available? There are thousands of organizations around the world that support postgraduate scholarships, so searching can take quite some time. It is not possible within this book to identify all or even a small proportion of them, so we shall look at the main sources of funding and suggest some ways of searching. We suggest that you look at all of these possible sources, and allow plenty of time for the search!

Scholarships from your own country

Government scholarships   Many national governments have schemes to award scholarships for excellent students to study abroad, usually as part of the country's strategy for economic growth. Examples include the Marshall Scholarships for US postgraduates to study at UK universities (see *www.marshallscholarships.org*). To find out about these scholarships you will need to enquire through your own government offices, your current university careers advice service or through the British Council offices in your own country.

Business/commercial scholarships   Both large and small businesses provide funding for scholarships. In many cases these are available only to those who work for or have been offered employment by those companies, as they are in effect part of the company's training programme. You may need to guarantee that you will return to work for the company for a specified period (perhaps one to five years) after graduation. Finding out about these awards will be through advertising from the companies or through a web search.

Charity organization scholarships   Both local and national charities provide funding for students to study abroad, particularly where the charity has an educational or development focus. Such scholarships may be limited in number and only available to students from certain backgrounds, perhaps to those from poor or difficult family circumstances, or to those seeking ultimately to work in development or teaching or healthcare fields.

Local scholarships   These are the most difficult to find out about yet in some ways are often the easiest ones to gain. Many local organizations or charities have small numbers of scholarships for the education of those from a particular town, city, school, church or university. The best way to find out about these awards will be through your own local contacts and organizations. Ask your local church or faith organization leader, or your local government office or your former school headteacher or the head of the local business guild or chamber of commerce.

Scholarships from international organizations

Some international organizations offer scholarships if they have an educational or development focus. For example, the European Union has scholarships to support students from Latin America wishing to study at postgraduate level in an EU country. Information on EU scholarships can be found at *www. welcomeurope.com*.

Scholarships from the UK

UK government scholarships   The UK government has always tried to encourage international students to study for their postgraduate degrees in the UK, and has a number of scholarship schemes to support this. More than 20,000 international students are funded each year through these schemes. The most significant ones are:

- **ORSAS (Overseas Research Students Awards Scheme) Scholarships.** The ORSAS Scheme provides scholarships to more than 140 different HE institutions each year. These are not full scholarships, but pay part of the fees for a Doctoral programme. They are intended to pay the difference between home fees and overseas fees so that international students only have to pay as much themselves as if they were UK students. In practice, many universities guarantee to pay the rest of the fee with their own scholarship for successful candidates, but you will need to check this with the universities you are applying to. Although the funding is from the UK government, applications and decisions are managed by individual universities, each of which will have a quota of ORSAS scholarships each year. Further information can be found at *www.orsas.ac.uk*.
- **Chevening Scholarships.** Chevening Scholarships are perhaps the most prestigious scholarships awarded by the UK government. They are funded by the UK Foreign and Commonwealth Office and managed by the British Council. Scholarships are normally linked to specific countries and are open to competition between students interested in studying in any discipline. Further information can be found at *www.chevening.com*.
- **Commonwealth Scholarships.** The Commonwealth Scholarship and Fellowship Plan (CSFP) provides scholarships for students from countries that are members of the Commonwealth. They are funded by the UK government but administered by the Association of Commonwealth Universities (ACU). The scheme provides General Scholarships, but also provides scholarships for students who wish to

study either jointly between a university in the UK and a Commonwealth university or to undertake much of their study or research in their own country as part of a Doctorate at a UK university (Split-site Doctoral Fellowships). Further information can be found at *www.csfp-online.org.*

- **DfID Shared Scholarship Scheme**. These are funded by the UK government's Department for International Development and are for students studying in a field relevant to development issues. Further information is available at *www.dfid.gov.uk/ funding/sharedscholarships.asp.*

UK Research Council scholarships and studentships Each of the seven research councils in the UK that fund university research has scholarship schemes. These are only open to UK students and EU students, and not postgraduates from outside these areas. Full-time scholarships, which are highly competitive, cover fees plus living costs of a least £10,500 per year. Applications for scholarships from the research councils have to be made through a university and directly to the research council. Further information is available on the websites listed in Appendix I.

UK business scholarships Most UK businesses that provide scholarships provide them for their own sponsored employees. Companies with an international profile with offices and bases around the world may therefore offer some of these awards to students from outside the UK. These may be available for study in a university in your own country, but may also be available for study in the UK.

Charity organization scholarships Just as with charitable organizations in your own country, UK-based charities may be able to offer scholarships for international students. Some charitable trusts, for example, see the sponsorship of international students as a key aim, and may have a small number of awards available each year. Further information on charitable trusts and scholarships can be found on the websites listed in Appendix I.

University scholarships Scholarships awarded by individual universities are an important source of funding for international students. These may include scholarships paid by the university or by an individual department. Universities use such scholarships as an important part of their marketing – some may be paid for by the university itself, while others may be paid for from endowments or donations made to the university to support international student scholarships. Examples include the Rhodes Scholarships at the University of Oxford and the Gates Scholarships at the University of Cambridge. Information on these scholarships will be published in the university's prospectus or on its website or, often, in a separate booklet on scholarships.

Professional association scholarships

Professional associations, and particularly those with strong international links, sometimes provide scholarships to enable international students to study in the UK. These will be restricted to those studying within one of the fields covered by that professional association – so it is worth looking at the websites of any UK professional body in your academic field to see if they have a scholarship scheme.

To assist postgraduate students in finding a suitable scholarship or other financial support, there are a number of websites that can be used for on-line searching. These include the British Council scholarships website, the Gradfund website at the University of Newcastle, and the Studentmoney searchable website. The web addresses for each of these are listed in Appendix I. In addition, the publication *Prospects Postgraduate Funding Guide*, available from Prospects UK, is an excellent publication providing guidance on funding for postgraduate studies.

There are a number of things to remember about scholarships, though, which are important when you are planning your application:

- They are always very competitive, and you need to present a strong case to persuade the sponsor that you are the best choice.
- If the scholarship is for more than one year you will need to show that you are making good progress in your studies at the end of each year before the scholarship will be confirmed for the following year. The sponsor will always ask the university for an annual report on your progress.
- Scholarships rarely cover all your costs, so you will need to have a plan to provide the additional funds you need – either from savings or by working while you are a student.
- Most scholarships will not fund students who are already receiving a scholarship from somewhere else. This means that it is unusual to receive two or three different part scholarships that together provide all the funding that you need.
- Some scholarships are available to students who are already in the UK starting their second or third year of study on a Doctorate, so do not stop applying for scholarships even after you start your programme.
- Universities will not award a scholarship to a student who is already on their Masters or Doctoral programme simply as a way of helping them through a financial problem. Poverty once you have started your programme will not in itself get you a scholarship, however sympathetic the university is to your problems.
- Wherever possible, plan to cover your costs from your own finances so that you are not dependent on a scholarship.

How can I transfer money to the UK?

As an international student you will need to make arrangements to access your money and funding while you are a student. Transferring money around the world is usually fairly straightforward, but each national government will have its own rules about the ways you can transfer money and how much you can transfer. It is important therefore that you investigate this at a very early stage of your planning. The best way to do this is to make enquiries with your own bank, which will be able to advise you about international banking and money transfer. There are a number of important things to think about though:

- You will need to have a bank account with a bank in your own country that has the facilities to arrange international money transfers.
- Once you arrive in the UK you will need to open a bank account with a UK bank. Almost every university will have branches of the four main UK banks (HSBC, Barclays, NatWest and Lloyds TSB), either on the campus or very nearby, but there are many other banks that you can use. You would be advised to find out from your own bank in your own country whether there is a particular bank in the UK with whom they have special arrangements or with whom they prefer to work. It is also helpful to use a bank near to the university, not just for convenience, but also because they will be experienced at dealing with international students and their financial needs. Some large branches may even have an international student adviser.
- Remember that it can take two or three weeks to open a bank account in the UK. The bank will need to see your passport, confirmation that you are a registered student and confirmation of your address in the UK before you can open an account. This means that you should be sure you have access to money for this time, and you might think about one of the following – using a credit card, checking that your own bank's cashcard will work in the UK, or bringing travellers cheques with you.
- Bank systems vary from country to country and bank to bank. Do not assume that you will be able to arrange financial matters in the same ways in the UK as at home, and always check with your UK bank in good time if you need to make special arrangements.
- You will need to make all your payments in the UK – your fees, your accommodation costs etc. – in sterling.

How easy is it to get a job?

Most students around the world have experience of working in a paid job as well as being a student. Sometimes this may be through a job during vacations, but often students have jobs to support themselves. It is very likely therefore that you may want to get a job to earn extra money while you are a postgraduate student. Most UK students have a part-time job alongside their studies. There are a number of issues you need to think about though if you are planning to work while in the UK.

First, what jobs will be available? Students work in a very wide range of jobs – from serving in fast food restaurants, bars, supermarkets or shops, to working as a cleaner, to being a part-time classroom assistant in a school. You may well have experience in some type of job, which will be helpful in getting a job when you are in the UK. You will also have some idea of the sorts of job you are willing to do and the sorts that you are not willing to do.

Of course, which jobs are actually available will be a matter of chance. In recent years the UK economy has been strong and there have been many jobs available for students. Most students who wanted a job have been able to get one, although this can change at any time. You need to remember, too, that there will be a lot of other students looking for jobs near to the university, so you may find that it is very competitive. Be prepared to act quickly if a job is advertised – call the employer as soon as possible.

You can find out about jobs from a wide range of places. Some will be advertised in local newspapers, some will be advertised on notice boards at the university, some will simply be advertised by a sign in the shop or bar window. Many will be advertised by word of mouth only – a student may tell his or her friends that there is a vacancy where they work. Many students get jobs by simply asking employers directly whether they have a job; if you want to work as a waiter or waitress, for example, then visit all the local restaurants and ask them directly. Some university Student Unions have now developed websites where local employers can advertise jobs that would be suitable for students, so it will be useful to find out if your chosen university does this.

Secondly, there is the question of how much you will be paid. Obviously, this depends on the job and how experienced you are. In the UK, though, there is a minimum wage for those over 21 of £5.25 per hour. This means that most of the jobs that postgraduate students do are likely to pay between £5.25 and £7.00 per hour.

Thirdly, as an international student you need to be aware of laws about working in the UK. If you are from a European Economic Area (EEA) country, then there are no restrictions on you getting a job and working for as many hours as you choose to each week. However, if you are from one of the countries that joined the EU in May 2004 (the eight 'accession' states) there are some restrictions in place, which you should check on the Home Office website at *www.workingintheuk.gov.uk*.

If you are from a country outside the EEA, there are a number of limits that you need to be aware of. You will have come into the UK with a student visa entitling you to stay in the UK as long as you are a full-time student. With a student visa you can get a job that employs you for up to 20 hours per week during university semesters (or terms) and full-time during the vacations without needing to get a work permit. If you have come to the UK with your family, then your husband or wife will only be allowed to work if you will be in the UK as a student for more than 12 months.

Getting a job as a student in the UK is like getting a job as a student anywhere else in the world. Act quickly when you hear about a job, try to give a positive impression when you enquire about a vacancy and try to show you have useful relevant experience. It is worth preparing in advance a short curriculum vitae (resumé) about yourself – no more than two sides of paper, containing personal details (name, address, contact details etc.), a list of the work skills you have and a list of the jobs you have done, with information on the employer and the dates you worked for them. Ask somebody in advance if they will be a reference for any applications you make – this might need to be your university tutor, but could be a previous employer if you have already worked in the UK. Add their contact details to your CV.

Once you have started work you will need to apply for a National Insurance (NI) number. You can do this by contacting the local Benefits Agency office, whose contact details can be found in the telephone directory. You will need to make an appointment to complete the required form and show them documentation including your passport and a letter from your employer confirming your job. Some employers, particularly small businesses, may not know that international students can *start* work without an NI number (UK citizens cannot!), so take with you to any job interview a copy of the leaflet on 'International students working in the UK' which you can download from the DfES website (*www.dfes.gov.uk/international-students/workleaflet.pdf*).

Are there any other ways of reducing the costs or earning money?

Once you are in the UK you may want to think of ways of reducing your cost of living or earning extra income to make your money stretch further. A good way to start with this is to talk with other students on the programme, other students in the university and also the Student Union. They will be able to give you a lot of information on things like where to do your shopping to buy food or clothes at low cost, and how to get a reduction on charges (a discount) for many goods and services. In all university towns and cities there will be many shops and services who will give a discount to students if they can show a Student Union card to prove they are a student – and this could include anything from 10% off the cost of a haircut to half-price cinema tickets to reduced costs in local restaurants. The best advice to help keep your costs down is:

- Join the Student Union so that you can use your student card to get discounts.
- If you need to travel by bus or train, then buy a student travelcard from the bus company or the rail station – this could reduce your travel costs by up to 33%.
- Buy goods and services from shops recommended by the Student Union.
- Many Student Unions have special sales for everything from stationery to pictures to fruit and vegetables, when outside suppliers come to sell goods at special low prices to students.

Above, we described ways of earning extra income by geting a job as an employee on the open job market. However, there are a number of other types of employment you might like to consider.

- If your English is very good, then consider offering conversation lessons in your own language to other students. Most universities have a language centre which teaches a wide range of languages to academics and students, and there may be international language schools in some of the larger cities. You could, of course, simply advertise this yourself on the 'jobs' notice board in the Student Union.
- If your keyboard skills are very good or you have excellent IT skills then consider whether other students might be willing to pay you to type their thesis for them or provide advice on using statistics software.
- Many universities use postgraduate students to work on research projects that academic staff are doing. This will normally be straightforward work like putting data from questionnaires into a database, or doing telephone interviews. Ask the academic staff in your department if they have any need for such support, and look out for advertisements on notice boards or on e-mail for such work.
- Consider working for the university services – perhaps as a catering assistant in the Student Union building, or as an office cleaner. These are often jobs the university finds difficult to fill – and it has the advantage of being a job that is very close to where you work.
- The university often has casual work available at some times of the year for students. This might include:

  (a) Acting as a 'tour guide' for students when they visit the university for open days.
  (b) Acting as a guide or helper for graduation ceremonies.
  (c) Working in a telephone call centre answering enquiries from applicants for courses.
  (d) Helping with summer schools or activity days run by the university for local children and the community.
  (e) Acting as a translator of academic papers in your own language.
  (f) Acting as a translator to help academic visitors to the university who speak your own main language.
  (g) Helping to prepare advertising mailings for the university or your department by 'stuffing envelopes'.

- An opportunity that may be available to Doctoral students is to do some academic teaching within the department you are based in. Many departments use Doctoral students to teach, either as 'demonstrators' providing support in practical classes in science or engineering, or to teach undergraduate course units. Sometimes, if you are awarded a scholarship there will be an expectation that you will do a small amount of paid teaching as part of the scholarship.

In connection with this last point, you will obviously have to have shown the academic staff that you have excellent knowledge in your field, and also that you have the basic skills to teach – for example, you will need to have the confidence to teach a class and the English language skills to communicate well. Many universities will provide some training and may require you to attend a short course before you are allowed to teach. Others build teaching skills courses into the training they give to *all* research students, as they believe that teaching and communication are essential skills for any Doctoral student. Teaching will be well paid compared to typical student jobs, and may be paid between £20 and £40 per hour – so it is worth doing. It is also very useful experience if you feel you might want a career as a university teacher after finishing your postgraduate programme.

● ● ●   *Pause for thought*   ● ● ●

If you think you will need to work to earn money while you are in the UK, think in advance of the jobs you might do.

(a) *List all the jobs that you already have experience of doing.*
(b) *List the skills you have that you think may be marketable, e.g. language skills, IT skills, secretarial skills, working with children, sport coaching etc.*
(c) *Think whether you have any contacts with family and friends who are in the UK. Can they help you with getting employment? If so, then make contact with them.*

What if I get into financial difficulties?

Wherever in the world you go to study for a postgraduate degree, it is unlikely that you will feel very wealthy during your time as a student. However, most postgraduates cope well on a limited budget – and even those who come to the UK with some concerns about finance usually find that they are able to find a part-time job to help support them. However, there is a risk for some students that they will get into financial difficulties – perhaps because money from home is delayed, or because changing exchange rates mean that you have less money than you expected, or perhaps because you lose your job or have unexpected costs or ill-health. While universities cannot solve all your financial problems, they can give a great deal of advice and support if you get into financial difficulties.

- All universities will have expert advisers in the Student Union who have considerable experience of the sort of financial problems all students can face and particularly those that international students may face. So this is often the place to start if you need help.

- Most universities have hardship funds to help students in extreme difficulties. The Student Union advisers will be able to tell you how to apply for support from the hardship fund. The support may be as a loan that you have to pay back but might be a grant that you do not have to repay. However, hardship funds can usually only give you small sums of money for an emergency – perhaps up to £200. They will not be able to solve long-term financial issues. For example: many students from Thailand and Sri Lanka had difficulties receiving money from home, or built up large telephone bills seeking to find if their family was safe, following the Indian Ocean tsunami in December 2004. Hardship funds were used to support them until their own banks were able to send money again.
- Universities will normally be willing to find ways of paying your fees over a longer period of time if necessary. You will need to discuss this with the Finance Department or Fees Office, but most are very willing to help. But it is important to remember that you will eventually have to pay all your fees – and most universities will not allow you to be awarded your degree until you have settled all your university debts, even if you have successfully completed the course.
- You should also talk to your bank. Banks are very experienced with the financial issues international students may face and can give excellent advice. They may be able to provide you with a loan, or reschedule your debts.

The most important thing, though, is to talk about your financial problems *as early as you can* – do not wait until it has become a very serious problem. Financial problems do not disappear if you pretend they are not there, and it is usually much easier to get help if the problem is dealt with at an early stage.

KEY RISKS AND HOW TO AVOID THEM

Most students cope well with the financial issues of taking a postgraduate programme. They do this by thinking carefully about the financial issues in advance and planning ways of coping with them. The key risks and ways to avoid them are:

Risk 1: *Not having enough funding for your fees and living costs*   Be sure that you have funding for the fees plus at least £7,000 for yourself for living costs, and at least £2,000 for each member of your family who will be coming with you. You do not need to have all this before you leave home, but you do need to have a clear view of how you will get this funding during the academic year.

Risk 2: *Not having enough money at the start of your programme*   The most expensive part of your programme will be the start – you may have to pay a deposit for accommodation and to buy special equipment. So, although you may be able to spread some of the costs throughout the year, including fees and living costs, you should be sure to have at least £1,000 available at the start of your programme for the 'up-front' costs.

Risk 3: *Not having access to your money when you first arrive in the UK* You should open a bank account as soon as you can after arriving in the UK, but ensure that you bring enough money to support you for two or three weeks in case it takes some time to sort out your finance. This could be as cash, as travellers cheques or by using a credit card.

Risk 4: *Applying too late for a scholarship* Start your search for scholarships as early as possible, preferably up to a year before you want to start your studies. Then apply for as many scholarships as possible, making sure that you meet the closing date.

Risk 5: *Assuming you have got a scholarship* It is surprisingly common for students to arrive in the UK believing that because they applied for a scholarship from a sponsor they must have been awarded one – and then they discover that they have not. Do not assume you have been awarded a scholarship until you have a letter which confirms that you have.

Risk 6: *Getting into financial difficulties and not seeking advice and help* Make sure that you seek advice when problems first begin to appear – do not leave it too late.

Risk 7: *Deciding that you will pay for most or all of your studies from a job while you are a student* Some students manage to do this, but it is a risk because it is not possible to guarantee that you can get a job. Also, it is quite difficult to get a job you can only work for 20 hours per week by law, that will pay enough to cover fees and living costs. So by all means plan to get a job – but be realistic about how much you can earn.

Risk 8: *Not acting quickly enough when you hear about job vacancies* There are always many students looking for jobs, so ring the enquiry number or visit the employer as quickly as you can when you hear about a vacancy.

Risk 9: *Not seeing the university as a potential source of employment* Most universities employ hundreds or thousands of people in every sort of job, from teaching undergraduates to office cleaning. Your own department may have jobs to help on research projects or to show new students around the campus. Your friends and colleagues and the staff in your department may be looking for 'babysitters' or language conversation. Be aware of the opportunities.

Risk 10: *Being so frightened of financial worries that you do not do a postgraduate degree* Most students find ways of coping and surviving financially, and most manage to find a job while they are a student. So, just as you should not leave home without planning your finances, you equally should not feel that you cannot leave home unless every financial issue is planned down to the last pound, dollar or yen.

CHAPTER 6
MOVING TO THE UK

- What are the immigration processes for students?
- What will the authorities in my own country need?
- How can I arrange accommodation?
- How can I arrange schools for my children?
- Getting there: how do I travel to the UK and get from the airport to my university town and accommodation?
- How will I settle in and will I experience 'culture shock'?

First thoughts

Moving to live in another country is both an exciting and a frightening idea for most people. The excitement of discovering a new culture, a different climate, meeting new friends and studying for a postgraduate degree ought to be a real attraction for you. However, people live their lives differently and have different ways of doing things in another country – and many of the familiar parts of your life, from how to do your shopping to social activities to how services such as trains, buses or health provision work may be different. It would be unusual if you did not feel nervous about what this will all mean for you.

It is important to realize that another country is not another planet! People from every country always have more things in common than they expect and find there are more similarities than differences. For example, people are people – they have the same everyday concerns about where they live, shopping for everyday needs, finding a job, looking after their family, making and spending time with friends, following their interests and leisure pursuits and, for many, following their faith. Where people do these things in different ways it is exciting to compare lives and experiences and to learn from this. Making friends across the world and from different cultures is both an exciting learning experience for you but also, we believe very strongly, essential to build international understanding and trust.

At the end of your time in the UK you will know all this – but before you come there are many things that can help you make the move to the UK as easy as possible, and that is what this chapter is all about.

What are the immigration processes for students?

The UK welcomes postgraduate students from all over the world. Entering the UK is, for most students, fairly straightforward, but there are rules and regulations about immigration that you need to know about. The laws on immigration change from time to time, but we shall describe here the regulations that you need to be aware of. **But – it is important that you check the current regulations and identify exactly what regulations apply to you and your family by looking at the latest advice on the UK visas website (*www.ukvisas.gov.uk*) and seeking the advice of an entry clearance post (see below) in your own country.** The UK government announced in March 2006 new procedures (called the Points-Based System) for assessing whether a visa should be given to those from outside the European Economic Area who have applied for entry into the UK. The system will be introduced gradually and the changes affecting international students (to be called Tier 4 immigrants) will probably be introduced in 2008. It is very important therefore that you visit the UK visas website to check the current situation.

If you are a citizen of a country in the European Economic Area (EEA) you are entitled to enter the UK as a visitor, to work or as a student with few restrictions, and to bring your family members with you. All you will need is a valid passport that you will have to show when you enter the UK. The European Economic Area is the countries of the European Union (EU) plus Iceland, Liechtenstein and Norway. The European Union countries are:

> Austria, Belgium, Czech Republic, Cyprus, Denmark, Estonia, Finland, France, Germany, Greece, Hungary, Ireland, Italy, Latvia, Lithuania, Luxembourg, Malta, Netherlands, Poland, Portugal, Slovakia, Slovenia, Spain, Sweden and the UK.

In addition, while Switzerland is not formally a member of the EEA or the EU, it is regarded as a member of the EEA for most immigration purposes.

If you are a citizen of any other country then you will need a special student visa to enter the UK as a student if your programme is longer than six months. This visa entitles you to stay in the UK for the length of your postgraduate programme, and to work for up to 20 hours per week during term time and full time during vacations without needing a work permit.

Visas are issued by the British government at Entry Clearance Posts, which are usually the British Embassy or Consulate in your own country. If there is no British diplomatic mission, the entry clearance post may be through the embassy or consulate of a country that has agreed to carry out this role for the UK. The location and contact details of the entry clearance posts in your own country can be found on the British government websites-*www.ukvisas.gov.uk* and *www.fco.gov.uk*.

The UK visas website also provides detailed information on all aspects of immigration and applying for permission to enter the UK. Before applying for a visa you should look in detail at this website, and also at the website of the UK government's Immigration and Nationality Directorate at *www.ind.home office.gov.uk*, where you will be able to find information about individual questions that you have and how to make general enquiries about visas etc.

The visa will only be issued if you can provide clear evidence that:

1 You have a valid passport which will remain valid until after the date you will complete your programme in the UK.
2 If required, you have the permission of your own government to study in the UK.
3 You have a letter containing an offer of a place on a Masters or Doctoral programme at a recognized UK university. When the Points-Based System is introduced (probably in 2008) a visa will be issued for entry to the UK to study one specific programme only. Therefore, you will need to have decided which offer of a place that you wish to accept before you apply for a visa, and will need to have the formal offer letter from that university (which will be called your 'sponsor' by the visa authorities) to include with your visa application.
4 You have made financial arrangements to support yourself and, if necessary, your family and dependants, while you are in the UK. You will need to be able to demonstrate this with letters or statements from your bank, or with pay slips.
5 You agree that you will obey the rules on employment while you are in the UK that limit the amount of paid work you can do.
6 You confirm that you will leave the UK at the end of your postgraduate programme.

The procedure for applying for a student visa varies between countries. In some cases you need to fill in the visa application form and send it together with your passport, the relevant payment, a recent passport-sized photograph and any supporting documents needed to the nearest UK government entry clearance post. Often, though, you will need to arrange an appointment to attend the embassy or consulate in person. Detailed information about procedures in each country can be found on the UK government website at *www. ukvisas.gov.uk*.

The fee from 1 July 2005 is £85, payable in local currency. The application will be processed, and if it is approved, you will be sent the visa and your passport. The process can take several weeks, but is normally completed within a few days. You can find the current waiting time for visas in each country by looking at the website at *www.ukvisas.gov.uk*. You will need to be very careful to complete the application forms correctly and provide all the information that is requested to reduce the chances of your application being refused.

It is important to remember that if you are planning to bring any members of your family with you to the UK you will also need to obtain a visa for each of them. This can be done at the same time as making your own application.

Visas can be issued for varying lengths of time and also for single or multiple entries into the UK. A visa may be issued, for example, for only one year, even if you are planning to study in the UK for up to three years. In this case you will need to apply to the Home Office in the UK to have your visa renewed for further years, and you will need to do this in good time. Your university, either through the Student Union or the university's own student services department, will be able to assist you in making an application for a visa extension once you are in the UK. Every university is required by the government to have a named individual who is responsible for student-related immigration advice, and you will be able to find out who that is and how to contact them from the Student Union.

Be sure to check whether your visa is for single or multiple entry. Multiple entry means that you can enter and leave the UK as often as you like while the visa is valid. This means that you can return home for a visit for example, or travel on holiday to another country, and then be allowed to re-enter the UK. However, if you have a single entry visa, you are only allowed to enter at the start of your programme and leave at the end – and if you leave the country at any other time you will not be allowed to re-enter the UK without a new visa. A single entry visa will probably not be a problem if you are coming to the UK for a one year Masters programme, but if you need to stay longer than this to follow a Doctoral programme then you should certainly try to obtain a multiple entry visa.

In some cases your visa will be granted but with the requirement that you register with the police in the UK after you arrive. If this is required then it will say this clearly in your passport. If you need to do this you must register with the police within seven days of arriving in the UK. If you will be living in London then you will need to report to the office in central London that handles such registrations – the address can be found at *www.ukvisas.gov.uk*. Elsewhere in the UK you will need to report to the nearest police station. To register with the police you will need to pay a registration fee and take with you two passport photographs of each member of your family accompanying you into the UK.

There are two other important things to remember about visas and travel to the UK. The first is that you should not be confused by the fact that the parts of the UK (England, Scotland, Wales and Northern Ireland) are sometimes called 'countries'. While they have some different laws from each other, and Wales and Scotland have their own parliaments, all are part of the United Kingdom – so you do not need a passport or visa to travel between them, and there are no restrictions or immigration procedures at the borders between them. Entering one of them from outside entitles you to move freely within all of them.

The second is that we have only described here the visa regulations for entering the UK. If you want to travel outside the UK while you are here as a student you will still need to satisfy all the visa and entry requirements of any other country you enter, including other countries in the European Union. So do not assume you can travel to Paris for a week's holiday without needing to meet the visa and passport requirements of the French government!

What will the authorities in my own country need?

Many countries require their citizens to get permission before leaving the country to study. You should always check, therefore, what the procedures are in your own country, and begin these procedures as early as possible. Check with your own national government offices what the requirements are, or ask at the local British Council office. In some cases they will require evidence that you have been offered a place to study on a genuine university programme before they will give their permission, so you will need to have the confirmation or offer letter from your university. They may also want to interview you to check that you are qualified to study abroad, that you have the finance to study in the UK and that you have made suitable arrangements for any dependants such as your husband or wife, children or parents.

● ● ● *Pause for thought* ● ● ●

Do you have all the key documents you will need to apply for a visa and for a place at a UK university? You will need a passport, for example, so be sure that if you do not have one, you apply for one in good time. Have you got all your other documents, too – birth and marriage registration documents for yourself, your wife or husband and your children, all your examination certificates and transcripts, and translations into English if they will be required?

How can I arrange accommodation ?

An important part of moving to the UK will be finding accommodation for you and, if necessary, your family. Most universities provide international students with a lot of help to get accommodation, so it is almost certain that your accommodation will be arranged before you arrive in the UK. We shall look in Chapter 7 at the details of how to arrange accommodation and at the options that are open to you.

How can I arrange schools for my children?

If your family will be coming with you to the UK then you will need to find school places for any of your children who are between 5 and 16 years old. This will be something that needs to be arranged if possible before you arrive in the UK. We shall look in Chapter 7 at how to make these arrangements.

Getting there: how do I travel to the UK and get from the airport to my university town and accommodation?

Most international students arrive in the UK by air. For many this will mean that they come on an international flight directly from their own country into one of the major airports in the UK – often Heathrow or Gatwick near London, or sometimes Manchester, Birmingham or Glasgow airports. Most international airlines have direct flights to London, for example. If there are no direct flights to London from your own country, then you have two choices – make a short flight to a city or country that does have direct flights to London, or fly direct to another city in Europe such as Paris or Amsterdam then make a short flight to the UK.

If your university is in or close to one of the major cities served by these airports then you can complete your journey by local transport. However, if your university is a long way from one of the main airports you should think whether it might be better to fly to a regional airport closer to your university. Many regional airports have direct flights from London, Birmingham, Manchester or Glasgow, and many also have direct connections to European airports such as Paris or Amsterdam. So, check where the nearest airport is to your university city or town and also check whether you can choose a flight route that goes directly to that airport.

When your flight arrives in the UK you will have to pass first of all through Immigration Control, where you will have to show your passport and your visa to an Immigration Officer. You will also have been given an immigration form on the flight to fill in, which you will need to hand to the immigration Officer. You will then need to collect your baggage from the baggage area, and pass through Customs Control. At this stage you will have to indicate if you are bringing any goods into the UK that require you to pay duty. You need to be aware of the limits and regulations about goods that you bring into the UK. There are obviously some goods that it is illegal to bring into the country, including recreational drugs, firearms, endangered animal products and some foods. In addition there are limits about how much of other goods such as alcohol or tobacco that you can bring with you. The Customs and Excise website at *www.hmce.gov.uk* indicates what you can and cannot bring into the UK, and you should study this carefully before you plan what to bring with you.

After passing through Customs you will enter the Arrivals area of the airport where you can begin your journey to your university or university town.

Every university will give you detailed instructions about how to travel from the airport and where to come to when you arrive at the university or the university town. During late September, the time when most university programmes begin, many universities arrange for a representative to be at the nearest major airport to welcome international students and assist them with their journey from the airport. This may include providing a special bus to take you to the university, which obviously makes transport very easy for you. However, it is more likely you will need to make your own travel arrangements, and this will usually involve travelling by bus or train.

Major airports all have good bus connections, as part of the national bus network. You will be able to catch a bus to almost any city in the UK, although your journey may involve changing buses at some point. The websites at *www.nationalexpress.com* and *www.gobycoach.com* contain information on national bus networks and will enable you to plan your route from the airport. Travel agents will be able to book a ticket for you before you leave your own country.

Most airports also have excellent rail connections, and you may be able to travel to your university town by train. This may involve catching a train into the centre of the nearest city (for example from London Heathrow to central London) and then catching a connecting train to your destination. The website at *www.national rail.co.uk* contains information on national rail networks and will enable you to plan your rail journey from the airport. Travel agents will be able to book a ticket for you before you leave your own country. Rail travel is usually faster and more comfortable than bus travel in the UK, but is also more expensive.

You will arrive in your university town or city at either the railway station or the bus station, and you will need to then find your way to your arrival point. This could be one of several places, and your university should have given you clear instructions about where you should report to. It could be:

- A reception point at the university, where there are staff and students to welcome you and help you find your way to your accommodation.
- Your accommodation, if it is in university halls of residence. You will need to report to the reception office at the halls of residence, and they will direct you to your room or flat.
- If you are living in rented accommodation outside the university, then you may need to arrange with the accommodation owner (the landlord) or agent to meet them at the accommodation address.

To get to your arrival point, with all your luggage, you will probably find it easiest to get a taxi. Taxis are available at most bus stations and rail stations, and licensed taxis are clearly identified by their signs. Taxis in the UK are not cheap, and you will probably have to pay about £1 for each kilometre of the journey – the fare will be the amount you can see on the fare meter at the end of the journey, and in addition you should normally give the taxi driver a 10% tip, particularly if you had a lot of luggage the driver helped to carry. Remember you will have to pay this in cash, so have enough UK currency to hand for this.

There are three particular problems that new arrivals sometimes have to face, and we shall look here at how to deal with these.

Your flight/bus arrives late at night   It is important to check well in advance what the time will be in the UK when you arrive as a late arrival time may cause you some difficulties. (Sometimes, of course, flights are delayed and you may arrive in the UK late at night even if that was not your schedule.) While many airports are open 24 hours a day, trains and buses do not run through the night. Also, you will face problems if your schedule means that you will arrive at your university or university town at night, as the reception points are likely only to be open during normal working hours (9 am to 5 pm). We would recommend very strongly, therefore, that you arrange your journey so that you arrive at your reception point well within the working day (probably no later than 3 pm), and that you do not arrive at a weekend, for you may then have to wait until Monday to report to reception. If this is not possible, then arrange in advance to stay in a hotel or guest house for one night, either near to the airport or close to the rail station or bus station in your university town. This can be arranged in advance for you by your travel agent, and you can then simply get a taxi either from the airport or the rail/bus station to your hotel/guest house. This will allow you to rest, and you can then report to reception the following day.

Your accommodation is not available when you first arrive   It is quite unusual for accommodation not to be available for you, unless of course you have not arranged any. Providing you have been in communication with the accommodation office at the university, there should not be any problem.

They will have advised you about where you can stay temporarily if need be until your accommodation is available or until you have found somewhere to live. Universities often have temporary accommodation where new international arrivals can stay for a few days until they can move to their permanent accommodation, or can provide details of low cost hotels or guest houses where you can stay.

You arrive at an unusual time of year   Most programmes start in late September or early October, but it is possible in many universities to start a PhD programme at any time of the year. If you arrive at the university in time for the normal start of the academic year then there are usually careful arrangements to welcome you and help you, but if you arrive at another time this may be more difficult. If this is the case, then discuss with your university admissions staff and with your university department what the arrival arrangements will be.

The most important things to remember, though, are:

- Do not arrive at your university outside normal working hours, Monday to Friday, if you can possibly avoid it.
- If you must arrive outside these times, arrange in advance accommodation where you can stay until the university will be 'open'.

- Always be sure you have made arrangements before you leave home about where you are going to be staying for at least your first three nights in your university town or city, even if this needs to be in a hotel or guest house.
- Make sure that you have UK currency with you before you leave the airport to pay for taxis, telephone calls or food and drink.

How will I settle in and will I experience 'culture shock'?

Everybody at the university will understand that you are new to the UK, new to the university and new to postgraduate study, and you can be confident that there will be many ways in which the university will try to help you 'settle in' as quickly as possible. You should receive information before you leave home about your programme of 'induction' or 'welcome', but you will also receive this information when you first arrive. You should expect that there will be a number of parts to your induction/welcome:

- **Programme and department activities**. Your programme or department will have arranged a number of events, which will include the chance to meet academic staff (particularly the programme leader and your personal tutor), support staff and other students, and the chance to familarize yourself with the department's facilities. This may well include some social events in the first week or so to help you to get to know staff and students.
- **University activities**. The university will also have a welcome and induction programme. This will partly be to help you find out about the services of the university – how to use the library, the computer system etc.
- **Student Union activities**. The Student Union organizes and manages the student social facilities in the university, and they will organize a range of events to welcome you. Some will be specifically for international students, others will be for all students. This will give you a chance to make friends and socialize. At the start of the academic year, too, there will be a 'Freshers Fair' organized by the Student Union, where you will have chance to find out about all the clubs, societies and organizations within the university that may interest you – the football club, the drama society, the Chinese society, etc. You will find there is an organization or society to cater for a very wide range of interests.
- **Registration**. This is the formal process of registering you at the university, and includes registering on your course, registering for library membership and e-mail and arranging payment of your fees. Many universities now ask you to register 'on-line' rather than in person, and it is often possible to do this before you leave your own country. The university will provide you with details of how to do this.

So your first few days at the university are going to be busy. You should think of this time as time for 'discovery' – finding your way around the university, around your department, around the library and around the student social facilities. This is a time when you should talk to other students – those on your programme, those on other programmes, new students like yourself and those who have been at the university for some time. Also, get to know the university town or city; you could arrange a visit to the town/city centre, and even visit some of the 'tourist' sites in the town. Think of these first few days almost as a working vacation, and do not worry about trying to do any studying at this stage.

Although you will get very tired, from the journey to the UK and the busy programme of settling in and the effort of living in a new environment, you will not have much time to feel homesick. However, you will probably want to contact friends and family at home just to let them know how you are settling in.

Once your programme starts, then you will begin to establish a work and life routine. We have looked in an earlier chapter at how you might expect to spend your time as a postgraduate student. After a few weeks you will be quite familiar with the university, your programme and your new town or city. Most students are very comfortable at this stage and enjoy their life as a postgraduate student, but a small number may start to feel homesick, feeling they are a long way from home, family and friends. In particular you may feel that the strangeness of language, lifestyles and social interactions are very tiring and challenging. There are a number of ways to try to cope with this feeling:

- Spend time with new friends and try to develop a good social life.
- Try to get a job, even if you do not desperately need the money – this will be interesting and enable you to meet people.
- Plan a trip. This could be a trip home at the end of your first term, or it might be a weekend trip to London or to see a friend at another university.
- Try to have at least one event each week to look forward to – meeting your friends, going to the cinema, or going for a walk.
- Do not speak with your family and friends at home too frequently. Hearing their voices might increase feelings of homesickness. Phone them once a week, perhaps.
- Keep in regular contact with family and friends by e-mail or text, or chat to them on-line.
- Talk to somebody about your feelings – your friends, your classmates, your tutor, the Student Union international officer. Most will understand how you feel (they may be feeling the same themselves!), and together you will cope with the challenge.

● ● ● *Pause for thought* ● ● ●

Is there anybody you know who has been a student in the UK recently? This might be a friend or a member of your family or somebody you knew a year or two ahead of you in university. Your university tutors may know students from earlier years who have been to the UK or who are still there. The university you plan to go to in the UK may also be able to put you in contact with former students (alumni) from your own country. Try to make contact with anybody who has come to the UK as a student to find out about their experiences.

And what about the weather?

British people have a reputation for always talking about the weather – and the popular image of British weather is that it is always raining. Be assured that neither of these is true! Wherever in the world you come from to the UK, though, you will notice that the weather and climate are different from home. Experiencing the British weather is part of experiencing Britain. There are two main things to know about it:

- It is very changeable. It is quite common for a single day to have a wide variety of weather from rain to sunshine to cloud and for the temperature to change from cool to warm or the other way round. It also changes a lot from day to day. This means that you need to be ready for almost any weather at any time.
- It does not tend to have extremes. British winters are not usually too cold, and the summers are not usually either very hot or very wet. Also, there are very few extreme or violent events, such as hurricanes.

So what is it like? Well, it depends a little on where in the UK you are going to be living, as the weather in Glasgow, for example, in Scotland, is different from that in London, or on the south coast at Brighton. The further north you live the colder you will find the weather, both in summer and winter. The driest part of the country is the south-east, and the annual rainfall increases as you go west or north from there.

We can look at the weather for each season of the year, and there are four seasons recognized in Britain: winter (December to March), spring (March to June), summer (June to September) and autumn (September to December). As most students arrive in the UK in September, we will look at the weather through the year from autumn onwards.

- **Autumn** sees the weather change from summer to winter. At the start temperatures are typically 15–20 Celsius during the day and 5–10 Celsius at night. By the end of autumn, daytime temperatures will be 5–15 Celsius, while night time temperatures will be 0 to 5 Celsius. It will rain on about 50 per cent of days, but there may be drier spells of a few days, particularly in September. When it rains it will rain for 2–4 hours, often of showers rather than heavy rain.
- **Winter** is the coldest and wettest season of the year. Generally the weather is cloudy, with sunny spells, with daytime temperatures reaching 5–10 Celsius, and night temperatures between –2 and +5 Celsius. Frosty nights are common, but snow is quite rare in most of the country; it is more common in the north, but even here there will usually only be 5–7 snowy days each year. Rainfall is typically 2–5 cm per month with 15–20 rainy days each month.
- **Spring** sees the weather improving towards summer. It can include a mixture of winter and summer weather. By April daytime temperatures are typically 12–14 Celsius and night time temperatures are 5–10 Celsius, although there may still be occasional

night time frosts. Rainfall declines during spring, although most months have 5–15 days with rain.

- **Summer** is the warmest and driest time of the year, but there are no very dry months, and even in July and August there may be rain on 5–10 days each month. Daytime temperatures are usually 18–25 Celsius, with night time temperatures of 7–12 Celsius. Most summers, though, have one or more hot dry spells, usually of 5–10 days, when temperatures can sometimes reach 30 Celsius or occasionally more. Hot weather in Britain is often quite humid and sticky, though, and hot spells often end with a short period of thunderstorms.

You will need to be ready for any weather, therefore. How you feel about the weather will depend upon what the weather is like at home and what you are used to. If home is in a tropical or sub-tropical country you will find the winters cold, but if you come from Scandinavia, Canada or Russia then the winters will feel mild. So, you will need a waterproof coat and an umbrella for the wet weather, a few sweaters and a good coat for the cold weather, and light clothing and sunglasses for the warm weather. You may prefer to wait to buy some of this clothing once you get to the UK – the clothing here is obviously designed for British weather, and you can also see what you need once you are in the UK. However, you are probably best advised to bring a waterproof coat and at least one sweater with you in your luggage.

KEY RISKS AND HOW TO AVOID THEM

In this chapter we have looked at questions about coming to the UK for the first time as a student. The key risks that we have identified, and the ways of avoiding them are:

Risk 1: *Not having the right paperwork to get a visa when you apply*   Ensure that you have all your personal documents such as a passport, birth and marriage registration documents and a formal letter offering you a place at a UK university.

Risk 2: *Not having the right paperwork to enter or stay in the UK*   Make sure you have the right immigration documents, including a passport and student visa. Plan this well in advance so that you have plenty of time to sort out the paperwork. In some countries this can take many weeks, so start the process at least six months before you want to come to the UK.

Risk 3: *Having a difficult journey to the UK*   Plan your journey and travel to the UK very carefully, and use a travel agent with experience of travel to the UK. Get advice from your university about how to travel there and the arrangements for welcoming and meeting new international students.

Risk 4: *Losing your luggage*   Fortunately this is quite rare, but it is worth taking precautions in case it happens. Carry essential documents, medication and money in your hand luggage, and spread your possessions between your suitcases so that you do not, for example, have all your warm clothes in only one suitcase.

Risk 5: *Arriving at your university town at a time when you cannot go straight to your accommodation or to the university reception point*   Avoid arriving in your university town at a weekend or outside normal working hours. If you do not have guaranteed university accommodation from the day of your arrival, arrange to book a hotel or guest house for your first few days.

Risk 6: *Not having enough cash to meet your needs in the first few days*   Do not leave the airport without enough UK currency as cash to support you for taxi fares, food and drink for three or four days.

Risk 7: *Not having suitable clothing for the first few days in the British climate*   Bring both a waterproof coat and a sweater with you, and check the current British weather through the internet a day or so before you leave home.

Risk 8: *Not making many contacts with family, friends and acquaintances who are or have recently been in the UK*   Make contact with these people several weeks before you are coming to the UK. They can provide lots of information and guidance and will be helpful contacts when you first arrive in the UK.

Risk 9: *Not knowing whom to contact in an emergency when you reach the UK*   It is worth carrying the contact telephone numbers of the key people whose help you might want if you have any problems when you first arrive. Your university and the Student Union may have emergency contact numbers, as will your embassy or consulate. Also have the numbers of the family, friends and acquaintances that you know in the UK.

Risk 10: *Feeling homesick*   It is natural that you will miss your family and friends at home, but get involved in university life, make friends, keep e-mail contact with people at home and you should be able to deal with it. Arrange a treat for yourself every week, such as a social event, and share your feelings with a friend.

CHAPTER 7
LIVING IN THE UK

- How welcoming is the UK to international students?
- What accommodation will be available?
- How will I find a school or childcare for my children?
- How easily will I be able to practise my religion?
- Will my personal attitudes and values fit in?
- What is shopping and entertainment like for students in the UK?
- What happens during university vacations?
- Is there anything else I should know?

First thoughts

Most students find that they settle into living in the UK quite quickly, and that they soon understand how the British way of life works. Western culture in general is quite well known and understood around the world as a result of global communications, and many international students coming to the UK are surprised by how much they already know and understand about the country, its people and their culture. You will also soon discover that some of the images you have of the UK are simply stereotypes or out-of-date, and there will be aspects of living in the UK that will come as a surprise to you. In this chapter we shall look at some of the main aspects of life in the UK that will affect you as an international postgraduate student.

How welcoming is the UK to international students?

The UK has a reputation as a country that welcomes visitors from around the world. It is a multicultural society into which people from a wide range of cultural backgrounds have settled, particularly in the past 30 years. There is increasing understanding and valuing of the contribution that these different groups make to British society and culture. The media, most businesses and most communities reflect the diversity of cultures in the UK. In the communities in which universities are located, therefore, you will find that international students are welcome as part of that diversity, and the community, businesses and public services have long experience of working with people from a wide range of cultures. If you walk around the shopping areas of any British city you will see people from many ethnic backgrounds; you will see shops selling a wide range of foods and goods from around the world and restaurants from many cultural traditions (Chinese and Indian food, for example, are very popular in the UK). All major cities will have a mosque, a Gurdawara and a synagogue as well as Christian churches. In smaller towns, of course, this diversity may be less obvious, and there may not be the range of cultural and faith services.

It would be naïve, of course, to think that there are never issues that international students face because they are recognized as coming from different cultural or ethnic backgrounds. But incidents of ethnic-related crime or abuse are relatively rare in comparison to many other countries, and every university will provide clear guidance if there are localities or particular sorts of behaviour in the city which should be avoided.

All this means that not only will you feel that you are welcome yourself, but also you that you have a real opportunity to get to know not just British culture, but also the wide range of other cultures that are found in the UK today.

What accommodation will be available?

Accommodation is an important part of your life in the UK. When you first arrive in the country you will want to be sure that you have suitable accommodation waiting for you, and you will want to be sure that your accommodation will be suitable to give you a comfortable life as a student. This is particularly important if you will be bringing your family with you to the UK. Universities recognize the importance of assisting with accommodation arrangements, and every university has an accommodation office to help with this. You will find information about the accommodation office in the prospectus and on the website of each university, and there will be information sent to you if you are offered a place on a postgraduate programme. It is extremely important that when this information comes you read it very carefully so that you understand the accommodation situation.

The accommodation arrangements are different for every university. Some will guarantee a place in a university hall of residence for all international postgraduate students. At the opposite extreme some will have almost no university accommodation for any postgraduates, so they will all need to live in private sector rented accommodation. For most universities the situation is somewhere between these two extremes.

If you are able to apply to live in a hall of residence then the accommodation offered will probably be a single study bedroom. This may have its own private facilities with a shower and toilet in a separate room leading from the study bedroom. This is described as 'en suite' facilities. Alternatively the showers and toilet facilities may be shared between several study bedrooms. In either arrangement there will probably be a kitchen that is shared by several students, and which is equipped with a refrigerator, a cooker and a sink.

The accommodation may be provided with a wide range of different arrangements. Most universities will have mixed halls of residence, which means that both men and women share the same hall. However, most universities will also have single sex halls of residence for those who prefer such arrangements. Similarly there will be variations in the provision of meals. Some halls of residence will be available on a self-catering basis, which means that no meals are provided. In such circumstances the halls will have kitchen facilities. Others may include meals in the cost, and you will be able to eat in the refectory or cafeteria in the hall of residence. Clearly, you can choose whichever arrangements you prefer.

Most halls of residence will have some communal facilities, including for example a common room, a television room, a small shop and laundry facilities. They will also provide cleaning services for the communal areas, including the kitchens, but you will have responsibility for keeping your own room clean. Washing clothes will also be your own responsibility. You will be able to do this using the self-service laundrettes which are available in most halls of residence or in the Student Union facilities in the university. You will also find private laundrettes in most localities, which you will be able to use.

If you are applying to live in a hall of residence then you will need to complete the application form by the deadline indicated to you. The university will then confirm back to you whether or not you have been allocated accommodation. Until you receive this confirmation you should not assume that you have been given a place in a hall of residence.

If you will not be able to get a place in a hall of residence then you will need to rent accommodation near to the university. All universities have lists of properties that students can rent from private landlords. In many cases these will have been inspected by the accommodation office to be sure they are of a suitable quality and that the rent is fair. However, the accommodation office will not usually make the arrangements for you – you will have to do this yourself by contacting the property's owner or landlord. The advantage of such private accommodation is that you can find something to suit your own needs and budget. The disadvantage is that it is difficult to make arrangements before you arrive in the UK. If you have to find private rented accommodation you may find it easier to make temporary arrangements for somewhere to live before you arrive, and then look for a permanent place after you have arrived. The accommodation office can usually give advice on finding temporary accommodation.

If you are bringing your family with you it is often more difficult to find a university that can accommodate you. Although some do have family flats, many do not. You will therefore have to find private rented accommodation. If you cannot arrange this until after you arrive in the UK, you may prefer to travel on your own initially and then arrange for your family to join you when you have found suitable accommodation.

● ● ●   *Pause for thought*   ● ● ●

Think about the sort of accommodation that you would like while studying in the UK. Would you prefer to live in a hall of residence or to share a house with other students? Would you prefer self-catering accommodation or would you like somewhere where your meals are provided? Do you have particular needs – for example, do you have mobility problems or some other disability? Would you prefer single sex accommodation? Do you want to live very close to the university or would you prefer to live a little further away? Write down a list of what you will be looking for in terms of accommodation.

How will I find a school or childcare for my children?

If your family and children will be coming to the UK with you, then finding a school or childcare will be an important issue for you. In the UK children must attend school between the ages of 5 and 16, and many of course stay in school or college until they are 18 and can go on to university. If you bring children with you who are of this age then they will be required to attend school. Most children attend local community schools – primary schools for 5 to 11-year-olds and secondary (or high) schools for 11 to 16-year-olds. These schools are free, and in university towns and cities will be quite used to taking children of international students. The accommodation office at the university you have chosen will be able to provide you with a list of local schools, and you will then need to contact the Principal of the school directly (known as a Headteacher in the UK) to arrange a place for your child.

Choosing a school before you actually arrive in the UK is quite difficult of course. Normally you would want to know what parents and the local community feels about each school before choosing. Also, you may not know exactly where your family will be living and what will be the nearest school. If you do know where you will be living, however, you can get ahead and apply for places before you arrive in the UK. If you wait until after you arrive, you need to use your first few days to approach local schools quite quickly to find a place for your child.

In theory, parents in the UK can choose which school to send their children to. Most tend to use the nearest school, particularly for their primary age children, but you will want to be sure that the school you choose is suitable for your children. Successful schools, of course, are popular and because schools have a limited capacity you may find your nearest school has no space for your children. However, you will normally be able to find a good alternative in a neighbouring area.

To help parents in choosing a school, the academic performance and quality of schools is carefully monitored by the government through a system of school inspections. Inspection reports for schools in England and Wales are published on the web. In England (but not in Wales, Scotland or Northern Ireland) the achievement of every school in examinations is also published in 'league tables'. You can view this information on the following websites:

For league tables: *www.dfes.gov.uk/performancetables*
For inspection reports: *www.ofsted/gov.uk/reports*

The British Council website (*www.britishcouncil.org*) has a useful leaflet on *'Choosing a state-funded school'* which you can download.

If you have children younger than 5 years old then you may want to find a nursery or childcare place for them. We have looked at the issues and costs involved in this in Chapter 5.

How easily will I be able to practise my religion?

As a multicultural society, the UK has members of every world religion or faith within the community. All universities recognize that their students will have a wide range of faiths, as well as having students with strong religious beliefs and those with none. University life itself is secular, but as academic communities universities value the range of beliefs that their students hold, and will provide opportunities for you to follow your own faith. Most universities have a chaplaincy service run jointly by priests/ministers from the main Christian denominations – Catholic, Anglican, Methodist, for example. The chaplaincy provides religious support, including services and pastoral care, but will always give advice and guidance to students of other faiths. In larger cities most universities will also have support from priests of other major faiths (including Islam, Judaism, Sikhism, for example), and will also be able to help students to make contact with their own faith groups. Many large universities have non-Christian faith groups that are very active in the university community, and may also have facilities for non-Christian faiths, such as an Islamic prayer room. University prospectuses and websites all have information about religion and faith within the university. If you have specific needs for your faith, then you should check with the university that these can be met.

It is important to note that the weekly and annual calendar of universities is basically the Christian calendar. This means that the working week is Monday to Friday, and the week's rest days are Saturday and Sunday. Holidays are centred around the main Christian festivals of Christmas and Easter. This can raise two particular issues for some students of non-Christian faiths:

- Will I have to attend classes or take examinations on my own faith's religious days? The answer to this is usually 'no'. You may choose to observe your own Sabbath on Friday, for example, if you are a Muslim, although this will mean that you will miss classes that are timetabled for Friday. If you have an examination timed for a holy day or the Sabbath you may ask to have it rescheduled for a different day, but this may mean that you will need to be kept isolated from other students if they have taken the examination at a different time. You should certainly discuss these issues with your tutor when you send in your application if you feel they are likely to be a major issue for you.
- Will I be able to observe religious periods or events, and will there be support for my faith needs at such times? For Muslims celebrating Ramadan, for example, the need for daytime fasting means it is important that meals are available at the correct times. Most universities understand and support the needs of students at such times and ensure that facilities are available either in halls of residence or in student cafeterias at the appropriate time.

As well as having specific needs in relation to religious festivals, many universities also seek to meet some of the dietary needs of students of particular faiths. Most will be able to provide, for example, halal or kosher food by arrangement with individuals or groups of students, either throughout the year or at specific festival times. If these issues are important to you then you should check the university prospectus or website, and also seek the advice of the admissions officer for your programme before you apply. All universities have advisers for international students who will be able to give you clear guidance on what facilities and services are available and, if necessary, which needs they cannot meet. The important thing to note, however, is that you are welcome as a postgraduate student whatever your faith or culture, and you should feel confident that your faith needs can be met within most universities in the UK.

Will my personal attitudes and values fit in?

The UK is recognized by many as a country that has a long history of tolerance and diversity, welcoming people from a wide range of backgrounds and nationalities. The culture is one which has strong traditions and values but a tolerant view of new ideas and varied lifestyles. Some of the important values that you will find in British society are those of religious and political tolerance, a strong belief in equal opportunities, but also a commitment to the rights and responsibilities of the individual within society. It is significant that, throughout history, Britain has been a popular destination for those seeking refuge or asylum from many of the political and military conflicts around the world – and this is not just because of the perceived economic benefits of coming to Britain, but also because of the open society, freedom and tolerance which are to be found here.

This is all reflected in the society and culture of the UK's universities. At every university there is a rich mix of people from across the full range of social attitudes and values. This means that whatever your views, beliefs, personal morality or sexuality you will find many like-minded people at your university, whether these relate to your views on politics, the roles of men and women in society, the importance of traditional codes of dress, or views on personal relationships, sex and sexuality.

This has two important advantages: a) you will be able to feel confident in your own views and beliefs, and have support from friends and fellow students who share them, and b) you will be able to see and hear at first hand a wide range of other views, which will be part of your own wider education. Perhaps more important, however, is the safety that you can feel in your views and values. Universities take great care to support the interests of all their students, be they minority or majority values or beliefs. So whether you have strong moral views based on your faith and culture, or very liberal views, you will feel free to practise and explore your own values and attitudes.

One note of caution must be sounded, however. You need to be aware of personal safety at all times. Students (whether they are UK or international students) can sometimes be a target for crime, particularly if they live in the parts of cities or towns where there is social deprivation or difficult community relations. International students are perhaps more at risk in this way, because they are a more identifiable group. It is important therefore always to think of personal safety, especially at night and in some parts of town (the Student Union will give advice on areas to be avoided). Many Student Unions provide safe transport at night for students who live some way from the university.

What is shopping and entertainment like for students in he UK?

Whatever your postgraduate programme, you will need to spend at least part of your time doing 'everyday' things such as shopping, and you will want to spend part of your time on leisure and entertainment. Many of the UK's major cities are increasingly developing a 24-hour society. Large shops and supermarkets have exended opening hours, in some cases for 24 hours per day, and entertainment venues such as bars and cinemas often have long opening hours too. Smaller towns do not yet have the same 24 hour culture, but this is slowly changing.

Shopping for food usually means that you must choose between the large supermarkets (Tesco, Sainsbury's, Asda, Morrisons) or smaller local shops, which will probably be more expensive. Shopping for clothes or other goods offers a similar choice – small local shops may be more convenient, but will not be able to match the range of choice or lower prices that larger shops can offer. Larger shops will be located either in the town or city centre or, increasingly, in shopping centres on the edge of town or on out of town retail parks. Out of town shopping can be a problem, of course, for students who do not have access to their own transport. Larger cities will have many shops with international brand names, and the full range of 'quality' from very expensive to very cheap.

Entertainment is often centred on the university itself and the Student Union, which runs everything from sports clubs to bands and music concerts to bars and discos. This is usually at much cheaper prices than those available in the local town or city, which is very helpful for students on a limited budget. However, most students will also use the entertainment in the town or city where they live, ranging from cinemas to restaurants to pubs and night clubs. What is available varies from university to university – but the prospectus and the university website will give a lot of detail on the entertainment on offer within both the university and the city. All universities, of course, will try to persuade you in their prospectuses that *their* town or city or campus has the best entertainment of all! If this presents a picture of a 24-hour entertainment world then be aware that for most students life is not like that, as money and the pressures of work and, of course, students' choices of how to spend their time, mean that it can be as hectic or as quiet as you want it to be. For most students their main entertainment is spending time with friends, whether at home or playing sport or in the bar or in the Student Union.

Many of the handbooks designed to help students choose a university have a lot of information on student life. Although many of these are focused on under-graduates, the picture they paint will be helpful to you. Details of some of these handbooks and guides are included in Appendix B, and you should certainly find out about social life in the universities you are considering applying to.

● ● ● *Pause for thought* ● ● ●

Are there particular facilities that you will want to have available near to your chosen university? For example, do you want your university to have a swimming pool or a gym? Are you a 'shopaholic' so that you need to be close to a major shopping centre or retail park? Do you want to be in or near a city that has good theatre or music available? Do you want to be able to go sailing every weekend? Spend a few moments thinking through what you want to be able to do in your leisure time while at university in the UK.

What happens during university vacations?

The traditional structure of the academic year in universities is that the year has three 10–12-week 'terms' – the Autumn term (October to December), the Spring term (January to March) and the Summer term (April to June). More recently, though, most universities have introduced a semester system, with Semester 1 from October to early February and Semester 2 from February to June. The main vacation periods are the Christmas vacation (3 or 4 weeks from mid-December to early or mid-January), the Easter vacation (2, 3 or 4 weeks in April), and the Summer vacation (12–14 weeks from June to the end of September).

Term time/semester time is the period during which formal teaching takes place and when examinations are held. This is the case for postgraduate programmes as well as for undergraduate programmes. During vacation times there will not usually be any teaching, and most undergraduate students will go home. This means that the university will be much quieter with far fewer students around. However, most academic facilities remain open, for this is the time when academic staff concentrate on their research, and when postgraduate students have the opportunity to focus on their individual assignments and research projects. This is when the university will feel most like a postgraduate community, since the students who are around will be those on Masters programmes or undertaking research for their doctorates. You can easily find a space in the library, and access to public computer workstations is always available. Student social and service facilities will all be open during vacations, too, although the opening hours of facilities such as cafeterias and bars may not be as long as during semester time. Most clubs and societies do not meet during vacations, but facilities such as the swimming pool and the gym will be open.

All universities, though, also have times when they close entirely. These are usually for quite short periods. The longest closure will be during the Christmas and New Year period between 23rd December and 3rd January, but there will also be occasional days when the university is closed, such as at Easter (usually the Friday before Easter, known as Good Friday, and the Monday after Easter, called Easter Monday) and on a small number of other public holidays (Bank Holidays as they are called in the UK) in May and August. These times are ones that you need to plan for as an international student, for you will not be able to have access to academic facilities, or your office or lab, and you will not be able to get meals at the university. If you are living in university accommodation (hall of residence or flat), as an international student you will probably be able to stay in your accommodation at these holiday times – but you should check this well in advance.

So how should you spend the time? Well, firstly, of course, it is a good opportunity to get on with your own work without any distractions. Many Doctoral students explain that they managed to write large parts of their thesis during the Christmas vacation. Secondly, you could consider using the opportunity to take a trip, either to go home or to visit friends in other parts of the UK. If planning to travel in the UK, remember, though, that the Christmas vacation is not a time for good holiday weather, unfortunately! Thirdly, many international students use this opportunity to organize a wide range of social activities themselves, and some university societies (for example the Chinese society) may take the lead in organizing these things. Fourthly, of course, you might try to get involved in the British social activities at these times of year. Many churches, for example, stage social events over Christmas and the New Year, and it is quite common for them to arrange for international students to have the opportunity to spend Christmas or New Year with a British family.

We have already indicated that the vacation periods are times when many academic staff concentrate on their own research, and attend academic conferences, as well as taking their own holidays, and they may not be around or as available as at other times of the year. However, they do recognize the needs of postgraduate students during vacation periods as well as during semester time, and will make arrangements for your work to continue. For Doctoral students, supervisors will normally continue to have tutorials with you and supervise your work, and for Masters students they will do the same over the summer period when you are working on your dissertation or project. You will find, though, that the arrangements to do this will have to be more flexible, and you will need to negotiate with your tutor about how you will work together during vacations – when you will need tutorials or other support, when you will submit drafts of your writing, for example, and how this will fit around your tutor's (and your own) other use of time over the vacation period.

Is there anything else I should know?

There are obviously many aspects of daily life in the UK that you will need to find out about. Here we mention some important things we think you ought to be aware of.

Local taxes   All residents in the UK pay an annual tax to the local council, known as Council Tax in England, Scotland and Wales. This pays for local services such as police, schools and refuse collection. However, if you live in a university owned hall of residence or flat, or in a rented house occupied only by students, then you will probably be exempt from payment. If you are not exempt, the amount you pay depends on the size of the property you live in, but is likely to be between £500 and £1,000 each year. Your rent may include this – but check with your landlord.

Driving   If you want to drive in the UK you will need a driving licence. If you are from an EEA country you can drive using your own national driving licence. For other countries you will probably be able to drive on your own national driving licence for up to 12 months, but at the end of that time you will have to acquire a full UK driving licence. For a small list of 'designated' countries (e.g. Australia, Canada, New Zealand, South Africa) you can simply exchange your national licence for a UK licence. For most other countries, though, you will need to take a UK driving test before you can have a UK licence.

It is also a legal requirement in the UK that the vehicle you are driving is insured, that it is roadworthy (this involves passing an annual inspection if it is over three years old, when an MoT certificate will be issued) and that the annual road tax has been paid for it. All this can be very expensive and many students find they cannot afford to run a car. You will need to cost this carefully. To find out more about driving in the UK, visit the UKCOSA website at *www.ukcosa.org.uk* and download their guide on 'Driving in Great Britain: a guide for international students'; or pick up the leaflet 'Driving in GB as a visitor or a new resident' from a Post Office in the UK.

Television licence   Public service broadcasting in the UK (the BBC) is funded through television licences. If you have a television you are required by law to have a licence, which currently costs £126 per year and covers all the television sets at the address on the licence. In halls of residence however each student needs a TV licence of their own. You can get a television licence by applying on the website at *www.tvlicensing.co.uk*. The fines for not having a television licence are very large!

Legal advice   Obviously we hope that you never need legal advice, but if you do, then it is worth seeking advice from 'free' sources before you talk to a lawyer. The best sources of advice are the Student Union (who may for example offer a service to check housing contracts), the Citizens Advice Bureau in every town (*www.nacab.org.uk*) and local free law centres (*www.lawcentres.org.uk*).

Welfare benefits   International students from an EEA country are normally entitled to the same welfare benefits as UK students, while those from a country outside the EEA are normally not entitled to any UK welfare benefits. There are some exceptions to this:

- Students from countries that joined the EU in May 2004 from Eastern Europe are not entitled to the full range of benefits.
- Students from other countries may be entitled to some short-term benefits in the event of their funding from overseas being held up or disrupted by factors outside their control.
- All students and their dependants are entitled to health care through the National Health Service on the same terms as a UK student.

More information is available by downloading the leaflet 'Welfare Benefits' from the UKCOSA website (*www.ukcosa.org.uk*).

KEY RISKS AND HOW TO AVOID THEM

For most postgraduate students, how well they achieve in their academic programme will be affected by how well they settle in to everyday life as an international student in the UK, and for most this is an easy and exciting thing to do – especially if you take some simple steps to reduce the risks of difficulties.

Risk 1: *Not seeing your time in the UK as an opportunity to sample and enjoy British culture*   If you stay detached from British culture, while you will still go home with a degree you will not have gained as much from the experience of studying in the UK as you could. See your time in the UK as a chance to share in how British people live – read British newspapers and magazines, make British friends, watch British television, visit the main cultural places in your own university town or city, go shopping, and at least visit a British pub, go to the theatre and try to visit a major sporting event such as a national level football, rugby or cricket game. There is no need, of course, to compromise your own values and beliefs in this, and you do not need to do *all* of these things – but do try to do many of them.

Risk 2: *Not seeing your time in the UK as a chance to get to know other cultures*
The UK today is a truly multicultural society. Take the opportunity to learn how those from other cultures and communities live. Again, this does not mean that you have to compromise your own feelings and beliefs, but it will extend your knowledge and understanding.

Risk 3: *Only mixing with those from your own country*   It is very easy as an international student to make friends only with those of your own nationality or background. Try to make friends with other students, both from the UK and overseas, and go along to events or organizations where you will meet people from other cultural backgrounds.

Risk 4: *Isolation*   The only way to avoid this risk is to make a strong effort to widen your circle of friends and to go to events and activities. Invite one or several of the other students on your programme to coffee, or to share a meal – organize a traditional meal from your own country and invite your friends of other nationalities to share it. Organize a trip to the theatre or cinema for a wide group of friends. And, most important of all, even if you feel nervous about it, go along to the social events in the first few weeks of the programme and join one or two clubs or societies whose activities you are interested in.

Risk 5: *Poor accommodation*   To avoid being housed in poor accommodation, ensure you apply early for the sort of accommodation you want, and keep in touch with the accommodation office until you have sorted out the most suitable place for you.

Risk 6: *Not ensuring any special or cultural needs you may have are met*   All universities are experienced in supporting the needs of international students, whether they be faith-based needs, particular diets, specific study needs or needs resulting from a disability. Talk to your tutor and to the Student Union for advice.

Risk 7: *Experiencing negative attitudes towards ethnic minorities or international students*   As in every country of the world, in the UK there are some risks of experiencing negative attitudes from some parts of the community towards ethnic minority groups or 'foreigners'. Such behaviour is illegal in the UK and is fortunately rare. In the university and the communities where students live you are very unlikely to experience problems. If you do, you should report them immediately either to the Student Union or your tutor. In the largest cities in the UK there may be areas where you would be advised not to go, particularly at night, but you will be made aware of where they are. Most international students have no problems at all with such issues and feel welcome in the UK and the university.

Risk 8: *Settling your children into school*   If you are bringing your children with you to the UK, find a school as early as you can. Meet the headteacher and your child's new teacher and talk to them about how you can work together to help your child settle in quickly. In the early weeks, keep in regular contact with the school to ensure your child is happy and making friends.

Risk 9: Dull vacations   Vacation periods can seem long and unexciting, particularly the Christmas vacation, when the days are short and the weather may be poor. To avoid this, plan the vacations carefully – organize some social events with your friends or some trips to other cities or places of interest, or plan a trip home if you can. Also, use it as a quieter time to write an important chapter of your thesis or to do an assignment for your programme.

Risk 10: Having such a good time socially that you don't do enough work to succeed academically   Providing you are well motivated and work hard as a postgraduate student this should not be a problem. However, you will find that there are very many interesting opportunities and activities available to you, so you will have to be disciplined and plan your work carefully to cope with the demands of postgraduate-level study.

PART 3
STUDYING FOR A POSTGRADUATE DEGREE

CHAPTER 8

STUDYING FOR A TAUGHT POSTGRADUATE DEGREE

- What does a taught postgraduate course involve?
- How do I make the most of my Masters course?
- How do I prepare and write assignments?
- How do I avoid plagiarism?
- How do I prepare for written examinations?
- How do I make the best use of IT?
- How do I make the best use of the library and learning resources?

First thoughts

Most postgraduate students are studying for a 'taught' Masters degree or a taught Doctorate. This means that they will study a number of courses or units taught by academic staff and assessed either by an assignment or through an examination, before starting a longer thesis, project or dissertation. Even those students on a traditional research MPhil or PhD, though, will be expected to attend some taught courses as part of their research training. This chapter looks in detail at the 'taught' part of postgraduate programmes, and at how to make the best of the courses and avoid the major risks.

What does a taught postgraduate course involve?

We have looked in Chapters 2, 3 and 4 at the ways in which taught courses are organized. Teaching units will cover particular topics within the academic field of your degree programme, but will also cover a range of research methods appropriate to what you are studying. So, for example, within a programme in Environmental Science you may study units on 'Hydrological Processes' or 'Population Dynamics' which focus on the science itself, but also units on 'Field

Methods in Environmental Science', 'Statistical Analysis' or 'Computer Modelling in the Environmental Sciences', which will focus on methods and techniques. Both types of course are important, for as a postgraduate you have to be able to show that you have both the knowledge and understanding of your field and the skills and knowledge of research and analysis methods.

Teaching methods will, of course, vary a great deal between different programmes and subjects. Traditional methods of teaching are still the most common ones, and you will probably have a significant amount of your courses taught through lectures, seminars and practical or laboratory classes – these will all be very familiar to you as a successful graduate. However, there has been a growth over recent years in the development of alternative teaching methods – so you may find that you experience a number of approaches with which you are less familiar. These might include the following.

New classroom approaches The use of a range of techniques from student presentations, to group decision-making exercises, to role play activities, to drama and workshop approaches is increasing. All require students to be more actively involved, and not simply listen to presentations by lecturers and professors.

IT-based learning The use of information and communications technology for learning and teaching has expanded rapidly, and there are almost no programmes that will not involve you in using IT in some way. This may, at a very simple level, just involve word processing your assignments, and using the internet for literature searching. More likely, though, you will find parts of your programme require you to use IT as an integral part of what you do. Any activity using IT as part of the learning is called 'e-learning', and where programmes use both e-learning and other more traditional methods such as lectures this is referred to as 'blended learning'.

Let us look at some examples of the sorts of e-learning you might be involved in:

- **Using a virtual learning environment (VLE) or managed learning environment (MLE).** Many programmes use IT systems such as Web CT or Blackboard to manage and organize the course. This will include all the course guidelines and handbook, instructions for activities, exercises and assignments, reading lists, including direct links to electronic journal articles or important websites, and copies of lecture notes. It will also include on-line discussion and an information board on which all messages about the course will be posted. In some cases you will also be expected to submit your assignment through the MLE, and this may involve your work being automatically checked for evidence of plagiarism. This means that the whole course revolves around the MLE, and you will be expected to log on to the site very frequently.

- **Using virtual case studies and examples.** To allow you to work through examples and case studies at your own speed and time these may be set up as virtual case studies. Using electronic resources, including video, websites, interviews and so on, a 'real' situation can be presented for study. This could include observations of a medical procedure or of an engineering or science experiment or of a visit to a field site in archaeology or geology. Virtual fieldwork is quite common in postgraduate courses, for example.
- **On-line discussion**. Many programmes will use on-line discussion to enable students to interact, talk about their ideas and views and share opinions. Sometimes this may be an interesting 'option' within a course, but it may also be a compulsory activity, to which everybody will be expected to contribute.
- **Using analytical and modelling software**. Most subjects have developed software programmes to support the analysis of data and also to help in designing and modelling new ideas and situations. In engineering, for example, most students will already be familiar with computer-aided design software. In the social sciences data analysis software for both quantitative analysis (such as SPSS) and qualitative analysis (such as NVivo) will often be used for exercises, assignments and problem-solving.

In addition to learning about your subject and about research methods, all programmes will include opportunities to develop general skills such as team working and communications. This is a requirement of the national benchmark standards for postgraduate programmes, and is included to give you a range of skills that will be valuable when you enter a job. You will probably not find that your programme has separate courses on 'team working', though, since these parts of the programme will be integrated into the course. So, for example, a unit on 'Planning Waste Management' may include an exercise where you have to work together as a group to solve a problem about choosing a site to dispose of nuclear waste, and then report back to the class using a formal presentation. Although the focus is on nuclear waste management you will be developing group, teamwork and presentational skills at the same time. You will probably be making friends, too!

How do I make the most of my Masters course?

If you have been successful as an undergraduate, then you will know most of the things that are needed to be successful in a taught postgraduate course. Some are very obvious:

- Organize your time well.
- Attend all of the taught sessions, classes and tutorials.
- Do all the exercises and tasks that are required of you by the course tutor.
- Meet all the deadlines for completing and submitting work.

- Keep good notes and records of the work that you do, so you can use them again later. This includes good lecture notes and notes from seminars and workshops.
- Ask for the help of tutors and fellow students if there are things you find hard or do not understand.

There are a number of other approaches, though, which are important if you are going to be successful, and which may be a little different from your experiences at undergraduate level.

First, **get involved** and participate actively in the programme. You will be expected to contribute and not simply to sit, watch and listen. Ask questions in seminars, add your ideas and views to discussions.

Secondly, **be critical** – which does not mean being negative. In academic study being critical means thinking carefully about ideas that you come across and deciding whether they are right, wrong, valid or not. There are very few theories or ideas in any field which are accepted by everybody as being always true and correct – and when you are dealing with new ideas or the findings of new research it is important that you look carefully at whether it appears correct and whether you agree with it. Just because an idea is in a book or well-known journal, or has been put forward by a well-known academic or scientist does not mean it is completely or even partially right. Developing criticality is an important skill at postgraduate level, therefore. Some new postgraduate students may feel it is rude or disrespectful to criticize ideas from tutors or professors – but be assured they will be expecting you to do this. In fact, you will not get a top grade in your work unless you show you can think independently. As a starting point, it is helpful to use a set of critical questions whenever you come across a new idea or the findings of a new piece of research:

- What is the evidence for this idea or conclusion, or is it just somebody's conjecture?
- If there is evidence, has it been collected and analysed in a valid and reliable way?
- Is there enough evidence to allow these conclusions to be drawn?
- Does the evidence support the conclusions, or are other interpretations of the evidence possible?
- How does this idea or conclusion compare with other or previous ideas on this topic? If it is different, why is this, and does this make sense?
- Does this idea or conclusion match what I would expect from my own knowledge or experience? If not, why not?
- Does this idea or conclusion help explain or interpret other situations?

Thirdly, **read and discuss** as much as you can. These are the two main parts of being a postgraduate student. As an undergraduate you may have had short reading lists for courses, and you were only expected to read a few of the items on the list. At postgraduate level you should try to read as much as you can, and even go beyond the reading lists on topics that really interest you. You should expect to spend a lot of your time reading, whatever your subject area. Discussion is just as important, since this allows you to test your ideas, hear the views of others, discover ideas that are new. Discuss different views in seminars, exchange opinions over coffee and lunch, talk about ideas in the pub in the evening. Remember that your fellow students and your teaching staff are some of the best thinkers in your field, so you should learn from them (and contribute to their learning!).

How do I prepare and write assignments?

For all the course units you study within your programme you will be assessed in some way, either through a written examination or through an assignment. We shall look at examinations a little later in this chapter, but here we shall focus on assignments, which are sometimes referred to as coursework.

Assignments can take almost any shape. A course might involve several small assignments or one large one. The assignments could involve any suitable activity, from writing an essay to answering 'problem' questions, to doing a small research investigation, to a decision-making or problem-solving task. Over the whole programme the assignments will probably be of different kinds so that you can show a range of skills and knowledge. Whatever the naure of the assignment, though, the preparation and writing needs to be done with care and thought to make sure you get the best possible grade. Below are some guidelines about planning and writing assignments.

Prepare a time plan as soon as you know what the task is

You will probably be given the instructions for each assignment at the start of a course unit. Divide the assignment up into the tasks that are needed, and plan when they need to be completed. Here are two examples.

For an essay you will need to do a literature search, read the literature you select, plan the essay, write a first draft, then write the final version. If you have ten weeks before the assignment is due to be handed in, then you might plan your work as follows:

Weeks 1–2	Literature search in the library and on the internet
Weeks 3–5	Reading
Week 6	Planning the assignment
Weeks 7–8	Writing the first draft
Week 9	Completing the final version
Week 10	Spare week in case you need it (!) – and submitting the assignment

For a laboratory-based project, you will need to plan the lab work and also schedule in the data analysis and the background reading on the topic. If you have ten weeks, then your schedule might look like this:

Week 1	Ensure you have booked your lab or workshop time
Weeks 1–2	Literature search in the library

Weeks 3–4	Plan the lab work procedures and data collection
Week 5	Undertake the lab work and collect the data
Weeks 6–8	Analyse the data and draft the first version of the investigation report
Weeks 9	Complete the final version of the report
Week 10	Spare week in case you need it (!) – and submitting the assignment.

Look carefully at the assessment criteria and mark criteria

Every assignment will have clear **assessment criteria**. This is a list of what your assignment will be marked for, and you need to write your assignment to match the criteria. For example, common assessment criteria are that you must:

'Show clear evidence that you know the research literature in the field'
and
'Provide a critical review of recent research in the field'

Both of these require you to show that you have done some research to identify the main literature on the relevant topic, and you will be judged by whether you have identified the most significant research from the past and the most recent research papers or books that have been published. To meet the first assessment criterion you will need to write about the main research ideas and through the use of references show that you are familiar with the sources – the papers, reports, books and authors where these ideas can be found. To meet the second one, though, you will need to show some skills of criticality by reviewing the research and being able to argue about which is strong and convincing evidence and which is not. We looked earlier at criticality and identified some questions you can use to show it – you should therefore show in your assignment that you have used this sort of critical questioning to review the research.

If you meet the assessment criteria then a judgement will be made by the marker about *how well* you have met them. So, for example, if you have read only five of the ten most important sources you may have met the criterion, but only just, whereas if you have read all ten and used some other sources as well then you will have met the criterion very well. The **mark criteria** therefore reflect how well you have to do against the assessment criteria to get a particular mark.

Judging what you need to do to get a good mark rather than only a satisfactory one is something that worries most students. So how do you find out? Some programmes may show you examples of assignments of different standards so that you can see the difference. In others you will be encouraged to show an early draft of your assignment to your tutor so that they can give you some feedback. Usually, though, you will be encouraged to meet with the course tutor to discuss exactly what is required to achieve the highest grades. If this is not offered to you automatically, do not be afraid to ask for a tutorial.

Finally, of course, discuss it with your friends and other students on the programme.

It is important to remember to check your assignment against the criteria several times, and particularly when you have produced a final draft. This is important because even though you think you know where your assignment is going, you might lose sight of this while you are writing. So check at the end, and check off each of the assessment criteria against your work. If there is anything missing then add it in, and if there is anything in there which does not help meet the criteria, then take it out.

Check that you are doing the correct assignment!

This sounds a very obvious thing to say, but before you start work it is always important to check two things:

- Check with your tutor and friends that it is the right assignment. It is not unknown for students to see last year's course handbook, which had a different assignment.
- Check with your tutor and your friends that your interpretation of what the assignment is asking for is correct, and that you have understood the instructions correctly and accurately.

Structure the assignment carefully

Most subject disciplines have particular traditions about the writing and presentation of different types of assignments. Whether your work is an essay, a lab report or a research project there will be particular models and structures of presentation which you should use. Typical models for these are:

- **Essay.** The essay will have a clear introduction in which the aim and organization of the essay is explained. There will then be a series of paragraphs which provide a logical sequence to the argument in the essay. Each paragraph will make a specific point, followed by an elaboration of the point and the evidence which supports the point it makes. The essay will end with two or three concluding paragraphs.
- **Research report.** A research report will have sections on

  1 The aim of the research
  2 The literature and existing research evidence
  3 The research methods
  4 The data presentation and analysis
  5 Discussion and conclusions

  Sections will usually be numbered and sometimes individual paragraphs may be numbered.
- **Experimental/fieldwork report.** An experimental or fieldwork report will usually be structured like a research report, as described above.

However, be aware that these are only models, and the exact structure that you need to use should be explained to you clearly in the instructions for the assignment or in your course or unit handbook. Check what is needed before you prepare your assignment, including simple presentational issues – should the assignment have double-spaced lines, for example; how long should it be; what should the title page or cover sheet be like? You may find further guidance on preparing assignments on a 'study skills' website in your university. Ask in the library or in the student services department whether your university provides such help.

Use a suitable referencing and bibliography system

If you have been successful as an undergraduate you will know how to use referencing systems within your written work. This means that wherever you are using the ideas of other people or are directly quoting their words from a book or a journal article you indicate whose ideas or words they are. The two main approaches used are:

- Author–date systems (for example, Kumar, 1999), where the author's surname and the date of publication are given in the essay or report and the full details of the publication appear in an alphabatical bibliography at the end of the assignment.
- Reference-by-number systems (Kumar[1], Butcher[2]), where full publication details are provided either at the bottom of the page (as footnotes) or in a numbered list at the end of the chapter (called endnotes), as in our example here (see p. 130).

If you do not do this there are two problems that will arise. The first is that you will not be showing the range of reading you have done and the range of ideas that you are using, and at Masters and Doctoral level this is an important part of the skills and knowledge you need to show – so you will not get a good grade for your work. The second, though, is even more important and serious, for if you use ideas or direct quotations without crediting their source you will be guilty of plagiarism, and this is a very serious academic 'crime'. This is covered later in this chapter.

Strictly speaking you should present a separate list of references (works you have referred to in your writing) and a bibliography (works you have read but may or may not have referred to in your assignment). In practice, most people who use an author-date system just have a single list and call it a bibliography. If you have used a reference-by-number and notes system then you will need to list the further reading separately. Which bibliography system should you use? There are several methods (see, for example, the list in Kumar, 1999, p. 245), and all are academically acceptable. However, most disciplines and most universities will be clear about what their preferred method is, and will explain this in programme handbooks. It will be best to use the method that is recommended to you. In the UK by far the most common bibliography system in use now is the Harvard system. This is the system we have used within this book (see, for example, Appendix A), but a full explanation can be found on the library website of almost every UK university.

There are now a number of software packages that will produce a bibliography for you as you work, for example EndNote, and this may well be available on the central computer network at your university. However, like all packages, they are only as good as the information you put in, so you still need to check the accuracy of the references in your bibliography.

Check for use of English

Checking that your written English is as good as it can be is an important step. Your English will not have to be perfect – even native English speakers rarely write perfect English! However, it will need to be good enough, which means it needs to be easy to read and to make sense academically and grammatically. Unless your written English is excellent, it is sensible to have your writing checked by somebody else – an easy system is to have reading circles amongst a group of friends where everybody agrees to read the drafts of everybody else's work. You should not expect your tutor to do this. They will perhaps agree to look at early drafts of your work to check the academic ideas and structure, but they will certainly not agree to check your English.

Do not leave it too late

This advice is very obvious, but it is surprising how often students run out of time to write their assignment, so that the finished product may not be of the highest quality possible. It is important to remember that while you may have a good idea of how long it takes you to prepare and complete an undergraduate assignment, there are three factors that will make your postgraduate assignment take longer – it requires wider reading; it should have more challenging ideas in it; and it is probably being written in a different language! It is wise, therefore, to have a target date for completion which is a week or two before the actual deadline, so that there is time for slippage if necessary.

Extensions and late hand-ins

Even with the most careful planning you may find circumstances where you have problems with time. For example, you may be ill, or there may be some difficult family events (your partner or child may be unwell), or there may be unforeseen problems with analysing the data in your work. All universities and programmes will have systems to enable you to apply for an extension to an assignment submission deadline – but the rules will be very precise and you will need to follow them exactly. There are a few important things to remember:

- *Never* simply hand your work in late without getting permission through the proper system. If you do this you may find that you score zero marks for the work, or that there is a mark penalty for every day it is late (typically 5% per day). Excuses offered after the hand-in deadline will not usually be considered.
- Make sure you know what the rules are on extensions and late hand-ins. Details will be in the programme handbook. Normally you will be required to submit a form as a request for permission for an extension, together with a clear explanation of the reason and, in most cases, evidence of the reason. For example, if you have been unwell, you will need to attach a medical certificate from the doctor to confirm your illness. This request will then be considered by the department, and you will receive a written response. Do not assume that your request has been accepted until you get that written confirmation.
- Ask for the extension to the deadline at the earliest opportunity – when you are first unwell or have problems which mean you may not meet the deadline. Tutors are often cynical that very late requests for extensions are simply because students have not planned their time carefully enough!

How do I avoid plagiarism?

'Plagiarism' is using the ideas or words of others as if they are your own. It occurs most commonly in written assignments when ideas are used without giving proper credit and reference to their source or when sections of text are copied from other books, journals or the internet without quoting their source or otherwise indicating that they are taken from another source. Plagiarism is regarded in all universities as a very serious issue and as a form of cheating. Students found to have committed plagiarism may be given a zero score for their work or, in extreme cases, asked to leave the programme.

When you submit an assignment you will usually be asked to sign a 'declaration' that the work is your own and that you have given proper academic credit to all sources you have used. It is important therefore that (a) you read the rules and guidance on plagiarism which will be included in your programme handbook or programme regulations and (b) you take every step you can to avoid plagiarism. Here are some of the things you can do:

- When taking notes from books, journals etc., never copy out sections of text, but always summarize them in your own words.
- Never 'cut and paste' text or diagrams from the internet.
- Where you want to use a particular phrase or quotation or diagram from a source, always put it in your own notes in 'quotation marks' with the precise reference next to it so that it is clear it is a direct quotation.
- Whenever you use a direct quotation or an idea or a diagram/table from another source in your work ensure that you give a reference for the source.

Plagiarism is very easy for tutors to detect. They are familiar with the research and ideas in their field and will know if you are quoting an idea without giving credit to its original source. They will also recognize the difference between your own writing style and the style of sections of text copied from other sources. In addition, some universities now use software linked to MLE/VLE systems which will automatically check assignments for evidence of plagiarism.

● ● ● *Pause for thought* ● ● ●

*Many of the ideas about studying that we have mentioned here will be familiar to you already through your undergraduate studies. However, you need to identify which ones will be more serious challenges for you when you become a postgraduate. For each of the following aspects of studying think about whether you feel it is a part of your work which is **Strong**, **Satisfactory** or **Weak**. The areas you feel are weak will be ones you have to work hardest on as a postgraduate student.*

Organizing your time	*Planning projects*	*Meeting deadlines*
Criticality	*Discussing ideas*	*Referencing*
Participation in class	*Writing assignments*	*Literature searches*
Wide reading	*Checking for plagiarism*	*Making notes*

Looking for alternative explanations for ideas

How do I prepare for written examinations?

Everybody who is a postgraduate student will be quite used to the process of taking written examinations, as they will have taken many examinations through their school and undergraduate years. Many Masters programmes still use written examinations to assess all or part of the course, although in recent years other types of assessment have begun to be used. It is quite rare now for the whole assessment of a Masters programme to be through written examinations, and in many cases there are no written exams at all. Some people like exams, some people hate them, so an important factor in your choice of course might be whether there are examinations or not in a particular programme.

If there are written examinations, of course, you will need to prepare thoroughly for them, and by now you will know the way of preparing that suits you best individually. Whether you revise best over long periods or all at the last minute, whether you simply read your notes or re-write them in briefer form, whether you practise exam questions or not, whether you revise best at night or in the daytime, are all things you will already know. The list below, therefore, is simply to remind you of a few important issues about preparing for written examinations at Masters or Doctoral level.

- Remember that the exam will be testing your thinking, analytical skills and understanding and not just your knowledge – so simply filling your answers with learned facts will not be enough at Masters level.
- Revise and learn *ideas*, with examples to illustrate them, and with evidence for and against the idea (or model or theory).
- Make sure you know the main sources on each topic so you can indicate where the ideas have come from and who the main thinkers and researchers are in the field.
- Plan your revision to give yourself plenty of time to revise before the exams.
- Do not rely only on lecture/seminar notes on each topic. Make sure you have read more widely and have included ideas from this wider reading.
- Make sure you know exactly what each examination will (and will not) cover. This should be clear in the course or unit handbook, but tutors should be able to tell you if you are not sure.
- Read the instructions on the examination paper very carefully so that you answer the right number of questions.
- Read each question several times to be sure you know exactly what it is asking you to do.

How do I make the best use of IT?

Earlier in this chapter we looked at the way in which IT has become an increasingly important part of teaching and learning on postgraduate programmes. Many postgraduate students are already very skilled with IT and use it effectively to help their studies. Others may be less familiar with it, though, perhaps because their undergraduate course used little IT or because it is some time since they were undergraduates. Developing good IT skills is an almost essential part of a postgraduate programme, however, and you will be expected to use IT as a key study skill – at the very least you will have to use the internet, send and receive e-mail, and write your assignments using a computer. There are a number of ways in which you can make the best use of IT, though, whatever your current level of skills:

- If you have never used computers, then it will be helpful if you take a basic computer skills course before you come to the UK. This should cover basic skills such as word processing, file management, the use of e-mail, and accessing and searching the internet. Courses such as this are available from IT training companies in most towns and cities around the world.

- Go to the IT services induction session in your first week or so at your university. Every university offers these sessions for new students, to show you how the university system works, what services are provided, where public access workstations are located, and what software is available. This may be provided by and for your own department, or may be provided centrally by the university.
- Study carefully what it says in your programme handbook about using IT, so that you know what will be expected of you.
- Identify what special training in IT is available in the department or university. This may range from highly specialized technical programmes to basic introductions to software and hardware. Talk to your tutor about your own needs and which courses will be most useful for you.
- If possible, have your own desktop or laptop computer. As a Masters student it is unlikely that you will be provided with your own computer, although as a Doctoral student you may be. In either case, having your own may be a better idea. This is, of course, an expensive thing to do and may not be possible. If you are able to buy your own computer, it is important that you plan carefully before you buy:

1 Find out in advance what system the university or department uses – does it, for example, use Microsoft or Apple software?
2 Find out what the minimum specification is that you will need to make your computer compatible with the university network or your programme's needs. What edition/version of Windows, for example, is expected, and how much memory will you need? Most programme handbooks will have information about this technical detail.
3 Find out if the department or the Student Union has special arrangements which will enable you to buy a computer at a large discount. Many students who buy before they go to their university are angry when they discover that they could have bought the same computer model 20% cheaper at the special sales in the Student Union during the first week of the course.
4 Make sure you take out insurance on your computer and buy basic security such as a padlock and chain to secure your computer to the desk to avoid theft.

● ● ● *Pause for thought* ● ● ●

*How good are your IT skills? For each of the skills or types of software listed below think about whether you are **Confident** in its use, have used but are **Not confident** in its use, or have **Never used** it. This will help you to identify your IT training needs.*

Word processing	*E-mail*	*Internet searching*
Spreadsheets	*Databases*	*Modelling*
Sending attachments	*Computer-aided design*	*Printing*
File organization and storage		*Managed Learning Environments*

How do I make best use of the library and learning resources?

An important part of your postgraduate studies will be the library or learning resources service within the university. You will be quite experienced in using libraries as part of your undergraduate studies, but the range of resources and services that most UK university libraries offer is very extensive. As a post-graduate student these services will be more important to you than during your time as an undergraduate. This is because more of your work will be individual work focused on topics of your own choice rather than simply following the themes and topics that everybody else on the course is doing. You will need, therefore, to develop good skills of searching for literature, research and resources to find the specialist research and materials on your chosen topic. This is particularly true in relation to your dissertation or project or, if you are a doctoral student, your thesis. You will need to be able to identify resources and literature that are available not only in your own university but also at other UK universities and in libraries and databases around the world, and then know how to obtain relevant and useful material. For example, you will have to be able to identify not just relevant books and papers in international journals, you will also have to find Doctoral and Masters dissertations on your topic from universities anywhere in the world. So there are a number of skills you will need:

- You will need to learn how to use your own university library. This will include knowing where the catalogues are, where the books and journals in your field are kept and how to order resources from other libraries through, for example, the system of inter-library loan.
- You will need to learn about the main bibliographic sources in your field – published bibliographies, on-line databases and search engines or catalogues. This will enable you to identify and access materials outside your own university.
- You will need to learn how to undertake internet searches for resources and materials in your field.

These skills will be demonstrated to you very early in your postgraduate pro-gramme, either through a general introduction by the library staff or through your programme tutors. This will show you how to use the physical and electronic resources of the library, and will also enable you to register for inter-library services through ATHENS. ATHENS is an electronic service which allows you access to a wide range of academic resources in the UK and internationally, and is an essential search tool.

However, this will only introduce you to the basic skills and resources, and you may need help from the professional library staff to help you locate and use the highly specialized materials in your field. Many of the library staff are highly experienced professionals in information services, not simply clerical or administrative staff. They have many years experience of supporting postgraduate students in their specialist information needs and will be expecting you to ask for their expert assistance. As an undergraduate you may not have needed to use this kind of support very much, but as a postgraduate it will be essential to you. So, at an early stage, get to know the specialist staff in the library who work in your academic field.

Developing your library and information skills is an essential step to postgraduate success. To develop these skills you will need to spend a significant amount of time using library services and facilities throughout your postgraduate programme, perhaps as much as 10–15 hours per week. In this way you will develop the academic resource and library skills that show you have reached postgraduate standard.

KEY RISKS AND HOW TO AVOID THEM

All Masters programmes and most Doctoral programmes will have some taught course units within them. Many of the challenges of taught courses will be familiar to you through your undergraduate studies, but as a postgraduate there are a number of risks you need to be particularly aware of:

Risk 1: *Failing to plan your study time*   You will have many activities to fill your time, from classes to computer and library time as well as social and leisure time. Plan carefully and try not to waste too much time.

Risk 2: *Not attending all of the taught programme*   Do not miss any of the programme – every session will be important and cover significant ideas and knowledge.

Risk 3: *Not getting involved and participating*   As a postgraduate you will be expected to contribute to debate in classes and develop skills of arguing and presenting ideas. So, do not sit quietly in your classes, but join in.

Risk 4: *Not developing criticality*   Being critical is an important sign of working at postgraduate level. Try to develop the skills for analysing, interpreting and being critical about ideas, research and knowledge.

Risk 5: *Not planning your assignment carefully and in good time*   Postgraduate assignments are more challenging than undergraduate ones, and you may be writing for the first time in English. So plan the assignment to give yourself plenty of time to complete it by the deadline.

Risk 6: *Writing in poor English*   Your English does not need to be perfect, but it needs to be good enough, so arrange for your assignment to be checked by friends or colleagues.

Risk 7: *Committing plagiarism*   Plagiarism will be treated as a serious issue, so you need to check very carefully that you have avoided it.

Risk 8: *Missing the submission deadline without getting an extension*   Plan to finish your assignment well ahead of the deadline so there is some room for slippage if problems arise. Seek permission for late submission in advance if you find you really need it.

Risk 9: *Not having adequate IT skills*   IT skills are essential now to be a successful postgraduate, so make sure you have the basic skills before you start your programme, and do as much IT training as you can as part of your programme.

Risk 10: *Not developing library and information skills*   The more advanced the work you do, the more specialized will be the knowledge and information you need and use, and the more advanced will need to be your library and information skills. Make sure you go on the training provided by your university or programme, and get to know and make use of the professional information staff in the library.

Notes

1   Kumar, R. (1999) *Research Methodology: A Step-by-Step Guide for Beginners*. London: Sage
2   Butcher, J. (1981) *Copy-Editing: The Cambridge Handbook for Editors, Authors and Publishers* (3rd Edition). Cambridge: Cambridge University Press

CHAPTER 9

PLANNING AND WRITING YOUR RESEARCH THESIS

- How do I plan a good research project?
- What's involved in writing a thesis?
- Can I publish my work?

First thoughts

Whatever your postgraduate programme, you will have to plan, undertake and write up a substantial research project as part of it. For a Masters programme this will take 33% of your study time, and will require you to write a dissertation of between 15,000 and 30,000 words. For a taught Doctorate it will take about half of your study time and will require a thesis of 40,000–50,000 words. For a PhD it will be almost all of your study time and will require a thesis of between 75,000 and 120,000 words. This substantial piece of research is given different names in different universities – it may be called a project or a dissertation (usually at Masters level) or a thesis (usually at Doctoral level). Whatever its size or name, though, it requires careful planning, independent research, reflection and analysis and a significant writing challenge. This chapter looks at how to plan, undertake and write a good research project.

How do I plan a good research project?

The sections that follow take you through the important issues to think about in planning your research project. If your programme is at Masters level then you will not need to think about the project in detail until you are part way through the programme, although it is never too early to start to have some initial ideas – but you probably do not need to worry about your choice until the Christmas vacation. If you are undertaking a Doctorate, however, your planning needs to start even before you submit your application for the programme, as you will be expected to have a clear idea of what your thesis will be about right from the start. Most Doctoral applications will need to include an outline research proposal (see Chapter 3) unless you are applying for a scholarship or studentship to undertake a specified project. If you are applying for a specified project, you will need to be sure that it is a project you are excited about and interested in, and also that you have some ideas about the research methods you will need to use and the existing literature and research in the field.

How do I choose a good topic for study?

Most Masters students and most self-funding students at Doctoral level will have an almost completely open choice about the topic for their research project. The only limitations will be whether your university can support you to do the project, i.e. whether it has the equipment, facilities and staff expertise to do the study. As a Doctoral student, of course, this will have been a factor in your choice of university, as there is no point applying to a university that cannot support your research topic.

So how do you choose what to do? The model below has been used successfully with large numbers of postgraduate students to help them choose their project topic. It works through a number of stages, which help you to narrow down your ideas from a broad field to a specific research question.

Stage 1   What are the broad themes that interest you?

Think broadly about what interests you in your subject. Write down a list of themes, by asking yourself the following questions:

- What themes particularly interested you in your undergraduate programme?
- If you are a Masters student or have completed a Masters degree, what themes interested you in your Masters degree?
- What are the current 'hot' topics in the field? In other words, what topics is there most discussion about either in the research papers or in the popular journals?
- If your field is a professional field (such as medicine, teaching, business, law), what are the current 'hot' professional issues that there is most discussion about?
- Are there any issues in the field which are particularly important to your own national setting – for example, if you are interested in agricultural botany, are there any particular agricultural issues in your own country that there is a priority to address?
- Are there any themes or topics that have interested you since you were young?

For each of these questions write down a list of the topics that come into your mind. This might be a long or short list, but it is helpful to have at least one topic under each heading.

Stage 2   What are the interesting topics within those themes?

Now narrow down this list to a smaller list of topics. You can do this, for example, by seeing if there are any themes that have come up in answer to more than one of your questions in Stage 1, or by trying to put the themes from Stage 1 into a rank order of interest for you. By doing this you should be able to narrow down your choice to a short list of two or three top topics of interest.

Stage 3   What questions might you ask about those topics?

Now think about the key questions that might be appropriate in relation to each of these topics. An important aspect of any research project is that it should be investigating a question, so try to think of all the questions of interest or importance in relation to each of the two or three topics you have considered.

Stage 4   Choose a question and check its viability

From the list of questions you now have it should be possible to identify two or three that are particularly interesting or exciting for you, and then to choose one that grabs your interest. This is a good starting point for checking whether it is a reasonable or sensible question. At this stage you need to check whether it is a viable topic. By viability we mean is it a question that needs answering and is it a question that can be answered in your size of project.

To check whether the question **needs** answering you have to find out whether the answer is already known – in other words, has research already looked at this question. To do this you need to undertake a literature search on the topic. Do not be put off if you find somebody has already looked at your question; it may be that their research has shown there are still some aspects of your question that need to be investigated, or it could be that you are not sure their research methods or conditions are correct and you might want to investigate the question again under different circumstances. It is at this stage of checking that your tutor will be particularly helpful, for he or she will be able to point you to research and literature that will tell you whether the question has already been answered.

To check whether the question **can** be answered in a project of the size you will be undertaking you need to consider the data that you might need to investigate it. If, for example, you might need to collect data over a very long period of time, or use a very expensive technique or piece of equipment that your university does not have, or use a very large sample for your study, or access data that is sensitive, then it is unlikely to be viable. If it does not seem as though you can undertake the study, you need to think about a different project.

Stage 5   Make your final choice

The last stage is to make your final choice of project. This may only be possible when you have been through Stage 4 several times, since there may be several possible projects you need to investigate for viability before you come up with a suitable topic. The final check to make when you are ready to settle on a topic or title is to ask yourself one last, but *very* important question: *Does this topic really interest me and excite me?* The answer needs to be 'yes', for you will be living with the topic for a long time. If it is your Doctoral thesis then you may be living with it night and day for three years. Even as a Masters dissertation topic it will be your life for at least three months, so you have to feel excited about doing it.

In the process of choosing a topic there are a number of important issues to think about, which will be emphasized to you by your tutor. The key issues are:

- Do not choose a project that is too large. Most postgraduate students' first ideas about a research project are too ambitious, involving large amounts of data collection and questions that are too general. Keep your project very focused on a very specific topic.
- Do not believe your research has to change the world. For a Doctoral thesis you do have to make a contribution to knowledge, but this is likely to be just a small advance in understanding. Masters and Doctoral theses are not large enough to contribute a new global theory to the sum of knowledge!
- Start your project with a research question. Having a single overall question that you are investigating provides a very clear focus for your work – and you can keep asking yourself throughout your research 'Is my work going to help answer my research question?' to check that what you are doing is relevant. Having a research question does not mean you have to use any particular methodology – it just keeps you on track.

Can I choose a topic that will be about my own country?

International students are sometimes very interested in choosing a research project that is relevant to their own country. This may be because they want to make a real contribution to their own country or because it focuses on an issue they know about or are interested in. In many cases this may be an excellent idea, but there are a number of things to think about if this is what you would like to do.

First, will your chosen study require you to collect data in your own country? If so, this may be very attractive to you, but you need to be sure that:

- Your own government will allow you to return to do this.
- You can do the data collection in your own country without supervision, as your tutor will not be with you.
- The regulations for your postgraduate programme allow you to be away from the university for a lengthy period of time.

Secondly, will you be able to get hold of literature and research that is relevant to your topic? For example, will your university library be able to get government reports or journals from your own country and in your own language?

Thirdly, will the university have the expertise to support your research in or about your own country? It may be that your topic is a general one which you will study in the context of your own country. However, if it is too specific will the university be able to support you? If, for example, you were to choose to do your PhD on the early history of Laos, or on the art of the San people of Namibia, would there be a tutor at the university or an external examiner in the UK who could support your work?

However, do not let these issues deter you, if there is a satisfactory answer to each of these problems. Undertaking a study related to your own country may be both rewarding and valuable to you, and many postgraduate students do their Masters or Doctoral thesis in this way.

● ● ● *Pause for thought* ● ● ●

You may already have some ideas about what you would like to research for your project. Think of three possible research projects and a research question for each. Then identify the advantages and disadvantages of choosing each one.

What will I need to put into my research proposal?

If your research project is part of a Masters programme, or a taught Doctorate, then you will probably need to get the approval of your tutor or the programme leader for your proposal. This will happen part way through the programme, and you will be given details of the timescale for submitting your proposal. For an MPhil/PhD the proposal will be part of your application to the programme and will be considered carefully in the decision about whether to offer you a place on the course. Whatever the timing, though, the proposal will need to include the same sorts of information:

1 A title.
2 The main research question that you will be focusing on, with, perhaps, a number of sub-questions.
3 The background to the study – why it is an important and interesting topic to study.
4 A brief background literature review. This should show that you have read a number of relevant books and papers so that you understand how your topic relates to the current knowledge and issues in the field.
5 A proposed methodology, that is, how you intend to undertake the study, what methods you will use, what data you will collect and how you will analyse the data. If this includes any form of experimental work or the use of any data collection or analysis equipment you need to provide a detailed and precise list of what you will need. You also need to explain why *this* methodology and *this* equipment is the best way to study *this* topic.
6 A proposed time schedule for the project, with key dates and the timing of each phase of the project.

The detail and depth of the proposal will need to be rather greater for a Doctoral proposal than for a Masters project. Typically, a Masters proposal will be submitted on a standard pro-forma from your department and may be 500–1,000 words long. A Doctoral research proposal is likely to be an individualized document (that is, not on a form), and will probably be 1,000–2,500 words long.

In writing your proposal, remember that its purpose is to enable the academic staff to judge whether what you want to do is practicable and realistic, and will be suitable to enable you to write a dissertation or thesis of the right standard. It also enables them to be sure that *they* have the right resources (library, IT, tutors etc.) to support your work. It is *not* a final, definitive guide to exactly what you will actually do. All research develops as you undertake it. You may find, for example, that the detailed literature review you do once you have started shows that there is a better topic for you to do or that somebody has already done your proposed project – or you may find that the data you thought you could collect is not available. So what you actually end up doing may be slightly (or sometimes radically) different from what you first proposed. This will not be a problem. Also, remember that if you are applying for a scholarship to do a particular research project then the outline and principles of what you will be expected to do will be given to you – but this does not mean that you will not be expected to show that you have thought carefully about exactly how you will do the work.

And what if your proposal is rejected? You should regard a rejection as saving you from big problems later on. Tutors have a very good idea of what will 'work' and what will not, what is achievable and what is not. If they suggest you think again it is because they believe you cannot produce a thesis or dissertation of the required standard from what you are proposing. So, take the advice they give, and submit another proposal.

How should I plan and organize my research project?

Whether your research is for a Masters dissertation or a Doctoral thesis it needs careful planning and organization – you will not be successful if you simply start work and then see where it leads. An important factor which makes it vital to plan is the time limit you will have. For your Masters dissertation the final date to hand it in will probably be the end of September, while for a Doctoral thesis there will be a maximum time you can spend on your work, probably four years. So you need to plan it carefully.

You need to start by thinking through what stages there are to your project. For most research projects we can identify ten stages:

Stage 1   Choosing the project
Stage 2   Initial literature review

Stage 3   Finalizing the research question(s)

Stage 4   Choosing and developing the methodology

Stage 5   Piloting the methodology

Stage 6   Organizing the data collection

Stage 7   Data collection

Stage 8   Data analysis

Stage 9   Drawing conclusions and interpretations

Stage 10 Preparing the final thesis

This looks a straightforward path to understand and follow, but there are a number of important points to remember with this model. First, your real project will not follow this path in a neat sequence:

- Some stages will overlap – for example, you will certainly start to develop interpretations and conclusions as soon as you start collecting data, and you may of course want to test some of your conclusions by collecting further data.
- You may need to return to earlier stages – for example, piloting may indicate you need to make changes to the methodology.
- Some stages will continue throughout the project – for example, you will need to keep reviewing the literature throughout the project to be sure that you have not missed anything important or that there have not been new publications on the topic. Even while you are preparing the final thesis you will need to do a last-minute literature check so that you do not miss the latest publications.

Secondly, you will need to be writing the thesis/dissertation from as early in the project as possible. Stage 10 is preparing the final version, not starting to write. We shall look in more detail at writing later in this chapter, but it is very important to recognize that you must start writing as soon as you can, otherwise it may become a major psychological barrier for you.

Let us now look at each of the stages in turn.

Stage 1 – Choosing the project   We have looked at this earlier in the chapter.

Stage 2 – Initial literature review   The literature review is a critical early stage in your project. A literature review has many purposes. It enables you to find out what research has been undertaken in the field, what is 'known' and what the important questions are that others are investigating or have suggested for research. It helps you to understand the history of your field, to know how ideas have developed, changed, appeared and disappeared over time. You will become aware of the range of methodologies that have been used to research your field, both in the past and in the present, and you should start to develop a critical view of the advantages and disadvantages of different approaches. It will also enable you to discover who else is working in the field and what they are working on. Most importantly, though, it will help you to look at your initial ideas for your research and develop and refine them to produce the project that you will undertake. It is almost the most important stage of the project, for if you do this thoroughly and well you will be saved many potential problems later on.

Stage 3 – Finalizing the research questions   Ideally your research questions will emerge from the literature review. The literature review will have shown you what is already known in the field and what important topics need to be researched.

Stage 4 – Choosing and developing the methodology   Whatever your subject and field, there will be a range of different research methods available to you. At this stage you need to choose the best approach to enable you to answer your research question. Many students though, unfortunately, start with an idea of the methods they want to use and then apply them to their research question whether or not they are the best way forward. The correct way forward, of course, is to read and reflect very broadly on possible research methods and then choose what is most appropriate, even if this involves you in learning new approaches or techniques.

There are two levels at which you will need to make choices about methodology. The first is the philosophical level, the second is the operational level. The philosophical level refers to the broad theoretical understanding of how knowledge is developed and of the nature of knowledge. For some students this is often a stage that is not considered, because their subject disciplines have a long history of working in one particular philosophical approach. This is true of many science and engineering disciplines where the empirical, experimental, quantitative, positivist approach is the norm and it would be very difficult to step outside this approach to research. In the arts, humanities and social sciences, however, there is a strong tradition of different philosophical approaches to research, ranging from strongly positivist approaches as in science to much more qualitative, phenomenological approaches. In this case, deciding on and justifying your approach is an important stage of choosing a methodology. For more on the philosophical dimensions of research you should consider looking at a text on research methods such as:

Schutt, R.K. (1999) *Investigating the Social World – The Process and Practice of Research.* London: Pine Forge.

The operational level involves choosing the precise methods and approaches you will use to investigate your research question. This might range from laboratory experiment to field data collection to social survey to the use of documentary evidence. Every discipline has a very extensive literature on research methods, and one characteristic of achieving Masters or Doctoral level is that you can show you know and understand about research methods in your field. You may be able simply to use existing research tools (for example a well-established experimental technique), or you may need either to modify an existing technique or develop a whole new technique. Whatever you choose to do, though, it is essential that:

- The technique has validity, i.e. it is the correct method to measure or test what it is you are trying to examine.
- Your use of the technique makes the data reliable, that is to say you have used it correctly and somebody else using the same technique in the same circumstances would get the same results.
- You have considered alternative methods/techniques and can justify your choice of method.

There are two other important aspects of choosing your methodology. The first is to think through the ethical aspects of your research. In all disciplines there will be sensitive research topics. For example, in biological sciences there will be issues about live animal experiments or the implications of genetic research. In engineering there may be issues about nuclear or military-linked topics. In medicine and the social sciences there will be issues of working with human subjects. Every discipline will have ethical codes of practice which you should ensure that you are familiar with. Your supervisor will be able to provide you with detailed guidance on ethical issues, but a helpful source is:

Lee, R. (2003) *Doing Research in Sensitive Topics.* London: Sage.

Secondly, and more important, are the health and safety issues. Whatever your research topic there will be health and safety issues. In laboratory or workshop disciplines there are strong legal frameworks for health and safety that you will be required to observe, from safe practice to the handling and storage of materials. In field disciplines (social or environmental) there are health and safety risks in working away from the university. The university will have clear guidelines for preparing and updating a Risk Assessment for your work, and you should check this carefully with your tutor. Your programme handbook should have clear guidelines on health and safety in your discipline.

Stage 5 – Piloting the methodology Whatever method you use, you will need to pilot your methodology. Piloting is practising, checking that you can use the method correctly and that it will work in the circumstances in which you are using it to provide usable data. Piloting usually suggests changes and modifications to the methods you are using, sometimes large, sometimes small, and so is an essential process. Not piloting the methodology is a very common cause of failure for postgraduate students.

Stage 6 – Organizing the data collection   Do not be put off by the word 'data'. By data we are talking about the evidence you will use to arrive at your conclusions, and there are many types of data. Your data could be experimental results, field data or survey data or they could come from direct observations of social situations. The data could be quantitative, qualitative or a combination of both types. Stage 6 involves making the arrangements to collect that data.

In a science or engineering context this stage might involve booking laboratory or workshop time and space, assembling the experimental equipment and experimental materials, and undertaking the full range of health and safety checks. In a social science context it may involve identifying the sample for a survey and making arrangements to send out and receive back questionnaires, or organizing interviews with key individuals. This stage is often rather longer than many postgraduates expect, since it involves making organizational arrangements, so it is worth starting this stage as soon as possible within your project.

Stage 7 – Data collection   Collecting the data can be a short or a long process – for example a project on the behaviour of apes may take many months of detailed observation and recording, while some experimental projects may take only a few weeks or even days to complete.

Stage 8 – Data analysis   Data analysis includes the systematic organizing of the data and its presentation in a form that readers of your project can understand. It also includes the interpretation of the data to identify the important ideas or new bits of knowledge that they reveal. Each discipline will have descriptive and analytical techniques, ranging from statistical analysis to computer modelling to presentational methods to qualitative analysis. You will need to choose the methods best suited to the data you have collected, and will need to be able to *justify* your choice of methods.

At postgraduate level, simply describing the information and data that you have will not be enough, however well you present them. Analysis and interpretation is what makes a piece of work demonstrate Masters or Doctoral standard. This means that you will need to use techniques to interpret and manipulate the data to see what it is telling you – what are the underlying ideas, models, pictures, theories or interpretations that are revealed from your data? A common problem with postgraduate projects is that they are not analytical enough. This may be partly because students who have collected the data believe they are close to finishing and simply do not spend enough time trying to see what the data really show, so it is important to allow enough time for analysis and thinking at this stage.

Stage 9 – Drawing conclusions and interpretations   Stage 8 involved very detailed analysis and interpretation, working with the detail of the data and drawing out important ideas about every part of the topic that has been studied. Stage 9 is the 'big picture' stage of the research, where the detailed interpretations are drawn together to try to 'answer' the overall research question. It will certainly involve a critical reflection on the conclusions you have drawn and the methods you have used, and will probably make recommendations for future research in the field. In social science fields it may include recommendations for policy-makers and practitioners about future practice and policy.

Stage 10 – Preparing the final thesis   We shall look at the writing of the thesis in more detail later in this chapter. The final stage of the project, though, is assembling the final version of the thesis. You will have produced drafts of individual chapters throughout the project, and these can be assembled into the first draft of the overall thesis or dissertation. At this stage, though, the work needs to be prepared for submission – making sure the whole work is coherent; writing, re-writing and editing; assembling diagrams, tables or charts; completing and checking the bibliography and appendices; preparing the contents and the abstract; printing and binding the work. This all takes a significant amount of time, which needs to be built into the planning of the project.

You will see from reading through the stages of the project that there is much to plan and prepare for. While it is not possible to plan precisely how long each stage will take, and unforeseen things may arise, it is very helpful to plan as carefully as you can. There are two simple techniques you can use to plan your time and your project – a **time line** and a **Gantt chart**.

Planning using a time line   A time line (Figure 9.1) is simply a line that represents the duration of the project, against which you mark the times at which you will undertake different activities. To produce a time line you will need to take the following steps:

1 On a large piece of paper draw a line on to which you mark the periods of the year (months, terms, semesters or quarters). The line should start from the beginning of the project (probably October of Year 1 for a PhD project, or April for a Masters project) and run to the submission date (probably April of Year 3 for a PhD, or the end of September for a Masters).
2 Separately, estimate how long each of the ten stages of the project (see above) will take, and note this down.

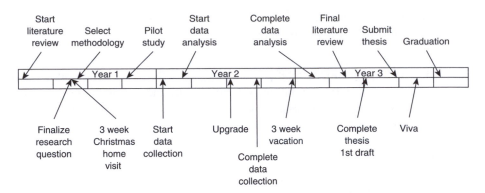

FIGURE 9.1   *Planning using a time line*

3   Mark on to the time line any fixed or immovable dates. These may include the date of the graduation ceremony you want to attend, and dates on which the university is closed (e.g. at Christmas). More importantly, it should include critical dates for data collection. Some data collection can be done at any time, but in some cases it is very precise – if you are doing research on a solar eclipse its date will be fixed, for example, or if you are researching students' adjustment to university life in their first week at university then that too will be fixed.

4   Then, working backwards from the end of the project, mark on the timings of the stages of the project.

This will give you a clear picture of how the project will operate, and will enable you to identify the dates by which particular stages or activities have to be started and completed. It will also help you identify any timing problems – and help you identify when, if at all, you might be able to take break or a holiday.

Planning using a Gantt chart   Gantt charts (Figure 9.2) are a technique for planning projects which are used extensively in business. They are similar to time lines except that they enable you to show the precise timings of particular activities and to see the overlaps between them. To plan using a Gantt chart:

1   Across the top of a large piece of paper draw a time line.
2   Down the side of the paper list the stages of the project in as much detail as you can.
3   Shade in on the chart the time duration of each stage, applying the same principles we outlined in looking at time lines above. In our example we have distinguished 'active phases' when that particular activity is a main focus, and 'intermittent phases' when the activity will carry on but at a much lower level.

The advantage of using planning techniques such as these is that you can monitor your progress week by week and month by month. Some times will

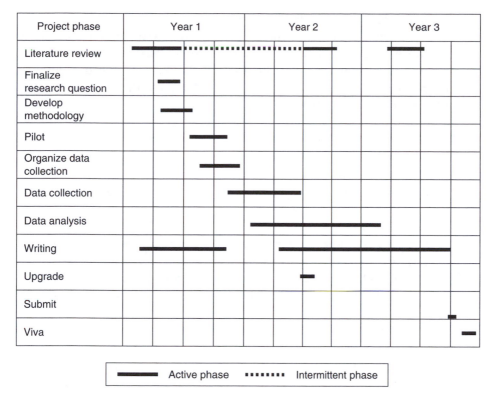

Project phase	Year 1			Year 2			Year 3		
Literature review									
Finalize research question									
Develop methodology									
Pilot									
Organize data collection									
Data collection									
Data analysis									
Writing									
Upgrade									
Submit									
Viva									

——— Active phase   ▪▪▪▪▪▪▪ Intermittent phase

FIGURE 9.2   *Planning using a Gantt chart*

change, as some stages take longer or less time than planned, but you can then adjust your plan to reflect this.

What's involved in writing a thesis?

For most postgraduate students the idea of writing a dissertation or thesis is quite daunting. It will certainly be the longest writing task they have done, and many will feel nervous about how they will cope with it. In this section we shall look at a number of aspects of writing to show how any concerns you have can be dealt with, so that you can write a good quality thesis or dissertation.

How should a thesis or dissertation be organized?

There is no single formula for a thesis or dissertation. It is important at an early stage to look at some examples in your field just to get a 'feel' for what they are like. The easiest way to do this is to visit the university library and look at some examples from previous students. If you are not currently at university then you can still arrange to visit the library of your nearest university. One of the decisions you will have to take is how your own thesis/dissertation should be organized. However, we shall outline here a common structure that is likely to be suitable almost whatever your field – and you can at least use this as a starting point for designing your own thesis. A typical thesis or dissertation might have the following structure:

- **Title page**   One page with the title, date, degree the project was submitted for and your full name.
- **Abstract**   A brief summary of the project, no more than a single page in length, summarizing the aims, background, methods and findings. This should be the last part of the work that you write!
- **Contents**   Tables listing the chapters, the figures and the diagrams.
- **Chapter 1 – Background and context**   A discussion of the background to the study and the reasons for its importance and interest as a research project.
- **Chapter 2 – Literature review**   A summary of the findings of the literature review.
- **Chapter 3 – Research methodology**   A description and justification of the methodology you have used.
- **Chapters 4–6 – Data presentation and analysis**   Chapters presenting, interpreting and analysing the results.
- **Chapter 7 – Discussion and conclusions**   The 'big picture' chapter, presenting the overall findings, the 'answer' to the research question and a critique of the research.
- **Bibliography**   A list of the references and wider reading that you have done.
- **Appendices**   Additional information you want to include. This could be some of the detailed data, or samples of some of the 'raw' results such as computer printouts or interview notes or a sample questionnaire.

The exact number of chapters will be for you to choose. You may need one or several data presentation and analysis chapters, particularly in a doctoral thesis. The chapters do not all need to be the same length. It is very hard to give guidelines on how long each section should be, because it will be unique for each thesis or dissertation. For example, the literature chapter length may depend on how much has been written in the field, and the research methodology chapter length will depend on how simple or complex the research method actually was. As a rule of thumb, though, the proportions given in Table 9.1 are a rough guide.

When should I start writing?

You should start writing as soon as you can. There are a number of reasons for this. The most obvious one is that the writing will take a long time and the sooner you get started the better. However, there are a number of other aspects of writing that are important. First, writing is a skill that develops and

TABLE 9.1   Word length guidelines for dissertations/theses

Section	Proportion of dissertation/ thesis	Word length for a typical Masters dissertation	Word length for a typical PHD thesis
Background and context	5%	1,000	5,000
Literature review	20%	4,000	15,000
Methodology	15%	3,000	12,500
Data presentation and analysis	45%	9,000	35,000
Discussion and conclusions	15%	3,000	12,500

improves with practice. You will probably find that your first sections of writing take a long time and need a lot of revision and re-writing. Indeed, you may choose to discard some of your earlier efforts. However, over time you will become better and the quality of your writing will improve.

Secondly, it is important to write things as you do them. You should be able to write the first draft of your Background/Context chapter almost as soon as you start the project, and the Literature Review chapter can be written as soon as you have done some wide reading. The Methodology chapter can be drafted as soon as you have decided what you are going to do. The advantage of this is that the thinking you have done is still fresh in your mind. This does not mean that you will not need to rework or add to these chapters – but at least you will have a good first draft of what you want to say.

Thirdly, getting an early first draft of some of the chapters is a good thing to do psychologically. You will feel you are making progress and will have something to show for your efforts.

Fourthly, and most importantly, though, is recognizing that thinking and writing are very strongly connected. By writing you will be forced to get your ideas sorted into a logical order and to clarify why you think what you do. You will need to bring the evidence forward to back up your ideas. This means that as you write, your ideas and thinking will improve and develop. It will also raise new questions in your mind, which you will be able to go back to the literature or data to check and work through.

How many drafts will I need?

This depends on how good you are at writing, but you should plan to produce a first draft and a second draft of each chapter together with a first draft of the whole thesis or dissertation and a final draft of the whole work. This will enable you to get each chapter to a good standard and then draft it further so it fits as part of the whole work.

How can I develop and improve my writing?

The only really effective way to improve your writing is to practise, and you will see your own skills develop as you progress through the work. Your tutor will give you some feedback on writing style and skill each time you submit a draft of a section for him or her to look at. There are three other approaches you can use to improve your writing:

- Read as much as you can. Reading academic writing in journals or books will make you increasingly familiar with good (and poor) writing style.
- Share your writing with friends and fellow students and give each other feedback on style, grammar, English language and academic writing.
- Most universities will offer courses or support on academic writing for international students. Find out if your university does this, and try to attend a course if you can. Your tutor may ask you to attend such a course if they feel you are having problems with writing, but even if they do not suggest it, you could still look for such a course.

● ● ●   *Pause for thought*   ● ● ●

Think about your own academic writing skills by thinking of a major project you did as an undergraduate, perhaps your undergraduate dissertation. How easy did you find it to write the dissertation? What aspects of the work did you need help or guidance with, and which areas were identified by your tutors as the strengths and weaknesses of your writing? This should help you identify aspects of your writing skills in which you might need support as a postgraduate.

If you have significant problems with writing, then your university will have support services to give you guidance and help. Your tutor will be able to tell you whom to contact.

How should I keep track of the sources I have used?

In Chapter 8 we looked at the importance of keeping a careful record of your sources and references as you prepare assignments. For your dissertation or thesis, reference management is even more important. If you do not do this properly as you go along then you will find you have an almost impossible task at the end to identify your sources and references. All universities will have software on their computer network to enable you to manage references, the most common one being EndNote. Learn how to use this before you start your literature review and your writing, and then use it carefully – when you complete your dissertation or thesis you will be very grateful that you did this.

How can I make sure that I avoid plagiarism?

It is important that you check your work to avoid plagiarism. In the previous chapter we looked at what plagiarism is, and at a number of strategies you can use to make sure you do not commit this academic crime. You should read that section again now. If you commit plagiarism unintentionally as part of an assignment you might be allowed to resubmit the work, or you may even pass the taught part of the course despite the fail mark you will get for that piece of work. Plagiarism in your thesis or dissertation, however, will almost certainly guarantee that you fail and are not awarded a degree.

How should I present my work?

The exact format for presenting your thesis or dissertation varies from university to university, and in some cases it varies between different subjects/disciplines in the same university. You will be given guidance on presentation and submission, probably in the programme handbook. It is important to read this guidance carefully before you start your thesis so that issues such as layout, font size, margin size etc. can be organized in the correct way right from the start. You should then read the guidance again when you start to prepare your final draft of the whole thesis to check, finally, that you will be presenting it in the right way.

Can I publish my work?

Although the main aim of your postgraduate programme will be for you to be awarded a Masters degree or a Doctorate, it will add considerably to your achievement if some or all of your work is eventually published in a journal or as a book. For a Masters degree dissertation there is no formal expectation that you will publish, but one of the indicators of the best work at this level is that it is seen as being of publishable quality. Where a distinction award is made this will usually indicate that your dissertation has work in it that should be published. For a Doctorate the standard required to pass is that your work and findings are of publishable quality, so you will find that there is some expectation from your university that you will try to publish some or all of your work. If you are planning to progress from the postgraduate course to a career as an academic or as a researcher then having some work published from your research is almost essential.

What you can publish and when, though, will depend on your own university's regulations. In some universities you are not allowed to publish work from your thesis or dissertation until after it has been submitted for examination for your degree. This means that you cannot publish as you go along. In other universities there is more flexibility on this, and providing you do not publish the final version of any sections of your work before you are examined then there is not a problem. You need to check this very carefully with your tutor before deciding whether to publish any of your findings, therefore.

As a Doctoral student you will be encouraged to attend academic conferences in your discipline, particularly as you get towards the end of your studies. This enables you to meet and mix with academics and other researchers in your field and to listen to their ideas. It may also be possible for you to present papers on your developing ideas from your research and get some views and ideas from others. Care needs to be taken with this for the same reasons that publishing may be a problem as you go along. But discuss this with your tutor to see if it is possible or a sensible idea.

After you have finished, though, you will be encouraged to publish. In many disciplines there is a tradition of post-Doctoral studies, when students spend time after their PhD to prepare papers from their research and take their research on a little further. However, this is not easy for Masters students, unless they progress to a Doctorate, and it is also not easy for those who leave academic life after their postgraduate studies and enter a different career. Whatever your circumstances, though, you should consider carefully trying to get one or more papers from your work published. This will raise the profile for your work, which will then be more easily accessible than your thesis. It will also demonstrate to yourself that you have truly produced some research that has made a 'contribution to knowledge'.

One final point to consider in all this is that you may not wish your work to be published either because it contains controversial ideas or because it contains findings that are of commercial value. Universities are sensitive to both these problems, and all have systems for ensuring your work stays confidential if necessary – your tutor will be able to provide advice on this. If your ideas are of commercial value then the university will be able to provide expert advice on such things as registering patents or setting up a company to exploit the discovery. While it is not common for students to become wealthy from their Doctoral research, it is not unknown – in which case you can both get a Doctorate and become a millionaire!

KEY RISKS AND HOW TO AVOID THEM

Writing a research project, dissertation or thesis is an essential part of a postgraduate degree programme. Most students find it a stimulating and rewarding part of their studies that enables them to focus in depth on a subject that truly fascinates them, and which also enables them to make a 'contribution to knowledge'. There are a number of key risks in this, however.

Risk 1: *Not choosing a topic that interests you*   It is essential that you choose a topic that will keep you interested and motivated even when the work is hard and there is still a long way to go to finish the project.

Risk 2: *Choosing a topic that is too large and unmanageable to carry out*   Most students overestimate how large a project they will need to do, and end up with too much literature to review and too much data to analyse. Take your tutor's advice on the size and scale of a suitable project.

Risk 3: *Not identifying a key research question* Whatever methodology you are going to use or whatever your philosophical view on research approaches, you must start with a research question. What is it that you are investigating or trying to find out? A research question keeps you focused.

Risk 4: *Not planning the project and its timings properly* Use a suitable method to plan your project meticulously, to make sure you finish by the deadlines.

Risk 5: *Not using the most suitable research methods* Choose a research method that suits the question you are investigating, do not just use something you feel confident about using. If you find you need to use a new approach to investigate your question then learn the techniques or methods it requires – or change your research question.

Risk 6: *Not managing the data in a suitable way* Whatever your project, you will have a large amount of data. Plan carefully before you start how you will store these data so that you can use them – whether that is in the form of notes or a database or some other method. If you do not do this you may find you will 'drown' in the data you have collected and not be able to use them properly.

Risk 7: *Not managing references in a suitable way* References are an important type of data. Keep your references up to date as you go along, preferably by using a software package such as EndNote. If you do not do this, you will spend a large amount of time at the end of your project trying to find references.

Risk 8: *Not piloting your methods* Whatever methods you use, you should pilot them. This enables you to check that the methods work, that they are valid and reliable and that you have the skills to use them.

Risk 9: *Not including sufficient analysis and interpretation in your thesis* A common weakness of theses and dissertations is that they are strong on description and weak on analysis and critical reflection. Ensure that you identify what your data are telling you about what processes and ideas underpin them.

Risk 10: *Not starting to write at an early stage* Writing a thesis or dissertation is a large task. It is important to start as early as possible. If you delay starting to write you will begin to feel that the 'research mountain' is getting higher and steeper each day. Remember another aspect of mountain climbing that is relevant here – every journey starts with the first step. So take the first step in your writing as early as you can.

CHAPTER 10

TUTORS, SUPERVISORS AND STUDENT SUPPORT SYSTEMS

- How do I make best use of my tutor or supervisor?
- What are the student life support systems?

First thoughts

For all universities, helping their students to complete their programmes successfully is a very important priority. The main way this is achieved is by recruiting intelligent, well-qualified and highly motivated students on to the programmes and employing academic staff who are leading experts in their field to teach them. But every student is an individual with their own particular background and needs, so universities have developed a range of systems to give help and support to students. For postgraduate students there are two important types of support: your tutor or supervisor, and the support services available from the university or Student Union. In this chapter we shall look at how you can make best use of both.

How do I make the best use of my tutor or supervisor?

As a postgraduate student you will have much closer individual support for your studies than you did as an undergraduate. Although the exact system varies between universities, you will find that there are a number of individual academic staff who you will work with closely, and who will provide you with support.

Masters students will usually be supported in the following ways, although the names and titles given to these roles may differ between universities:

- **A personal tutor**. Your personal tutor will be the academic who will support you both academically and personally during your programme. He or she will provide you with guidance on your work, and talk with you about choosing options and dissertation titles. Your tutor will also be able to provide you with guidance and support if you have any personal issues, and will be able to direct you to support services such as financial advisers, counsellors or careers guidance staff. You will probably meet with your tutor individually a number of times during the programme.

- **Course unit tutors**. These are the academic staff who lead or teach on individual teaching units. They will probably mark your assignments for their unit and may provide individual or group tutorials while you are studying their unit.
- **Programme leaders**. Each programme will have an academic who is the overall leader and is responsible for organizing the programme. You will meet these people at key times during the programme, particularly at the start, and will be able to talk with them if there are particular questions or issues you need to discuss.
- **Postgraduate tutor**. If an academic department has more than one postgraduate programme they may have a postgraduate tutor who has overall responsibility for the welfare and academic studies of all the postgraduates in that department. Although you will meet the postgraduate tutor occasionally, you are most likely to need to talk with him or her if you have a particular issue or problem.
- **Dissertation supervisor**. When you decide on your topic for your Masters dissertation you will be given a dissertation supervisor who will support you as you work on your project. Most programmes allocate dissertation supervisors only when topics have been chosen, so that you will have the academic who is most expert in your field.

It is likely that some of these roles may be filled by the same person. It is quite possible, for example, that your personal tutor will also supervise your dissertation, or that one of the course unit tutors will provide your supervision. Most departments, though, will ensure that there are several tutors who you will work with during your programme. This is for two reasons. First, it means that you will experience a variety of academic views, which is helpful in developing your expertise in the subject. Secondly, though, it means that there are several people who can provide you with support. Although it is quite unusual, there are times when students do not 'get on well' with their personal tutor or a particular unit tutor, so it is helpful if there is somebody else they can turn to for advice.

Doctoral students may have a similar range of tutors who they work with during their studies, particularly if they are following a taught Doctorate programme. For all Doctoral students, though, the key support is through their supervisor. MPhil/PhD students will be allocated their supervisor from the start of the programme, while taught Doctoral students may not be allocated a supervisor until the time when they finally choose their thesis topic. The supervisor will probably be your personal tutor too, because the individual nature of Doctoral research means that you will have a very close relationship with your supervisor.

In recent years the UK Quality Assurance Agency has developed guidelines for 'good practice' in supervising Doctoral students. One part of this is the expectation that each Doctoral student will have a supervisory team which looks after their progress, and not just a single supervisor or tutor. The exact way that these teams are organized varies between universities and sometimes between departments. You will still have a main supervisor who will provide you with most of your support and guidance week by week and month by month, but there will be one or two other academic staff who get to know you and your work and can provide support if necessary. The other members of the team might be a 'second supervisor' and the programme leader. You should have opportunities to meet with your whole team together at regular intervals (at least once a year), and they will have responsibility for assessing your progress each year and arranging any upgrade process.

In the sections that follow we will look at how you can make the most of your tutors and supervisor. We shall concentrate on the role of the supervisor, as he or she will probably be the most important of your tutors. However, most of what we say here will also apply to how you might work with other tutors too.

How should I try to work with my supervisor?

Supervisors come in all shapes and sizes! Most academic staff in UK universities are, of course, British. There are more men than women, they are more likely to be over 40 years old than under 40, and the numbers from ethnic minority groups are still quite small. Like all professional groups, they vary widely in personality, too, ranging from extrovert to shy and from serious to having a lively sense of humour. This means that there is a wide range of profiles amongst your possible supervisors, and your first task will be to get to know *your* supervisor personally.

The most important thing to remember about working with your supervisor is that now you are a postgraduate student you should expect a two-way relationship with him or her. You should not expect your supervisor simply to tell you what to do; you should see him or her as a partner to work with. A good supervisor will know how to support you in many ways but will aim to work with you to help in the ways most suited to your individual needs. Do not be afraid to ask for the things you need or to work in the way that suits you best. This does not mean, of course, that you can demand that your supervisor does exactly what you want, but you should see your working relationship as one that can be 'managed' as much by you as by your tutor.

What can I expect of my supervisor?

Your supervisor has responsibility for supporting you and guiding you through your research project. He or she will have expert knowledge in the field you are researching and also expertise in research methods and techniques. The supervisor's role will be to advise you on each part of your project – research proposal, literature search, methodology, data collection, data analysis and writing the dissertation or thesis. At each stage your supervisor will talk with you about what you are doing and planning, make suggestions for each part of the work, and read and review drafts of your writing. He or she will do this by having individual tutorials with you, and also by talking with you informally, whether in person or through e-mail.

An important part of the supervisor's role in the early stages of your work is to do a 'needs analysis' with you. This means that together you will assess the skills and knowledge that your project will require and then identify what particular training you may need. This could be training in particular IT skills or a particular research technique. It could involve arranging additional English language support. It might include arranging visits to organizations outside the university to meet experts in particular fields. Obviously, your exact needs will be unique to you – your requirements may be quite different from what another student on the same programme needs. There are many ways that such a needs analysis can be conducted, so check with your tutor how it will be done in your case.

It is important to understand, however, both what your supervisor *can* do for you and also what he or she *cannot*. As a postgraduate student you will be expected to be independent in the way you work, and your research will be expected to be your own work, that you have planned and undertaken. Your supervisor is not there to tell you what to do nor to be by your side in everything that you do. A supervisor rather should act as a guide, an academic colleague, somebody to test your ideas with and to seek advice from. It is also important to know the limits of your supervisor's expertise. At Masters level it is likely that whatever you choose as your research topic your supervisor will know most of what your dissertation will discover in outline. At Doctoral level, though, it is likely that you will soon know and understand more about your particular subject than your supervisor. Doctoral level work is about contributing something new to knowledge, so your research ought to be discovering ideas or knowledge not yet known to your supervisor. His or her role, therefore, is to support you in the process of discovering that knowledge, as your supervisor will be an expert in research in the field.

How often should I meet with my supervisor?

This is a difficult question, for it depends on many things. As a Masters student you will probably have four or five tutorials during your dissertation period – one or two at the beginning to help you get started, one or two during the research to discuss progress and research issues, and one or two towards the end to discuss the writing of your dissertation. You may find that your programme gives you an **entitlement** to supervision – a certain number of hours of supervision which is guaranteed as a minimum amount of time with your supervisor. You may need more support than this, of course, and this minimum can usually be increased. However, some programmes also have a maximum amount of support they will give you. You should check with your programme what the 'entitlement' for support is.

As a Doctoral student you will meet with your supervisor more frequently, and this will happen over the whole time period of your research. As a full-time student you might expect *on average* to meet formally with your supervisor once every two weeks, although the frequency of tutorials will vary a lot throughout your studies. There will be times when you may need to meet more often – perhaps in the early stages when you are developing your proposal or at the time when you are trying to develop your research methods and techniques. At other times you may need to see your supervisor less often. When you are doing the literature review or writing draft chapters of your thesis it may be that you only need to see your supervisor every four or five weeks. You may also, of course, have informal meetings. Some departments try to give their Doctoral students an office close to their supervisor. Some have common rooms which both academic staff and postgraduate students use. In laboratory-studio-or workshop-based disciplines you may have your own work space in or very close to the lab, studio or workshop your supervisor uses. In these circumstances you may meet your supervisor informally quite frequently, and can talk about your work almost continuously.

How frequently you meet will depend very much on you and your needs. You should not expect that your supervisor will always be the one to arrange to see you. You should seek a meeting with him or her if and when you need it. It is a good idea to make an appointment for your next meeting every time you have a tutorial, but if issues arise in the meantime you can contact your supervisor for advice or, if necessary, an earlier appointment. Obviously you cannot simply demand to see your supervisor whenever it suits you. All academic staff have busy schedules, and also have times when they may be away at conferences or on holiday. Most will usually try to see you as soon as they can, particularly if there is an 'emergency' issue.

What will my supervisor expect from me?

Your supervisor will expect you to show that you are a good postgraduate student. This means that you will need to be independent in the way you work, that you will work hard and be well organized. At postgraduate level your supervisor will not expect to have to guide you through every step of your work and will expect you to have clear ideas about what you need to do and how you will do it. This means that you should expect to:

- Be punctual for tutorials and meetings.
- Meet deadlines for submitting work to your tutor.
- Listen to and act on your tutor's advice. This does not mean that you must do everything your tutor suggests; no one will be impressed by this because you need to demonstrate criticality and reflection. However, most of the advice and guidance your tutor will offer will be based on long experience of supporting postgraduate students, so it is likely to be very useful. Your tutor will not be impressed if you never listen to advice or take up suggestions.

- Come to tutorials well prepared for the discussion, and having completed all the tasks you agreed to do by that time. For example, if you agreed you would write a draft of a particular chapter by the time of the tutorial, then you should have completed it if at all possible.
- Be active and positive in tutorials. Although there will be times when you have particular problems that you want your supervisor to help you resolve, you should always go to the tutorial with some ideas for how the problem might be dealt with. 'Always bring solutions not problems' is good advice about tutorials.
- Negotiate with your supervisor a way of working together that suits both of you. This means deciding, probably at your first meeting, how you want to arrange:

(a) The frequency of tutorials and meetings.

(b) How tutorials and meetings will be organized, and what will be expected of you in tutorials.

(c) How you will communicate – will it be by e-mail, telephone, or notes and messages?

(d) How you should submit your work. Some academic staff are happy for you to send work by e-mail because they can read it on-screen and send it back to you electronically with comments (perhaps using 'Track change' software). Others prefer you to give them hard copy, so they can read it on the page and write comments on it. Most will *not* want you to send them work electronically that they then have to print out themselves before they can work on it.

(e) How far ahead of tutorials they will want you to send in your work. Your tutor will need to have time to read your work before a tutorial and so will certainly need it a few days before. When you are at the stage of writing whole chapters you may need to submit it a week or so in advance, and with drafts of the whole work they may need two weeks to read it.

(f) When they are available for you to see them. Academic staff organize their time in many ways. Some may be willing to see you at any time they are 'free' during the working week. Others may have particular 'office hours' that they use for seeing their students and having tutorials (perhaps one or two mornings or afternoons each week). Some may be happy for you to simply 'call in' to see them if you need to. Others may want you always to make an appointment.

Most importantly, though, your supervisor will expect you to be enthusiastic, energetic and interested in your work. Most will want to have a friendly and positive relationship with you, for that makes their work and your work more enjoyable and rewarding. Particularly for Doctoral students, but often for Masters students as well, you will develop a friendly professional relationship with your supervisor that will last for many years, and long after you have finished your programme. Many academic staff continue to work on projects and research with their former research students as they develop their academic career in other universities around the world.

What should I do if things go wrong?

In a survey by *The Times Higher Education Supplement* (THES, 12 August 2005), most Doctoral students rated the supervision they received from their tutor as very good and as one of the strongest aspects of their time on their programme. It is important to be aware, however, that while for most of the time you will be happy about how things are progressing, every Masters or Doctoral student has times during their work when things are difficult and challenging. There is a difference between the normal 'ups and downs' of postgraduate life and when things are going wrong and problems are occurring. One of the main ways your supervisor can help you is in telling you whether the challenges you are facing are simply 'normal' ones, or ones where some additional support may be helpful. So it is important always to keep your tutor aware of when things are going well or not so well. Your supervisor will know that everything will not be perfect for you all the time and will expect you to raise issues and problems – so there's no need to be afraid that you are showing yourself to be a poor student when you do.

Your supervisor (or other tutors) should be able either to guide you on how to deal with issues, whether academic or personal or, perhaps more importantly, to direct you to somebody else in the university or outside who can help you.

The biggest challenge is if the problem you have is with the tutor or supervisor themselves. Although it is unusual, occasionally students find that they have a poor relationship with their supervisor or tutor or feel they are not getting the support and help that they need. It is important if this happens to you that you try to deal with the problem as soon as possible, for such a problem will certainly make it difficult for you to work effectively on your research. So what should you do?

First, you should keep a written note of the issues that you have, together with details of the times of meetings or events and the problems that you felt were occurring.

Secondly, try talking to your supervisor or tutor directly about it. It might be, of course, that he or she is not aware that there is a problem and can resolve the difficulty with you very quickly.

Thirdly, if talking with your supervisor does not help, then talk to one of the other academic staff who you work with. (We listed the main academic staff who are responsible for you earlier in this chapter.) You could perhaps talk to another member of your supervisory team or to the programme leader. They will try to resolve your problem or offer help. In extreme cases it may be possible to change supervisors, although this is not always easy since you will need a supervisor with particular expertise.

If the steps listed above do not resolve the problem, then your university will have formal procedures for dealing with complaints. Information on the procedures will be available from your department or from the Student Union, who will also be able to offer advice.

● ● ●   *Pause for thought*   ● ● ●

*Think about how you worked with your supervisor or tutors when you were
undertaking projects as an undergraduate. Did you have a good working
relationship with them? Try to identify the reasons why you did or did not work
well with them, and think about what you might need to work on in terms of:*

(a)   How you manage yourself and the way you interact with your tutor.
(b)   How you might try to ensure your tutor can best meet your study needs.

*Most problems between tutors and students arise from poor communications or a
lack of clarity about the expectations that each has of the working relationship. Plan
to raise these two issues with your tutor at your first meeting.*

What are the student life support systems?

Most of the support for your academic studies will come from the academic
staff, administrative staff and fellow students in your department. However,
every university also has a wide range of support for postgraduate students
that you can use. In the first few days of your time at the university you will
find it useful to get to know what other services are available. In this section
we shall look briefly at what those services might be and how you can
use them. In Chapter 7 we looked at a range of services that might support
your personal life in the UK, so here we shall focus on those that might support your academic studies and related issues, both within and outside the
university.

Services within the university

The Student Union   Every university has a Student Union, although its exact
title will vary from place to place. Its purpose is to provide a full range of social
and welfare facilities and services for students, and you will automatically be a
member of the Student Union when you register as a student at the university.
For you as an international postgraduate student it can provide a wide range
of advice and services to support your academic studies. Most Student Unions
will have specialist advisers who know and understand all of the issues about
life and study as a postgraduate. Most Unions will also have at least one international student adviser who knows and understands the issues of being an
international student in the UK and within the particular university. These
advisers can give you advice on both minor and major issues. With major problems they can often talk with your department or supervisor on your behalf or
represent you or accompany you in meetings with academic staff.

In addition to the Student Union, which is run by and on behalf of students, the university itself will have many services to support you.

The International Office   You will probably have had some contact with the International Office when you were enquiring or applying to the university. While their main task is recruiting international students, they will also be able to provide you with support and guidance while you are in the university. They will be very knowledgeable about the sorts of issues international students may face, and will be able to give advice or direct you to somebody or an organization who can help with any issues you have. In large universities the International Office may have specialist staff who know particular countries or regions of the world very well, perhaps as an expert, for example, on China or South America. They will have an excellent understanding of your culture and background, and of the economic, social, political and educational systems in your own country. They will therefore have a good understanding of some of your issues and can provide good advice or guidance.

Study support and disability services   Every university has services to support students with specific study needs. They will be able to provide programmes or training in study skills, ranging from note-taking to essay writing to the use of IT. They will also be able to provide testing for learning issues such as dyslexia, and then provide guidance on what individual needs you may have to overcome such problems. Your own tutor or programme leader or the Student Union will be able to provide information about these services.

Over the past 20 to 30 years there has been a strong move in UK society to support the needs of people with disabilities. Universities are generally very good at providing support for students with disabilities. Legislation by the UK government under the Disabilities Discrimination Act 2005 now means that universities are obliged to meet the needs of most disabled students so that they can study. Each university, therefore, will have a Disability Service, which can provide advice to current students and to applicants about how their individual needs can be met. They will also work with individual academic departments to arrange for particular students' needs to be met. If you are aware of a disability or study need that is likely to affect how you work as a student then it is important that you contact the Disability Service at the earliest opportunity, and probably before you submit an application for a place at the university. They will be able to give excellent advice on how well your needs can be met. Details of the university Disability Service will be in the prospectus or on the website or, if issues arise after you have started your programme, you will be put in touch with them by your department.

Careers service   Towards the end of your time as a postgraduate student you will be faced with the question of 'what shall I do next?'. We shall look at this in detail in the final chapter of this book. An important source of help and guidance will be the university Careers Advisory Service, who have experience and expertise in supporting students in thinking about a career. Thinking about your career should start early on and most universities encourage students to use the Careers Service from the start of their course. You will find that the Careers Service often run work experience schemes, career planning courses and sessions with employers to provide information about different jobs. Do make contact with them early on to find out about the range of services on offer.

Counselling service   Every university will have a counselling service. This will be able to provide independent support to students who feel they have personal or academic problems that they cannot resolve easily themselves. The main purpose of the counselling service is to provide support through listening to students and, if appropriate, helping them to develop a strategy for dealing with issues or providing guidance on additional support and help. All counselling services will be free of charge, totally confidential and staffed by trained counsellors with substantial experience of dealing with the issues that students face. Your tutor, your programme handbook, the Student Union or the university website will be able to tell you how to contact the counselling service.

● ● ● *Pause for thought* ● ● ●

Are there any particular needs that you already know you will have while you are a postgraduate student in the UK? Use the list below to check what you might need. Use the websites of those universities you are considering applying to to identify how they might be able to meet those needs:

(a) Mobility needs (for example, do you use a wheelchair?)
(b) Other disability needs (for example, are you hearing-or sight-impaired?)
(c) Medical needs (for example, are there particular medications you need regularly, such as insulin for diabetes, or particular treatments you need, such as physiotherapy?)
(d) Learning needs (for example, are you dyslexic?)

Services outside the university

Outside the university there are a number of services that you will be able to use to support your academic studies, and we shall look briefly here at the most useful ones.

Public library and information services   In every town or city you will find that there is a local library and information service. These are usually owned and operated by the local government – the city council or the district or county council serving the city or region. Although you will be able to get books and other resources from these libraries through your university's inter-library loan service, it is probably better to visit and use these libraries yourself. They will usually have very good collections of local materials – publications on local and regional geography, history, society, business and politics, and special collections of local materials. They will also have good information on local organizations and how to contact them. You will be able to join these libraries at no cost as a local resident, and in many cases your university library card will be enough to allow you to use their services.

In some of the larger cities, and in particular London, Cardiff, Belfast and Edinburgh, you will find national libraries and museums which are an important source of information. For example, if you are a student in London then it will be worth visiting the British Library. This is one of four copyright libraries that hold every publication within the UK. If you live outside London you can access their materials through your own university library through the inter-library loan service.

Embassies and consulates   For international students an important source of guidance and advice is their own national embassy or consulate. Larger countries and those with a large number of students in the UK will have a specialist education advice section. This can provide you with advice and guidance on a wide range of issues, from visas to travel to funding. If you are being funded by your own government or by an organization in your own country they will also ask the university for regular reports on your progress. Perhaps most importantly, though, they can provide advice if there are particular issues that you face. The staff in the education advice section will often know the academic staff and international office staff in your university or department, and they will certainly know the way in which UK universities work. This means that they can sometimes speak on your behalf to the university to seek help for you or can give advice on how you might deal with an issue.

Many countries will require you to 'register' with their embassy or consulate when you are in the UK. Even if they do not actually require this, you may find it useful to make contact with them soon after your arrival in the UK so that you can find out what support and services they can provide, and how to contact them in an emergency. Details of the locations and contact details in the UK of the embassies and consulates of every country can be found on the internet at *www2.tagish.co.uk.*

KEY RISKS AND HOW TO AVOID THEM

We have been looking in this chapter at how to work with academic staff and other services inside and outside the university to make the most of your academic studies as an international postgraduate student. Most students find that they are well supported and that this means they are successful in their programme. However, there are a number of risks that you need to be aware of, so that you can try to avoid them.

Risk 1: *Not developing a good working relationship with your tutor/supervisor*   This relationship is very important to you as a postgraduate student. Try your utmost to build a good working relationship with the supervisor you are assigned.

Risk 2: *Not building an academic relationship with several members of staff in your department or school*   You need to have more than one academic colleague who you can talk with and work with. This provides you with a range of views on academic issues but also means that there is somebody else you can talk to if you have issues with another tutor or your supervisor.

Risk 3: *Not identifying with your supervisor the best ways of working together*   Find out at an early stage how your tutor would like you to work with him or her – but also discuss your own needs and ways of working. In this way you can find the best ways of working together.

Risk 4: *Not taking responsibility for your own work and study time*   As a postgraduate student you must realize that you have responsibility for all that you do, and you will be expected to be in control and lead the way in your own work.

Risk 5: *Doing everything your tutor/supervisor suggests without thinking about it critically*   Listen to your tutor's advice, but always reflect on whether it is the right thing to do. Taking advice uncritically is a sign that you are not working at postgraduate level.

Risk 6: *Not taking enough notice of your supervisor's guidance*   Tutors and supervisors are experienced academics and researchers. Their advice will be intended to help you make progress, and you should not take it as being a personal criticism. Think about it and act on it.

Risk 7: *Not keeping regular contact with your supervisor*   The amount of contact you need with your supervisor will vary throughout your programme. However, it is your responsibility to make contact if it is some time since you met. Do not wait for your tutor to call you.

Risk 8: *Not finding out what services are available for international postgraduate students from the Student Union*   The Student Union will have excellent advice and services for postgraduate international students, so find out what they can offer at an early stage in your programme.

Risk 9: *Not finding out how your embassy/consulate can support you*   Your embassy or consulate will have a lot of knowledge about your university and about education and life in the UK, so make contact with their education support and advice section.

Risk 10: *Not seeking help and advice as soon as you need it*   All students have times in their programme when things are going well and times when there are difficulties or challenges. Problems that start off small can become large and difficult if ignored – and most issues can be resolved. So seek help and advice as soon as you are aware of any issue or problem. Seeking advice is not a sign of weakness – it is a sign of a mature professional view of your needs as a postgraduate student.

CHAPTER 11
EXAMINATIONS AND VIVAS

- How are Masters examinations organized?
- How will my Doctorate be examined?
- When should I submit my thesis?
- How do I submit my thesis?
- Who will the examiners be?
- What do the examiners do?
- What will happen in the viva?
- How can I prepare for the examination?
- What are the possible outcomes?
- What happens if things go wrong?

First thoughts

Whatever your postgraduate programme, you will have to be assessed by examiners to decide whether you have met the standard for a Masters or Doctorate. For most Masters programmes the assessment is partly based on written examinations to assess your achievements on the taught course units, and partly on your project or dissertation to assess your research and enquiry skills.

For taught Doctoral students, the assessment of the taught units is a qualifying stage before you can start the thesis and the research; the final decision about the award of the Doctorate will depend on the quality of your thesis. For PhD students, it is the examination of the thesis alone that is used to decide whether you should be awarded a PhD.

For most Doctoral students, therefore, one of their largest concerns when they start their programme is the oral examination at the end of their research. The oral, known in most universities as a *viva voce examination*, or usually just called a 'viva', is a key part of the examination used to judge whether a student should be awarded their Doctorate.

In this chapter we shall focus on examinations and vivas and explore the best ways to try to ensure you pass.

How are Masters examinations organized?

In Chapter 8 we looked at how you should prepare for assignments and examinations in a Masters programme. Most Masters programmes require students to pass the 'taught' part of the course before they can move on to the project or dissertation stage. When the examinations and assessment for the taught course have been completed, usually in May or June of a one-year programme, an Examination Board will meet to consider the performance of each student. Those who have passed each of the taught units will be allowed to 'proceed to the dissertation stage' – in other words, they will be allowed to complete and submit their project or dissertation. In reality most will already have started work on their project at this time. Those who have not passed all their taught units will often be given a chance to retake the examination or re-submit an assignment for those units they have failed. The examinations will be in August or early September, and the deadline for any re-submitted assignments will be about the same time.

The dissertation will have to be submitted by a specified date, often at or close to the end of September. The work will then be marked by the supervisor and either 'second marked' or 'double marked' by another tutor. Second marking means that the second tutor knows what mark has been awarded by the first marker but reads the work to judge whether they agree with the mark given. Double marking means that the work is marked by a second marker without knowing the first mark awarded. The system used varies between universities and sometimes between programmes within the same university. When the work has been marked a second time, if there is a disagreement between the two markers they will meet to discuss the mark and agree on a final mark to be awarded. If they cannot agree then a third marker may be asked to look at the work.

The final quality check is that a sample of the marked work is looked at by an external examiner. The 'external' is a senior academic working in the field but who works for a different university, and their role is to confirm whether the standards of the work are being judged correctly and consistently.

The final mark for the project or dissertation is then considered by an Examination Board, usually in October or November. The Board will agree the marks and decide who has passed and who has not, and whether any candidates should be awarded a distinction or merit, if the university has such categories. Those who have not passed may be given an opportunity to resubmit their dissertation later in the year. In many universities students may pass 'subject to minor corrections'. This means that the work is good enough to pass on its academic content but that there are minor changes needed, often corrections to spelling, grammar or layout. In this case you will be given a short period of time, perhaps two to four weeks, to make the minor changes, before resubmitting your work. Those who have passed the 'taught' part of the programme but who either do not submit or who fail the dissertation/project will usually be awarded a Postgraduate Diploma instead of a Masters degree.

In some universities you may be asked to attend a viva for a Masters programme. This is not something all students will need to do, for a viva is only used for a small number of students, usually those whose marks are at the borderline of pass/fail or pass/distinction. It will normally be a short interview with a small group of academic staff, including your supervisor and the external examiner. They will ask questions about your dissertation or to test your understanding and knowledge of the taught course, and will judge from your answers which side of the borderline your mark should be placed. You should check the regulations for your programme, which will be in the programme handbook, for information about whether vivas may be part of the examination or not. If they are, you should check how they will be arranged and how you will be informed whether you have a viva.

How will my Doctorate be examined?

To be awarded a Doctorate you will be judged by the quality of the thesis that you submit for examination. The thesis will be read by two examiners, and you will then attend a viva with the examiners. Following the viva the examiners will decide whether your work has reached the standard for you to be awarded your Doctorate. For the rest of this chapter we shall look in detail at this examination process.

When should I submit my thesis?

PhD programmes are normally three years long, while taught Doctorates might be three, four or five years long because of the length of the teaching programme. However, the length of time it takes to complete your thesis will vary from student to student. This is because people work at different speeds, projects vary in how difficult they are, and some projects produce more problems than others. To finish in three years means that you will need to work very hard and that you will not have any major problems to overcome.

Obviously, you should submit your thesis when it is finished! Every university will say in its regulations that it is you, as the student, who must decide when it is ready to submit. However, your supervisor will advise you whether your work is ready, and you should take his or her advice on this. If your supervisor says that your work is not ready or still needs more to be done to it, then it is probably unwise to submit it, as you are not very likely to pass. Usually your supervisor will want to read a final draft of your whole thesis and will then indicate that, perhaps after you have made few changes, you should submit your final thesis.

It is important to remember that handing in your thesis is not the end of your programme. There will be a period of time of at least one month and perhaps as much as three months between the time you submit and the date of your viva. After your viva, if you have passed, you will need to make arrangements for the thesis to be properly bound and resubmitted, which will take a week or two. You may also have minor corrections to make to the work, which could take up to a month or so. This means that you need to allow a period of at least three months between submitting your thesis and the time when your programme will be completely finished. Of course, as we shall explain later, it is also possible you may be asked after the viva to do more work on your thesis and resubmit it before the examiners will agree to award the degree – so there may be an even longer time period before you have finished.

Although you can only submit when you are ready, you will want to set yourself a target for completion. This may be because you only have funding for three years or because you want to be sure you can go to the graduation ceremony at the end of your three years. To identify the target date, work backwards from the final date by which you want to have completed everything and submit your work at least three months and preferably four months before that date. If you must be back home by, say, the beginning of September, then you should aim to submit your thesis no later than the end of May, and preferably by the end of April. If you need to have finished by the end of June to be able to go to a graduation ceremony in July, then you should submit no later than the end of March. You can build this into your project planning at the start of your research project (see Chapter 9).

How do I submit the thesis?

Most universities will have a clear procedure for submitting a thesis. The first stage will probably be that you have to complete a form that is an indication of your 'Intention to Submit'. This normally has to be completed at least three months before the date on which you think you will be ready to submit. This starts the procedures within the university of making arrangements for an external examiner to be appointed.

When your thesis is ready, you will have to print several copies and have them bound. The number of copies varies between universities, but the university usually requires three – one for each of the examiners and one for your supervisor. However, you will need one more copy – for yourself! These copies must be softbound, not hardbound. The theses you see on the library shelves will be bound in an impressive hardback cover, but you can only get your work bound like this once you have passed. You should submit your thesis for examination in soft paper or card covers, and your university will give you detailed guidance on how it should be bound. They will also recommend places where you can get the work done.

The next stage is to hand in your work, in the way and to the place that is indicated in your university's regulations. All you can do then is sit and wait for the examination – but submitting your thesis is often a time of great relief and celebration!

Who will the examiners be?

Most Doctoral programmes require you to have two examiners. The internal examiner will be an academic from within your own university and probably from within your own department. Your supervisor cannot be your internal examiner. The external examiner will be from a different university and will be a senior academic with expertise in your research field.

It is your supervisor's job to choose the two examiners and invite them to be examiners for your thesis. The examiners have to meet the university's requirements as examiners in terms of experience and expertise, and will have to be approved by a committee of the university. However, many supervisors will discuss with their students who might be suitable as an examiner – and you may have the opportunity to indicate if there is anybody you feel would be particularly suitable, or even particularly unsuitable. The final choice, though, is your supervisor's.

What do the examiners do?

First, they read your thesis. This may take them several weeks. From reading the thesis they will decide whether they feel at this stage the work meets the standard for a Doctorate, but they will also identify a range of questions they might want to ask you at the viva. These questions might be to test your knowledge, or they might be to clarify anything that is not clear in the thesis. They might want to find out more clearly your thoughts behind particular ideas or conclusions, or test whether your evidence matches the conclusions you have drawn. They will then write a report which describes their views of the written thesis.

The second stage is the viva. The two examiners will meet, usually on the day of the viva, and compare their initial reports. They will then reach a conclusion about how good they feel the thesis is, and the questions they want to ask you in the viva. This will include deciding who is going to ask which questions and in what order, and will lead to the viva itself (see below). After the viva they will make the final decision on their judgement, taking into account both the thesis and your discussions in the viva. They will then tell you the outcome and, if necessary, provide details on any further work that needs to be done.

What will happen in the viva?

The viva examination usually takes between one and two hours. In some universities in addition to yourself and the two examiners there may be a senior member of academic staff present to act as chair of the examination. Your supervisor may also be present, although some universities do not allow this. However, even if there is a chair or your supervisor is present, they are not allowed to ask you questions or to take part in any of the discussion about the outcome.

The examiners will probably start by trying to make you feel comfortable, perhaps by welcoming you and having some polite 'social' conversation to start with, for they will understand that you are nervous. However, they will soon move on to start to ask the range of questions they have planned. The questions could cover anything about the thesis. They might ask you about the methods you have used, the results and findings or the conclusions you have drawn. They may ask very detailed questions or they may ask about the overall methods or findings. They will certainly want to explore any areas they feel you have not explained clearly enough or in enough detail in your thesis. You may be asked to justify some of the conclusions you have made and to show exactly how your data have led you to draw those conclusions. In the area of methodology you may be asked to justify your choice of the overall method you used, as well as explaining the decisions you made about the detailed methods you chose. You may also be asked to show how well you know the range of literature and previous research in your field and how your findings add to the literature. In most vivas you will be asked to explain carefully what you believe to be your distinctive 'contribution to knowledge' from your research.

A helpful way to think of the viva is as a serious academic discussion. It is an opportunity to sit and talk about your work and your field with two senior academics who know the field well. As such, it should be challenging and stimulating, and should give you a chance to show that you can engage in serious academic discussion and debate at a very high level. After the examination many students look back on their viva and see it as a stimulating and enjoyable experience, and they forget the nerves they felt when they first entered the viva room.

How can I prepare for the examination?

Like any examination, you should try to prepare as thoroughly as you can for your viva. After you hand in your thesis you will have at least a few weeks to prepare. An important part of that preparation is to start by taking a break, and leaving your thesis alone for two or three weeks. This is because the last stages of completing the thesis will have been very tiring both physically and emotionally, so you will need a rest. You will also have become so involved with the detail of the thesis (checking references, refining your English, checking data etc.) that you will not have a clear view of the whole work. A few weeks of rest away from the thesis will enable you to feel better and to gain a more balanced view of the whole research project and thesis.

When the date of your viva has been fixed, you should then arrange a practice viva with your supervisor for a week or two before the examination date. Most supervisors will actively offer and arrange this, but if your supervisor does not do so then take the initiative and ask him or her for a 'mock' viva. This practice is very important. It gives you a chance to get used to answering the sort of questions you will be asked and allows your supervisor an opportunity to give you advice on how to improve your performance in the viva. Your supervisor may also be able to give you guidance on possible areas of questioning. The mock may also help you to feel less nervous for the real viva, as you will have a view of what to expect.

In preparation for the mock viva and then also in preparation for the real examination there are a number of things you should do to help your performance.

Know your thesis   This sounds obvious, but you need to read and re-read your thesis so that you know it in every detail. You need to know the *'what'* of your thesis, and be able to find particular parts of the work very quickly if asked a question about some specific point. But more importantly, you need to know the *'why'* of your research – why did you choose the research method, why did you feel that particular parts of the literature were important, why did you draw the conclusions from the data that you did?

Mark up your thesis   Your thesis will be a very important tool for you in the viva. 'Marking up' the thesis means adding labels to sections or writing notes at key parts of the work to help you. Many students have found the following ideas helpful:

- Add index labels to the start of each chapter which stick out from the thesis so that you can quickly find it.
- Add index labels in the same way to important sections, diagrams, models or tables so that you can easily turn to them.
- Add notes to the text. You can do this either by writing in the margin or on the opposite page, or by using sticky notes (such as Post-its ®). Use these where you feel there is more you could have said about an idea, section or diagram.

List your own corrections   As you go through your thesis you will certainly find some corrections that you would like to make – spelling errors, grammatical mistakes, sentences you would want to make clearer. Do not panic about this; every Doctoral student in history will have found mistakes in their thesis, and, unless there is a large number of these errors, it will not affect the outcome of your examination. Keep a note of them all, because you can make these corrections before you submit your final bound thesis.

Be able to summarize your thesis   It is very easy to get lost in the detail of your work and forget the 'big picture'. However, you are quite likely to be asked questions like 'What is the overall conclusion from your work?' or 'What is the main theme of this chapter?'. To help you to answer, write a few brief notes for each chapter summarizing the main points of that chapter – perhaps five to ten 'bullet points' for each. Do the same thing, then, for the whole thesis, perhaps by asking yourself 'What are the main ideas from my thesis that I hope other researchers will still be referring to in five years time?'.

Identify possible questions   It is very hard to know what questions you will be asked in the viva. There are some obvious general questions, such as:

* Why did you choose this topic for your research?
* What are the main contributions to knowledge that your research will make?
* What were the most difficult parts of the research?
* What do you think the main future research questions are that come from your research?
* What would you do differently if you could do the research again?

However, beyond these questions you could be asked anything at all. It is important to think of the parts of your work which you are least confident about, or where your findings are surprising or controversial, for these are likely to be areas for questioning. You may also identify, when you re-read your thesis, sections that are not as clear as you might have hoped – you may be asked to clarify these themes. You should also ask your supervisor to suggest questions that he or she would ask if they were your examiner. You could do the same with any friends or colleagues who are willing to read the whole thesis for you.

The important thing with all of these questions is that you need to know what your answer will be, so spend some time thinking about your response.

Practise 'good' answering   Knowing what the answer to a question should be is only part of giving a good answer. There are a number of important 'rules' of answering questions, which you should think about. You can then use them to practise answers, both in the mock viva and with friends, family or colleagues. These 'rules' are:

- Do not talk for too long in any answer. Some students simply keep talking once they have been started by the examiner. A good answer is likely to take between one and three minutes to give – if you talk for much longer than this you have probably strayed away from the question. If you have not said enough, the examiners will prompt you to say more or ask you to clarify some more detail.
- Do not say too little. Even if you are very nervous, very short answers will not be enough. Do not just say 'yes' or 'no', even if that is what you really are trying to say. Add some detail – remember that you should make your answer take at least one minute.
- Speak clearly and slowly. Nerves make people speak quickly, so practise your talking speed in the mock viva or with friends.
- Make eye contact, and smile. Look directly at the examiner who is asking you a question, and then look at both examiners as you provide your answer. An occasional smile while you listen or answer makes you look confident in what you are saying.
- Do not rush to give an answer. When you are asked a question take at least a few seconds to check that you understand the question and to think about your answer. A good spoken answer is structured like a good paragraph of writing, in that it has three parts: point – expansion – example.

  Point – this is the specific idea that you want to cover or the point you want to make, expressed in a simple way.
  Expansion – this is where you go into detail to show where that idea has come from and to add some further information about the point.
  Example – this is where you give the example that illustrates your point. This could be a reference to some of your results, or to the literature, or to some of your analysis, or to one of your samples or case studies.

- When you have finished your answer, be quiet. If there is a silent pause then it is for the examiners to fill it by asking you for more detail or by asking you a further question.
- If you do not understand the question then ask for it to be repeated or clarified.
- If you do not know the answer, then do not try to 'bluster'. It will be obvious that you are blustering. Simply say that you do not know how to answer the question and explain why – for example, your data do not cover that; you have not investigated this aspect of the topic; you have not read that particular source. Do not assume that not knowing the answer is a weakness or a problem – by not giving an answer you may be showing that you understand very well the limits of your research and are not being drawn into giving answers about things you really do not know about.

●●● *Pause for thought* ●●●

Discussing your work in a viva is really only like explaining your ideas and work to a friend or colleague. Being able to explain something orally is regarded by many as the ultimate test of whether you really understand something. How good are you at explaining ideas? Practise the skill by explaining a topic from your undergraduate studies to a friend or relative and see what their response is. Do they understand what you have explained? Was it clear what the main ideas were? Practise the skill, too, throughout your postgraduate programme, either through discussions with friends and colleagues or by making formal presentations at seminars.

Practise creating thinking space   You will be asked many questions that are simple to answer, but you may be asked questions that are more difficult. For these questions you may want to take a few moments to think about your answer, so it is helpful to create some 'thinking space' for yourself during the viva. There are a number of ways of doing this:

- Ask for the question to be repeated, even if you actually understood it fully the first time it was asked.
- Take a few moments to find the place in your thesis which covers the topic you have been asked about.
- Take a longer pause before answering than normal.
- Start by saying 'That's an interesting question – I'd just like to take a moment to think about this.' You can then take a few moments longer than normal before starting your answer.

Pausing like this before answering does not indicate that you do not know what the answer should be. Instead, it shows the examiners that you are thoughtful about your work and are not willing to rush to give a quick answer.

Prepare to defend your thesis   Some universities describe the viva as 'defending your thesis', which is the phrase also used in Europe and North America. It is helpful to remember this, for in your viva you need to be able to defend your findings and also to defend the research methods you chose to use. Throughout your research you will have had to make decisions – which literature to use, which research techniques to use, what interpretation to make of the data, and what exactly to include in your thesis. You will have thought long and hard about each of these decisions – and you must be able to explain your decisions to the examiners during the viva.

You should be clear and robust in this. The examiners may be testing your confidence in what you have done. Do not assume that because they challenge you on something you did that they think you were wrong – they are probably just pushing you to explain clearly and defend what you decided to do. Sometimes a decision in research is also just a matter of opinion or preference. There are very few absolute 'right' and 'wrong' decisions in research, and providing you can explain why you chose as you did then the examiners will be satisfied. This means that you should not easily say, 'Oh, yes, perhaps you are right, I should have done this a different way.' Rather, be prepared to defend your thesis.

Of course, you must not be stubborn in defending a research choice which it becomes clear in the viva was an incorrect one. Be prepared to say, 'If I was doing the research again I might do that part a little differently', or 'Perhaps that is an alternative interpretation of my data'. This shows a willingness to think carefully about your research and findings. And it is important to remember that your examiners will not be expecting you to have made no errors at all in your work, since the 'perfect' PhD has probably never been written. Equally, remember that there are always several ways of doing research, several possible interpretations of data, and that all 'knowledge' is questionable. The examiners just want to be sure that your work is good enough to meet Doctoral standards.

Think about last minute preparation   In the final day before your viva you will need to make your last minute preparations. Everybody does last minute examination preparation in their own way. Some people read and re-read their work until the moment the viva starts. Others prefer to do no last minute work and find it more helpful to relax, go to the cinema, or meet friends. By the time you are a postgraduate you will know what type of preparation for examinations suits you best – so plan to do that, whatever it is!

● ● ●   *Pause for thought*   ● ● ●

> *How do you prepare best for examinations? Think through the strategies you have used in the past for preparing for examinations, and identify which ones were helpful and which were not. Are you somebody who needs to be revising right up to the moment of the examination or are you somebody who needs to relax for a day or so beforehand? Talk to your friends about their strategies and see if they have any tips that might work for you.*

What are the possible outcomes?

After the viva has finished you will be asked to leave the examiners to make their decision. This could take anything from 10 minutes to an hour or so. It is important to understand that the length of time it takes to make the final decision does not indicate what that decision is. Some examiners reach decisions quickly, whether it is 'pass' or not, others take longer because they discuss every detail of the viva. Once they have reached their decision though, you will be asked to come back to see them, and they will tell you their decision.

There are several different decisions they can make. The precise range of possible decisions varies a little between universities, as do the exact phrases or words used to describe the decisions. You should therefore check with your own university regulations about this. However, the range of decisions is usually as follows.

Fail, with no right of resubmission

This decision is very rare. It happens usually only when there is evidence of cheating or plagiarism. This is an outright fail with no opportunity offered to improve and resubmit the thesis.

Fail, but with the possibility of resubmission

If the examiners think your work is not of a good enough standard even for the award of an MPhil they may decide to fail you but give you the right to do more work on the research and thesis and resubmit it at a later date for consideration for an MPhil. In this case they will give you detailed guidance about what would be necessary to raise the work to MPhil standard, and will give you this information in writing after the viva.

Award of an MPhil

If the work is felt by the examiners to be of Masters but not Doctoral level then they can award an MPhil for your work (or in some universities an MRes). There are two ways that this decision could be reached. If the examiners feel there is nothing you could do to your work to raise it to Doctoral standard then they may simply award an MPhil. Alternatively, they may give you the option of choosing an MPhil rather than doing further work and resubmitting it (see below) for consideration for a Doctorate. Some candidates who have found their research particularly hard or who have no further time (or sometimes finance) to do more work on their thesis may choose to take the MPhil under these circumstances.

Resubmission

The examiners may feel there is a lot of good work in your thesis but that it is not yet at Doctoral standard. They may therefore ask you to do further work and resubmit a revised thesis for re-examination. In this case the examiners will indicate to you very clearly:

- What needs doing to the thesis. You will receive in writing after the viva a detailed description of the further work that is needed. This may be further analysis of your data, the rewriting of some sections, the addition of further work or the collection of some additional data.

- How long you have to resubmit your work. This could vary between one month for small-scale extra work to a year or even two years if there is a lot of work to be done.
- How you will be re-examined. It is possible that you may have to have a further viva (with the same examiners). More likely, though, you will have to resubmit your thesis and the examiners will simply read your work to check you have made the changes they have asked for.

Some universities distinguish between 'minor resubmission' and 'major resubmission'. Minor resubmission would be work that requires only a month or two to do. Major resubmission would be work that requires more than three months or so to do.

If you are asked to resubmit then it will be normal for your supervisor to support you while you do the further work, but you will have to pay fees to the university for the additional time that you will need to be registered as a student. When you finally resubmit you should do so in the same way as when you submitted first time. However, it is helpful at this stage to include with your resubmitted work a set of notes indicating exactly what changes you have made to your thesis and where in your work the examiners will find the changes. This helps you to demonstrate that you have done all the things the examiners asked of you, and will enable them to find the changes more easily.

Pass subject to minor corrections

This decision means that your work is of Doctoral standard but that a small number of corrections need to be made – usually corrections to spelling, grammar, diagram titles, headings etc. You will be given a short time scale to correct your thesis, usually up to one month, and you will also be given a written list of the corrections needed. When you have made the corrections you should then submit your thesis to the internal examiner who will check that you have made the corrections required. He or she will then give you a signed note to confirm that the corrections have been made, and you can then hand in the finally bound thesis with the corrections confirmation note.

Pass

This is the best decision. It means that the examiners feel your work has met the standard for a Doctorate and needs no additional work or corrections. All you need to do is to get the thesis bound into its final form and hand it in. You can then celebrate in whatever way you wish!!!!

The most common decisions are the last three in the list – resubmission, pass subject to minor corrections and pass. However, most examiners will find something that needs further work in your thesis, so the most likely decision is resubmission or pass subject to minor corrections. While these decisions will be disappointing for you in comparison to a straight pass, they really mean that your work is almost there in terms of standard. Everybody who has minor corrections to do will eventually pass, and almost everybody who has to resubmit will eventually pass too, providing they do the corrections they have been asked to do by the time deadline. So with any of these three decisions you will almost certainly end up with your Doctorate.

What happens if things go wrong?

Occasionally candidates are unhappy with either the outcome of their viva or with the way the examination was conducted. Every university is required to have an appeals procedure that enables you to raise your concerns and to have any issues investigated. Details of the procedure should be in your programme handbook or on the university website, and your programme leader or the head of department will provide you with the information too.

You will not, however, be allowed to appeal against the academic judgement of your examiners. There have been a number of legal cases that have confirmed that academic judgement cannot be questioned. So, however good you thought your thesis was, if the examiners did not agree you cannot challenge their decision.

You can appeal however about the process of the examination. If you felt the examination was not conducted properly you may be able to appeal to be examined again. However, you will have to have clear evidence of the irregularity that you believe created the problem and that it made a significant difference to the outcome of your examination.

If you make an appeal it will be heard by a panel of academics within the university, and if you are not content with their decision you can ultimately appeal to an independent external organization, the Office of the Independent Adjudicator for Higher Education (OIA). The website of the OIA is *www.oiahe.org.uk*. If your appeal is upheld, though, the best decision that can be made is that you should be re-examined, perhaps by a different set of examiners, since they cannot overturn the academic judgement of the examiners.

KEY RISKS AND HOW TO AVOID THEM

The examination of your Masters or Doctoral programme is probably the part of the course that will cause you most worry. To reduce the worry and to try to increase your chances of success there are a number of risks you need to be aware of, so that you can plan how to avoid them.

Risk 1: *Failing to meet the submission deadline for your Masters project or dissertation*   The submission deadline for your Masters dissertation is like the time of a written examination, and you must not miss it. If you think you may not be able to meet this date discuss the problem with your tutor as soon as possible so that you can apply for permission to submit late (if that is allowed). If you simply do not hand your work in then you risk getting a zero score for it.

Risk 2: *Submitting your Doctoral thesis against your supervisor's advice*   The decision to submit your thesis is actually entirely yours. However, your supervisor has considerable experience of research projects, and if you are advised that your thesis is not ready – then it is not ready. The risk is that you will not be awarded a Doctorate for your work.

Risk 3: *Forgetting to give notice of your intention to submit your thesis*   This is easy to forget. Most universities require you to give formal written notice of your 'intention to submit' at least three months before the date you want to submit your thesis. If you forget to do this then you may find that your examination may be delayed by several months when you do finally submit.

Risk 4: *Failing to read the detailed instructions on how to prepare your thesis for submission*   You will be given very detailed written instructions on preparing your thesis for submission. This will include information on matters such as type spacing, paper margins, types of binding etc., but also information on exactly how to submit – how many copies, who they should be given to, how you get a receipt for them and so on. Follow these instructions carefully to avoid any technical problems with your thesis or the examination.

Risk 5: *Not checking your final thesis for spelling and English grammar errors*   You will want your thesis to create a good impression with the examiners, so you will want there to be few English language errors and for it to be easy to read. Check the English language yourself, but also ask somebody else to read the thesis and suggest improvements and corrections to you. This could be a family member or a friend. However, do not expect your final thesis to have absolutely no spelling errors – you will find some when you read it to prepare for the viva, and you will probably find some more when you read it again in five years' time!

Risk 6: *Failing to prepare thoroughly for the viva*   The viva is an examination, and you need to prepare for it thoroughly over several weeks. This will mean that you know your thesis thoroughly and are prepared for a wide range of possible questions.

Risk 7: *Not having a practice or 'mock' viva*   A practice or 'mock' viva will help you to practise your answering skills and to be clear about what the viva will be like. It should help to make you less nervous about the real viva. Talk to your supervisor about arranging a mock viva.

Risk 8: *Having a poor answering style in the viva*   A Doctoral viva is as important as an interview for a job you really want. You want to impress. Answering questions is a skill you can develop and practise. We have looked at some of those skills in this chapter.

Risk 9: *Not being prepared to defend your thesis*   Remember that you are there to defend what you have done. You will need to be able to explain many of the choices you made while doing your research project, and be able to justify them to your examiners. You made each of the decisions after careful thought, so be confident about what you have chosen to do and be ready to make your case. The examiners will expect you to understand that good research involves making judgements and decisions, and that there is rarely one single best way of doing something. However, while you should defend your thesis robustly, be prepared to acknowledge that there may have been things you could have done differently. Defending your thesis is not the same thing as stubbornly refusing to recognize any alternative views or ideas.

Risk 10: *Failing to meet the deadline to resubmit your thesis*   If you have to resubmit your thesis with corrections or changes, then make sure that you meet the deadline that has been set. If problems arise that mean you may not meet the deadline, then talk with your supervisor at the earliest opportunity.

PART 4
MOVING ON AFTER YOUR DEGREE

CHAPTER 12
BEYOND YOUR POSTGRADUATE DEGREE

- Will I be able to attend a graduation ceremony?
- What are the issues about returning home?
- Will I be able to get careers guidance?
- How can I keep in touch?

First thoughts

Whether you have thought about it before you applied or whether you start considering it during your programme, you will eventually have to think about life after your postgraduate studies. There are some immediate questions you need to consider, such as graduation ceremonies and arranging to return home to your own country. There are also some important long-term issues, about your career and future life, and about what you might wish to do with your postgraduate degree. In this chapter we shall look at each of these issues.

Almost every student who makes it to the end of their postgraduate programme will pass and be awarded their Masters degree or Doctorate. This does not mean that if you start a postgraduate course you are guaranteed success – it just means that most people who are not going to succeed decide to finish the programme early and 'drop out', so they do not get to the end of the course. For most students, therefore, finishing is a time for celebration, for recognizing their excellent achievement and for sharing their pleasure with friends, family and colleagues. This is both the finish of your programme but also the start of the next stage of your life, whatever it is that you choose to do.

Will I be able to attend a graduation ceremony?

Most postgraduates choose to attend the university's formal graduation ceremony. Graduation is a spectacular event, with processions, academic robes and great ceremony, and is an opportunity for the university, the students and their families and friends to celebrate together. If you attend graduation you will be presented to a senior member of the university, often the Vice Chancellor or Chancellor, and in some cases you will be presented with your degree certificate or even presented with your academic 'hood' in a public ceremony.

Graduation ceremonies vary enormously between universities. Some are very large ceremonies, some are small; some are on campus, some are in a large venue near the university. Some are in the summer, in July or August, while others are spread throughout the year. You will need to find out about the arrangements in your own university.

For many international students graduation raises some interesting personal questions. Most would very much like to attend graduation, and bring their family and friends to watch the ceremony. Particularly with a postgraduate degree it is seen as the pinnacle of academic achievement, and a real cause for pride and celebration. However, there are two important issues. First, *will you be able to attend yourself?* Unless the ceremony is held at a time shortly after you have finished your degree programme you may find that you will have had to return home to your own country before it takes place. There will then be questions about whether you can afford the time and the money to return to attend graduation. Secondly, *will your family and friends be able to attend?* You will almost certainly want them to be there, but the cost of them coming from your home country or finding the time to come may be a problem.

With these two issues in mind, you need to plan very carefully as far in advance as possible if you want to make the arrangements to be there. Most universities publish the dates of their graduation ceremonies 6–12 months before they occur. This means that some advance planning is possible. You can plan at an early stage for flights and hotel accommodation for your guests, and your family and friends can plan to cover their financial costs.

It is also important to check how many guests you will be allowed to bring to the ceremony. In some universities graduands can only bring one or two guests, and in all universities there is some limit, probably no more than three or four. You will therefore need to decide who you want to there. In many cases the ceremony is relayed by close-circuit TV to another hall so those who cannot be present at the ceremony can still watch it 'live'. In addition, most departments will hold a reception or lunch for their new graduates, and you will probably be able to take more guests to that event.

There are a few practical issues to remember about graduation:

- You do not have to attend graduation at all. If you have passed your postgraduate programme arrangements can be made for you to be sent your degree certificate by mail.
- You will have to give notice of your intention to attend graduation several months before the event and probably quite a long time before you have actually passed your programme. If you do not complete the programme then you can withdraw from the graduation arrangements. Check what your university requires you to do. As a Masters student you may receive a graduation information pack early in your

course. However, as a Doctoral student where the final date of completion is not as easy to predict, you may have to make enquiries yourself as you begin what you hope will be your final year of study.

- You may have to pay a small fee to attend graduation and will have to meet the cost of hiring academic dress. Fees for graduation vary greatly between universities, and many universities do not charge at all.

You will need to make your own decision about whether you want to or are able to attend graduation, of course. For some it is a very important mark of a major achievement in their lives. For others the achievement and the degree are reward enough.

What are the issues about returning home?

Most international postgraduate students return to their home country very soon after finishing their programme. After one, two or three years away this is usually a very exciting time, and most students, and their family and friends, look forward to the return. There are a number of issues that students face at this time, though.

First, you may feel you do not wish to return to your own country except to visit family and friends. It may be that you have made many friends in the UK and have settled into British life. It may be that you feel you would like to stay and work in the UK. Or you may feel that, although you do not necessarily want to stay in the UK, you would like to follow your career in a different country. Many postgraduates are attracted by the opportunities in countries such as the USA, Canada or Australia, for example.

Staying in the UK is not usually an option for most postgraduates, so if you wish to stay you need to plan this carefully. In granting you a visa to come to the UK as a student the British government will have required you to confirm your intention to leave the UK at the end of your study programme. When your student visa expires, therefore, you will have to return home unless:

- You accept a place on a new study programme and apply for a new student visa. You may be able to do this while you are here in the UK, but you may have to return home to do this anyway.
- You get a job and your employer is able to apply for a work permit for you. We looked at the issues of getting a work permit in Chapter 5. To be given a work permit your employer will need to show that there was no suitable applicant from the UK or the EU for the job, so you are likely to get a work permit only if you are employed in a skilled or professional job or where there is a shortage of qualified people in that field in the UK.
- You apply to stay in the UK under one of the government schemes designed to use the skills of overseas postgraduates in fields where there are shortages of UK graduates. There are three schemes available in the UK:

(a) The *'Highly Skilled Migrant Programme'* (HSMP), which enables those with skills or training in specific areas (for example in the medical field) to work in the UK.

(b) The *'Science and Engineering Graduates Scheme'* (SEGS), which enables international students with a good first degree, a Masters or a PhD in some fields of physical science, engineering or mathematics to remain in the UK for up to 12 months to pursue a career opportunity.

(c) The *'Fresh Talent: Working in Scotland Scheme'*, which enables those with a good first degree, a Masters or a Doctorate from a Scottish university to apply to stay to work in Scotland for a period of up to two years.

In March 2006 the UK government announced that it will replace its current regulations on granting visas to those wishing to come from outside the EEA to work in the UK. The new regulations will be introduced over a period of time from 2007 onwards. The new regulations will allow international postgraduate students who have studied at UK institutions to apply for a visa to work in the UK for 12 months after completing their studies. The new regulations will replace the 'Science and Engineering Graduates Scheme' and 'Fresh Talent: Working in Scotland Scheme'. Details of the new arrangements will be available on the Home Office 'Working in the UK' website at *www.workingintheUK.gov.uk* which is a useful source of detailed information about all aspects of seeking to remain in the UK to work.

- You get a visa as a visitor. This will only allow you to stay in the UK for a short period of time, and does not give you permission to get a job. However, it is a way of staying for a while to be with friends and perhaps take a holiday.

Moving to another country, of course, depends upon the entry and work regulations for that country. To find out information about this you should contact the embassy or consulate of the country that you are considering moving to.

Secondly, you will be aware that you have been away from home for some time. Family life, your friends, your own town or city, and the national economic and political scene will have 'moved on' while you have been away. This means that you will need at least a short time when you return to catch up with the changes. It may take a few meetings for you to settle back into the relationships you have with friends and family. Some of the changes will have been exciting and positive ones. Others may be less easy to adjust to. The important thing, though, is to be prepared to take a little time to adjust.

Thirdly, you will have changed in yourself. Whether you have been away for one year or three years you will have changed in many ways. You will, of course, have your postgraduate degree, but you will also have had many new experiences, both from living in the UK and from being a little older. You need to be aware that you will have changed and that it is a different 'you' who is going home. This may change the way you see life in your own country and may also change the way that friends and family see you. Most postgraduates report that this is all a very positive aspect of studying abroad, and the changes make them value very much their own country, life, friends and family.

If you came to the UK with a family, then readjusting to life in your own country will be a challenge for your partner or children, too. They will need to re-establish their routines and friendships, just as you will have to. Children are often very concerned about returning home. For them, even a year away is a very long time, and they will have settled into school and made close friends in the UK. However, they often find it very easy to settle back into life at home, just as they usually adjust quickly to life in the UK when they first arrive. Most children make friends easily, and the experience of living in another country often gives them confidence in dealing with changes. They will certainly find that their achievement in their English language classes back home is very high!

Finally, whether you want to stay in the UK, move to another country, or return home you will be faced with the critical question of what to do next. We shall look at this next.

● ● ●   *Pause for thought*   ● ● ●

It is often useful to talk with people who have had the experience of studying abroad and have then returned home. You may have friends, colleagues, family or acquaintances who have done this, or the academic staff at your undergraduate university may have experience of this. Another good contact is the local alumni association of your postgraduate university. They will be delighted to talk with you about their experiences and will be able to provide good advice. Talk to any or all of these people to get their views, insights and thoughts on returning home.

Will I be able to get careers guidance?

Your decision to do a postgraduate degree will in some way have been part of your plans for your career. Whatever your subject or professional field you will expect that a postgraduate degree will provide opportunities for you after graduating. For example, you may have chosen to do a Masters degree as a way of getting an essential qualification to enter a career of your choice, or to give you the opportunity for promotion or more rapid advancement in your career. You may have chosen to do a Doctorate for the same reasons, or perhaps to enter a research or academic career path. Whatever your postgraduate degree, you will expect that it will give you higher status and an advantage in competition for jobs.

Some students who take postgraduate degrees, therefore, do not need much careers guidance. They know what they want to do next, and will have been seeking out opportunities in that field while they have been completing their postgraduate degree. Others, though, may need considerable assistance. This could be because they are not aware of the opportunities there may be for postgraduates or because they do not know in detail how to pursue those opportunities and make the right contacts. Even those who think they know exactly what they are going to do, though, may find careers guidance useful. There may be many interesting opportunities for postgraduates that they had not been aware of and which might be more interesting or attractive than their original plans. It is important to think broadly about careers, for having a postgraduate degree is a real opportunity both for advancement and for taking new career pathways.

There are three main sources of careers advice that you can use. The first is the Careers Advisory Service in your university. Every university has one, and you will find information on what they do and how to contact them in your course handbook or on the university website. Most Careers Advisory Services will have either a specialist adviser for postgraduate students or an adviser who specializes in your academic area, and some may have both. Some also have a specialist careers adviser for international students. They can give you individual advice, or suggest people or organizations you might contact. Also, they will probably organize each year a specialist careers fair for postgraduate students where you can meet a wide range of employers or professional organizations to discuss careers. Even if you think you know exactly what you are going to do in your career and how to do it, it is well worth talking at least once to a careers adviser. They can confirm that your ideas or plans are possible and sensible, or alternatively may give you some ideas on other opportunities.

The second is the academic department in which you are working. The academic staff will have a lot of knowledge of careers for postgraduates in their field. They will know the academic opportunities in research or university posts, but they will also have strong professional links where the field has a professional aspect to it. Most importantly, they will be part of the national and international networks in their field, and will have many contacts. Businesses employing postgraduates will often have built strong relationships with university departments, partly to make sure they are aware of the best new postgraduates. They will advertise their opportunities on the departmental notice boards or may even e-mail you directly through mailing lists. Many postgraduate programmes will provide sessions on career opportunities, which will be useful to attend. In addition, though, you should talk with your tutors and supervisors at an early stage about the opportunities and career paths they know about.

There is one word of warning here, though. While the guidance you receive from academic staff may be very knowledgeable and detailed, you must always remember that they are not trained careers advisers. This means that there are two potential problems. First, they will not know everything about opportunities in the field, and may only know about employers or universities that they have personal experience or knowledge of. There will be many opportunities they do not know about. Secondly, they will not always be completely objective in their advice. For example, they will be trying to persuade the best Masters students to stay on to do a PhD or the best PhD students to do post-Doctoral studies. They may also feel that careers in their own specialist part of the field are more important or worthwhile than those in other areas. So, their advice is very important, but needs to be taken alongside other information and guidance.

The third is your own networks. Through your previous student life and through any employment or professional work you have done you will already have a network of contacts you can connect with. You should use this network to find out about career opportunities that might suit you.

For international students a particular issue is the problem of finding career and job opportunities in your own country while you are still away studying in the UK. This is a challenge because you may find it hard to learn about available jobs back home, or it may take longer for you to hear of them. In addition, there are problems with practical issues such as the time it may take to send an application form or the difficulty and cost of attending an interview. Some of the practical issues are now much easier to deal with than even five years ago, of course. Many employers now advertise their opportunities on websites that can be accessed anywhere in the world, and may be happy to receive applications via their website or by e-mail. It is now quite common, too, for interviews to be conducted by live video link, so that you may not need to return home for an interview.

There are a number of ways that you can plan to deal with this issue of distance:

- You could, of course, simply plan to wait to apply for jobs until after you have returned home.
- Friends and family can be asked to look for job advertisements or opportunities in the media or through local contacts at home, and to keep you informed.
- You can identify the professional or business organizations in your field in your own country and contact them to be placed on their e-mail or mailing lists so that you are kept aware of any opportunities.
- You can use the internet to search for opportunities.
- The Careers Advisory Service in your own university may be able to give you guidance on suitable careers websites or organizations in your own country.
- If you are looking for a career in business the UK branches of international companies will be able to advise you on opportunities within their organization in your own country.
- If you are a Masters student you might use the summer vacation before you start your programme to visit or contact potential employers or professional organizations in your own country. You can make sure they know that you will be finishing your programme the following year and looking for a suitable career opportunity at that stage, so that they keep you informed of any possibilities. This can have an extra benefit, too, in that it is possible that a potential employer may think about sponsoring you or giving you a scholarship for the course. If you are taking a Doctorate then it may be worth planning to have a vacation at home about a year before you finish so that you can make these contacts.

Most postgraduate students find that they move on into interesting and successful career pathways after they finish their programmes. Some Masters students, of course, decide to continue their studies and apply for a Doctoral programme. Whatever your plans though, it is important to start thinking quite early in your programme about how to pursue the opportunities that may be available.

●●● *Pause for thought* ●●●

Do you have any ideas about a long-term career yet? It is worth spending a little time thinking about the possibilities in your field. Talk with the careers advisers and academic staff in your current university about career opportunities for postgraduates in your field. Contact potential employers about their thoughts on postgraduate qualifications. Making some early contacts like this can be very useful for after you graduate and can also enable you to make sensible choices about programmes, universities, specialisms and options. Most importantly, think broadly about the possibilities, and even if you have a clear view of what you want to do, at least make yourself aware of the alternative careers you could consider.

How can I keep in touch?

Most international postgraduate students enjoy their programme and their time in the UK enormously. They make close personal friendships and strong professional links that last them many years and often for life. Keeping in touch after graduation is important therefore, particularly when friends and contacts may return to their homes around the world. You will certainly want to keep in contact with friends through ways you are very familiar with – e-mail and the internet are invaluable for keeping in touch. Also, many postgraduates enter careers that enable them to be part of international business, professional or academic networks, and it is always delightful to know you have friends around the world whom you can meet as part of those networks.

In addition, every university has its alumni association. This is an organization that tries to keep in touch with graduates after they have left to provide a network not just for the university to use but also to enable individuals to contact each other. Many universities have international branches of their alumni association in individual countries. These national branches organize events, meetings and social activities. They also provide a support network for current students, and advice for those considering applying to their university. Being part of the alumni association is both a good way of keeping in touch, therefore, and also a way of giving something back to the network that supported you in your planning and in your studies. Your university will certainly give you details about their alumni association when you graduate, and joining is usually free.

KEY RISKS AND HOW TO AVOID THEM

Although you may have some ideas about graduation, returning home and your future career by the time you apply for a postgraduate programme, there are a number of risks that you need to be aware of so that you can plan to avoid or reduce them.

Risk 1: *Forgetting to give notice of your intention to attend graduation*   Most universities require you to confirm several months in advance that you plan to attend graduation. Find out your university's dates and deadlines.

Risk 2: *Leaving family plans for graduation too late*   Planning travel, accommodation and finance for the family to come to graduation can take time. If you leave it late you may not be able to get flights for them or you may have to pay the most expensive prices.

Risk 3: *Leaving your plans to return home too late*   When you come to the UK you will have planned the move itself over several months. The return home will take as long to plan. You will need to book flights, and perhaps arrange for your belongings to be shipped home. Remember that you cannot stay after your visa expires, and that you might only have your accommodation rented until the last date of your programme.

Risk 4: *Finding it difficult to adjust to life back home*   Getting back to normal life after student life will take some time, and your own country, family and friends will have 'moved on' in many ways while you have been away. Allow time to adjust and settle back in.

Risk 5: *Forgetting that you will have changed personally*   You will have changed at least a little as a result of your experiences as a postgraduate student and of living in the UK. Try to be aware of how your confidence, knowledge, understanding and views may have changed during your programme, and use all of these changes as positive experiences.

Risk 6: *Forgetting that your family will need to adjust to life back home*   If you come to the UK with your family, remember that they will need to adjust to life back home too. Plan the changes with them, including children, and plan to take time to settle in again after you return.

Risk 7: *Not seeking careers guidance at university*   Even if you have a clear view of what your career path will be, the university Careers Advisory Service can be useful, perhaps by making you aware of alternatives. If you do not have much idea, then they will be very useful in helping you make some career decisions.

Risk 8: *Only taking the careers advice of the academic staff in your department or school*   Particularly for postgraduates, the academic staff in your department can be an invaluable source of ideas, information and contacts. But always remember that they do not have the breadth of knowledge or the objectivity of professional careers advisers.

Risk 9: *Not thinking widely about career opportunities*   It is quite easy to forget to think about careers when you are enjoying your programme and are very busy. But if you leave your thinking about careers too late you may find that you have missed the best opportunities. Also, think widely. Postgraduates are in large demand in many fields, and there may be interesting career directions that you had not thought about before.

Risk 10: *Not keeping in contact with employment networks and opportunities at home* Although you will be based in the UK for one to three years, if you will be returning home afterwards then it is important to keep in touch with the networks of possible employers while you are away.

APPENDIX A
GENERAL READING ABOUT POSTGRADUATE STUDIES AND POSTGRADUATE LIFE

Bell, J. (1999) *Doing Your Research Project: A Guide for First Time Researchers in Education and Social Science* (3rd edition). Milton Keynes: Open University Press

Blaxter, L., Hughes, C. and Tight, M. (2001) *How to Research* (2nd edition). Milton Keynes: Open University Press

British Council. *Studying and Living in the United Kingdom*. 92pp downloadable from *www.educationuk.org*

Clough, P. and Nutbrown, C. (2002) *A Student's Guide to Methodology*. London: Sage

Craswell, G. (2004) *Writing for Academic Success: A Postgraduate Guide*. London: Sage

Crème, P. and Lea, M. (2003) *Writing at University: A Guide for Students* (2nd edition). Milton Keynes: Open University Press

Cryer, P. (2000) *The Research Student's Guide to Success* (2nd edition). Buckingham: Open University Press

Dunleavy, P. (1996) *Authoring* a PhD. London: Palgrave Macmillan

Engineering and Physical Science Research Council (1997) *Research Student and Supervisor: An Approach to Good Supervisory Practice*. Swindon: EPSRC

Gatthorn, A. and Joyner, R. (2005) *Writing the Winning Thesis or Dissertation* (2nd edition) London: Corwin Press

Graves, N. and Varma, V. (eds) (1997) *Working for a Doctorate: A Guide for Humanities and Social Sciences*. London: Routledge

Hart, C. (1998) *Doing a Literature Review*. London: Sage

Hart, C. (2001) *Doing a Literature Search*. London: Sage

Hart, C. (2004) *Doing Your Masters Dissertation*. London: Sage

Higher Education Policy Institute (2004) *Postgraduate Education in the UK*. Available at *www.hepi.ac.uk*

Humanities Research Board/The British Academy (1997) *Guidelines on Support for Research Students in the Humanities*. Stanmore: HRB

Jackson, H. (2005) *Good Grammar for Students*. London: Sage

Lee, R. (2003) *Doing Research on Sensitive Topics*. London: Sage

Lowes, R., Peters, H. and Turner, M. (2004) *The International Student's Guide: Studying in English at University*. London: Sage

McCarthy, P. and Hatcher, C. (2002) *Presentation Skills: The Essential Guide for Students*. London: Sage

Murray, R. (2002) *How to Write a Thesis*. Milton Keynes: Open University Press

Murray, R. (2003) *How to Survive Your Viva*. Milton Keynes: Open University Press

Oliver, P. (2003) *Writing Your Thesis*. London: Sage

Oliver, P. (2003) *The Student's Guide to Research Ethics*. Milton Keynes: Open University Press

Particle Physics and Astronomy Research Council (1996) *An Approach to Good Supervisory Practice for Supervisors and Research Students*. Swindon: PPARC

Phillips, E. and Pugh, D.S. (2000) *How to Get a PhD: A Handbook for Students and Their Supervisors* (3rd Edition). Buckingham: Open University Press

Redman, P. (2005) *Good Essay Writing: A Social Sciences Guide* (3rd Edition). London: Sage

Rudestam, K.E. and Newton, R.R. (2000) *Surviving Your Dissertation: A Comprehensive Guide to Content and Process*. London: Sage

Rumsey, S. (2004) *How to Find Information: A Guide for Researchers*. Milton Keynes: Open University Press

Rugg, G. and Petre, M. (2004) *The Unwritten Rules of PhD Research*. Milton Keynes: Open University Press

Ryan, Y. and Zuber-Skerritt, O. (eds) (1999) *Supervising Postgraduates from Non-English Speaking Backgrounds*. Buckingham: Open University Press/SRHE

Shepherd, K. (2005) *Presenting at Conferences, Seminars and Meetings*. London: Sage

Tinkler, P. and Jackson, C. (2004) *The Doctoral Examination Process: A Handbook for Students, Examiners and Supervisors*. Milton Keynes: Open University Press

Trafford, V. and Leshem, S. (2002) Starting at the end to undertake doctoral research: predictable questions as stepping stones. *Higher Education Review*, Vol. 35 No. 1, pp. 31–49

Trafford, V. and Leshem, S. (2002) Anatomy of a doctoral viva. *Journal of Graduate Education*, Vol. 3 No. 1, pp. 33–41

Walliman, R. (2005) *Your Research Project: A Step by Step Guide for the First Time Researcher* (2nd edition). London: Sage

Wellington, J., Bathmaker, A., Hunt, G., McCullouch, G. and Sikes, P. (2005) *Succeeding with Your Doctorate*. London: Sage

Wilkinson, D. (2005) *The Essential Guide to Postgraduate Study*. London: Sage

Wisker, G. (1998) *The Postgraduate Research Handbook*. London: Palgrave Macmillan

APPENDIX B
GENERAL GUIDES TO UNIVERSITIES IN THE UK

The publications listed here are general guides to universities in the UK. They are annual publications, so are updated each year and often have a full title with the year named in it, e.g. *The Guardian University Guide 2006*. They are also written for students thinking of undergraduate studies. However, they give a detailed description of the universities, student life and the strengths and weaknesses of particular subjects and departments in each university. This means they are useful in providing a good picture as a background to your choice. However, remember that they are undergraduate guides!

The Guardian University Guide (London: Guardian Books)
The Times Good University Guide (London: Times Books)

KEY WEBSITES FOR GENERAL INFORMATION ABOUT POSTGRADUATE STUDIES IN THE UK FOR INTERNATIONAL STUDENTS

Department for Education and Skills

www.dfes.gov.uk/international-students

British Council

www.educationUK.org
www.britishcouncil.org

This website includes downloadable information sheets on a wide range of aspects of living and studying in the UK.

UKCOSA   The Council for International Education

www.ukcosa.org.uk

This website includes a series of downloadable Guidance Notes covering 27 different aspects of living and studying in the UK.

Prospects UK

www.prospects.ac.uk

Scottish International Foundation Programme

www.studyinscotland.co.uk

UK NARIC   The National Recognition Information Centre for the UK

www.naric.org.uk

HERO   Higher Education and Research Opportunities

Official website operated on behalf of the main HE organizations in the UK. Contains wide-ranging information about UK universities, programmes, research and funding.

www.hero.ac.uk

LEAGUE TABLES

Most league tables are published every year and are usually available both as a publication and on the internet. Always remember with league tables to look at the description of how it has been calculated, and remember too that most are about undergraduate studies and/or research, and not about postgraduate studies.

The Guardian League Tables

The Guardian University Guide (London: Guardian Books)

   www.EducationGuardian.co.uk/guides

The Times University League Tables

The Times Good University Guide (London: Times Books)

   www.timesonline.co.uk/student

The Sunday Times University League Tables

   www.timesonline.co.uk/student

The Times Higher Education Supplement League Tables

The Higher Education League Tables, *The Times Higher Education Supplement,* 27 May 2005

The Student Satisfaction Survey, *The Times Higher Education Supplement,* 23 September 2005

   www.thes.co.uk

The Times Higher Education Supplement World University Rankings

World University Rankings, *The Times Higher Education Supplement,* 5 November 2004 and 4 February 2005

   www.thes.co.uk/statistics/international_comparisons/2004/main.aspx

KEY WEBSITES ABOUT VISAS, ENTRY INTO THE UK AND WORKING IN THE UK

The Home Office

Visa applications

www.ukvisas.gov.uk

Immigration and Nationality Directorate

www.ind.homeoffice.gov.uk

Working in the UK website

www.workingintheuk.gov.uk

The Foreign and Commonwealth Office (FCO)

UK overseas missions and Entry Clearance Posts

www.ukvisas.gov.uk

www.fco.gov.uk

Embassies and consulates worldwide

The following website has the contact information for all overseas consulates, embassies and other diplomatic mission offices for every country of the world

www2.tagish.co.uk

Britain in China website

This UK government website is specifically for those potential postgraduate students who live in China

www.uk.cn

KEY WEBSITES TO ASSIST IN CHOOSING PROGRAMMES AND UNIVERSITIES

The English UK website list of National Agent Associations

Lists the contact details and websites of the national associations of educational agents in every country to enable you to identify whether an agent is 'recognized' in your own country

www.englishuk.com/agents/agent associations

The HERO (Higher Education and Research Opportunities) website

Official website operated on behalf of the main HE organizations in the UK. Contains wide-ranging information about UK universities, programmes, research and funding

www.hero.ac.uk

The TQI (Teaching Quality Information) website

Official website of the Quality Assurance Agency on which universities are required to publish information about the quality of their programmes, including external examiner reports, data on admissions, achievement and student profiles. Searchable database of all programmes at every university

www.tqi.ac.uk

The HERO RAE website
Provides detailed information on the performance of each university and each of its subject areas in the research assessment exercise in 2001

www.hero.ac.uk/rae

The Hobsons website

www.postgrad.hobsons.com

The UK Prospects website

www.prospects.ac.uk

The Studentmoney website

Searchable database of postgraduate Masters and Doctoral programmes

www.studentmoney.org/postgraduate

The Association of MBAs website

www.mbaworld.com

The Association of Business Schools website

www.the-abs.org.uk

The Graduate Management Admissions Council

www.mba.com

The Studylink website

www.studylink.com

The Guardian Education website

www.EducationGuardian.co.uk/courses

The Hotcourses website

www.hotcourses.com

The FindaMasters/FindaPhD website

www.FindAMasters.com
www.FindAPhD.com

KEY WEBSITES ABOUT ENGLISH LANGUAGE TRAINING AND QUALIFICATIONS

The British Council English Language website

Searchable database of accredited English Language Schools and programmes in the UK

www.englishinbritain.co.uk

The English UK website

Searchable database on English language schools and programmes

www.englishuk.com

KEY WEBSITES FOR INFORMATION ABOUT EVERYDAY LIFE AS A POSTGRADUATE STUDENT IN THE UK

The National Union of Students (NUS)

www.nusonline.co.uk

Miss Your Mum Website

www.missyourmum.com

***The Guardian* Newspaper**

www.EducationGuardian.co.uk/students

***The Times* Newspaper**

www.timesonline.co.uk/student

FINANCIAL INFORMATION

General information

British Council

www.educationUK.org
www.britishcouncil.org

UKCOSA   The Council for International Education

www.ukcosa.org.uk

Prospects UK

www.prospects.ac.uk

The Studentmoney website

www.studentmoney.org

The Royal Bank of Scotland Student Living Index 2004

http://image.guardian.co.uk/sys-files/Education/documents/2004/08/23/bank.pdf

Scholarships

The British Council Scholarships Database

http://ukscholarshipsdatabase.britishcouncil.org

www.educationuk.org/scholarships

Gradfund

www.ncl.ac.uk/postgraduate/funding

The Studentmoney website

www.studentmoney.org

The Chevening Scholarship website

www.chevening.com

The Overseas Research Students Awards Scheme (ORSAS) website

www.orsas.ac.uk

The Commonwealth Scholarship and Fellowship Scheme (CSFP) website

www.csfp-online.org

The DfID Shared Scholarship Scheme

www.dfid.gov.uk/funding/sharedscholarships.asp

Research Council Scholarships (for UK and EU students only)

BBSRC – Biotechnology and Biological Sciences Research Council

www.bbsrc.ac.uk

ESRC – Economic and Social Research Council

www.esrc.ac.uk

EPSRC – Engineering and Physical Sciences Research Council

www.epsrc.ac.uk

MRC – Medical Research Council

www.mrc.ac.uk

NERC – Natural Environment Research Council

www.nerc.ac.uk

PPARC – Particle Physics and Astronomy Research Council

www.pparc.ac.uk

AHRB – Arts and Humanities Research Council

www.ahrc.ac.uk

KEY WEBSITES ABOUT WORK AND LIFE AFTER POSTGRADUATE STUDIES

Prospects UK

www.prospects.ac.uk

The Skillclear website

Lists the areas of skills shortage in which non-EU postgraduates may seek employment in the UK

www.skillclear.co.uk/skilllist.asp

APPENDIX K
OTHER USEFUL WEBSITES

The Eurydice website

A European Union website with detailed descriptions of the educational system in each member state of the EU, including England, Scotland, Wales and Northern Ireland

www.eurydice.org

The International Association of Universities (IAU) website

The IAU World Higher Education Database provides information on the HE system in every country, including lists of universities. Operated and organized by UNESCO

www.unesco.org/iau

The AIESEC website

www.uk.aiesec.org

The Graduate Overseas website

This is a general website to provide advice, contacts and services for international students

www.graduateoverseas.net

Travel websites

Specialist Student Travel Agents

www.statravel.co.uk

Rail

www.nationalrail.co.uk

Bus

www.nationalexpress.com
www.gobycoach.com

Air

www.studentflights.co.uk

APPENDIX L
WEBSITES OF HIGHER EDUCATION INSTITUTIONS IN THE UNITED KINGDOM

Aberdeen, University of	www.abdn.ac.uk
Abertay, University of	www.abertay.ac.uk
Aberystwyth (University of Wales)	www.aber.ac.uk
Anglo-European College of Chiropractic	www.aecc.ac.uk
American Intercontinental University – London	www.aiulondon.ac.uk
Anglia Ruskin University	www.anglia.ac.uk
The Arts Institute at Bournemouth	www.aib.ac.uk
Ashridge Business School	www.ashridge.org.uk
Aston University	www.aston.ac.uk
Bangor (University of Wales)	www.bangor.ac.uk
Bath, University of	www.bath.ac.uk
Bath Spa University	www.bathspa.ac.uk
Birkbeck College (University of London)	www.bbk.ac.uk
Birmingham, University of	www.bham.ac.uk
Birmingham College of Food Tourism and Creative Studies	www.bcftcs.ac.uk
Bishop Grosseteste College	www.bgc.ac.uk
Bolton, University of	www.bolton.ac.uk
Bournemouth University	www.bournemouth.ac.uk
Bournemouth Business School International	www.bbschool.co.uk
BPP Professional Legal Education, Law School (London, Leeds, Manchester)	www.bpp.com
Bradford College	www.bilk.ac.uk
Bradford, University of	www.bradford.ac.uk
Brighton, University of	www.brighton.ac.uk
Bristol, University of	www.bristol.ac.uk
Brunel University	www.brunel.ac.uk
Buckingham, University of	www.buckingham.ac.uk
Buckinghamshire and Chilterns University College	www.bcuc.ac.uk
Camberwell College of Arts	www.camberwell.arts.ac.uk
Cambridge, University of	www.cam.ac.uk
Canterbury Christ Church University	www.cant.ac.uk
Cardiff University	www.cardiff.ac.uk
Cardiff (University of Wales Institute)	www.uwic.ac.uk
Central England, University of	www.uce.ac.uk
Central Lancashire, University of	www.uclan.ac.uk
Central School of Speech and Drama	www.cssd.ac.uk
Central Saint Martins College of Art and Design	www.csm.arts.ac.uk
Centre for Human Ecology	www.che.ac.uk
Chelsea College of Art and Design	www.chelsea.arts.ac.uk
Chester, University of	www.chester.ac.uk
Chichester, University of	www.ucc.ac.uk
City University	www.city.ac.uk

City College Norwich	*www.ccn.ac.uk*
College of Estate Management	*www.cem.ac.uk*
College of Law	*www.lawcol.co.uk*
Cornwall College	*www.cornwall.ac.uk*
Courtauld Institute of Art	*www.courtauld.ac.uk*
Coventry University	*www.coventry.ac.uk*
Cranfield University	*www.cranfield.ac.uk*
Creative Arts, University College for the	*www.ucreative.ac.uk*
Cumbria Institute of the Arts	*www.cumbria.ac.uk*
Dartington College of Arts	*www.dartington.ac.uk*
De Montfort University	*www.dmu.ac.uk*
Derby, University of	*www.derby.ac.uk*
Doncaster College	*www.don.ac.uk*
Dundee, University of	*www.dundee.ac.uk*
Durham, University of	*www.durham.ac.uk*
East Anglia, University of	*www.uea.ac.uk*
East London, University of	*www.uel.ac.uk*
Edge Hill College	*www.edgehill.ac.uk*
Edinburgh, University of	*www.ed.ac.uk*
Edinburgh Business School	*www.ebs.hw.ac.uk*
Edinburgh College of Art	*www.eca.ac.uk*
European Business School London	*www.regents.ac.uk*
ESCP-EAP London Campus	*www.escp-eap.net*
Essex, University of	*www.essex.ac.uk*
Exeter, University of	*www.exeter.ac.uk*
Falmouth College of Arts	*www.falmouth.ac.uk*
Glamorgan, University of	*www.glam.ac.uk*
Glasgow, University of	*www.gla.ac.uk*
Glasgow Caledonian University	*www.gcal.ac.uk*
Glasgow School of Art	*www.gsa.ac.uk*
Gloucestershire, University of	*www.glos.ac.uk*
Goldsmiths College (University of London)	*www.gold.ac.uk*
Greenwich, University of	*www.gre.ac.uk*
Greenwich, School of Management	*www.greenwich-college.ac.uk*
Harper Adams University College	*www.harper-adams.ac.uk*
Heriot–Watt University	*www.hw.ac.uk*
Henley Management College	*www.henleymc.ac.uk*
Hertfordshire, University of	*www.herts.ac.uk*
Heythrop College	*www.heythrop.ac.uk*
Holborn College	*www.holborncollege.ac.uk*
Huddersfield, University of	*www.hud.ac.uk*
Hull, University of	*www.hull.ac.uk*
Imperial College (University of London)	*www.imperial.ac.uk*
Institute of Advanced Legal Studies (University of London)	*www.sas.ac.uk*
Institute of Classical Studies (University of London)	*www.sas.ac.uk*
Institute of Commonwealth Studies (University of London)	*www.sas.ac.uk*
Institute of Education (University of London)	*www.ioe.ac.uk*
Institute of English Studies (University of London)	*www.sas.ac.uk*
Institute of Germanic and Romance Studies (University of London)	*www.sas.ac.uk*
Institute of Historical Research (University of London)	*www.icbh.ac.uk*
Institute of Musical Research (University of London)	*www.sas.ac.uk*
Institute of Philosophy (University of London)	*www.philosophy.sas.ac.uk*
Institute for the Study of the Americas (University of London)	*www.sas.ac.uk*
International Institute for Communication Excellence	*www.iice.org*
Keele University	*www.keele.ac.uk*
Kent, University of	*www.kent.ac.uk*

Kent Institute of Art and Design (now University College for the Creative Arts)	www.kiad.ac.uk
King's College (University of London)	www.kcl.ac.uk
Kingston University	www.kingston.ac.uk
Lampeter (University of Wales)	www.lamp.ac.uk
Lancaster University	www.lancaster.ac.uk
Leeds, University of	www.leeds.ac.uk
Leeds Metropolitan University	www.leedsmet.ac.uk
Leeds College of Music	www.lcm.ac.uk
Leicester, University of	www.le.ac.uk
Lincoln, University of	www.lincoln.ac.uk
Liverpool, University of	www.liv.ac.uk
Liverpool Hope University	www.hope.ac.uk
Liverpool John Moores University	www.livjm.ac.uk
London Business School	www.london.edu
London College of Communication	www.lcc.arts.ac.uk
London College of Fashion	www.fashion.arts.ac.uk
London External Programme (University of London)	www.lon.ac.uk
London Film School	www.lfs.org.uk
London Metropolitan University	www.londonmet.ac.uk
London School of Business and Finance	www.lsbf.org.uk
London School of Economics and Political Science (University of London)	www.lse.ac.uk
London School of Hygiene and Tropical Medicine	www.lshtm.ac.uk
London South Bank University	www.lsbu.ac.uk
Loughborough University	www.lboro.ac.uk
Luton, University of	www.luton.ac.uk
Manchester, University of	www.manchester.ac.uk
Manchester Metropolitan University	www.mmu.ac.uk
Middlesex University	www.mdx.ac.uk
Napier University	www.napier.ac.uk
National Film and Television School	www.nftsfilm-tv.ac.uk
NESCOT-North East Surrey College of Technology	www.nescot.ac.uk
Newcastle upon Tyne, University of	www.ncl.ac.uk
Newman College	www.newman.ac.uk
Newport (University of Wales)	www.newport.ac.uk
North East Wales Institute of Higher Education	www.newi.ac.uk
Northumbria University	www.northumbria.ac.uk
Norwich School of Art and Design	www.nsad.ac.uk
Nottingham, University of	www.nottingham.ac.uk
Nottingham Trent University	www.ntu.ac.uk
Northampton, University of	www.northampton.ac.uk
The Open University	www.open.ac.uk
Oxford, University of	www.ox.ac.uk
Oxford Brookes University	www.brookes.ac.uk
Oxford Centre for Mission Studies	www.ocms.ac.uk
Oxford Institute of Legal Practice	www.oxlip.ac.uk
Paisley, University of	www.paisley.ac.uk
Peninsula Postgraduate Health Institute	www.pphi.ac.uk
School of Pharmacy (University of London)	www.ulsop.ac.uk
Plymouth, University of	www.plymouth.ac.uk
Portsmouth, University of	www.port.ac.uk
The Prince's School of Traditional Arts	www.princesschooltraditionalarts.org
Queen Margaret University College	www.qmuc.ac.uk
Queen Mary College (University of London)	www.qmul.ac.uk
Queen's University of Belfast	www.qub.ac.uk
Ravensbourne College of Design and Communication	www.rave.ac.uk
Reading, University of	www.reading.ac.uk

Regent's Business School London	www.regents.ac.uk
Robert Gordon University	www.rgu.ac.uk
Richmond, The American International University in London	www.richmond.ac.uk
Roehampton University	www.roehampton.ac.uk
Rose Bruford College	www.bruford.ac.uk
Royal Academy of Music	www.ram.ac.uk
Royal Agricultural College	www.rac.ac.uk
Royal College of Art	www.rca.ac.uk
Royal College of Music	www.rcm.ac.uk
Royal Holloway College (University of London)	www.rhul.ac.uk
Royal Northern College of Music	www.rncm.ac.uk
Royal Scottish Academy of Music and Drama	www.rsamd.ac.uk
Royal Veterinary College	www.rvc.ac.uk
Royal Welsh College of Music and Drama	www.rwcmd.ac.uk
Salford, University of	www.salford.ac.uk
Sarum College	www.sarum.ac.uk
Schiller International University	www.schillerlondon.ac.uk
Scottish Agricultural College	www.sac.ac.uk
Scottish School of Herbal Medicine	www.herbalmedicine.org.uk
Sheffield, University of	www.sheffield.ac.uk
Sheffield Hallam University	www.shu.ac.uk
SOAS (School of Oriental and African Studies)	www.soas.ac.uk
Southampton, University of	www.soton.ac.uk
Southampton Solent University	www.solent.ac.uk
Staffordshire University	www.staffs.ac.uk
St Andrews, University of	www.st-andrews.ac.uk
St George's (University of London)	www.sgul.ac.uk
St Mark and St John, The College of	www.marjon.ac.uk
St Martin's College	www.ucsm.ac.uk
St Mary's College	www.smuc.ac.uk
Stockport College of Further and Higher Education	www.stockport.ac.uk
Stirling, University of	www.stir.ac.uk
Strathclyde, University of	www.strath.ac.uk
Sunderland, University of	www.sunderland.ac.uk
Surrey, University of	www.surrey.ac.uk
Surrey Institute of Art and Design (now University College for the Creative Arts)	www.surrart.ac.uk
Sussex, University of	www.sussex.ac.uk
Swansea (University of Wales)	www.swansea.ac.uk
Swansea Institute of Higher Education	www.sihe.ac.uk
Teesside, University of	www.tees.ac.uk
Thames Valley University	www.tvu.ac.uk
Trinity and All Saints College	www.tasc.ac.uk
Trinity College, Carmarthen	www.trinity-cm.ac.uk
Trinity College of Music	www.tcm.ac.uk
Ulster, University of	www.ulster.ac.uk
University College London (University of London)	www.ucl.ac.uk
Warburg Institute (University of London)	www.sas.ac.uk
Warwick, University of	www.warwick.ac.uk
West of England, University of the	www.uwe.ac.uk
Westminster, University of	www.wmin.ac.uk
Wimbledon School of Art	www.wimbledon.ac.uk
Winchester, University of	www.winchester.ac.uk
Wolverhampton, University of	www.wlv.ac.uk
Worcester, University of	www.worc.ac.uk
Writtle College	www.writtle.ac.uk
York, University of	www.york.ac.uk
York St John College	www.yorksj.ac.uk

INDEX